NO END IN SIGHT

*An autobiographical account
of his early years*

Jonathan Hall

MINERVA PRESS
LONDON
MIAMI   DELHI   SYDNEY

NO END IN SIGHT
An autobiographical account of his early years
Copyright © Jonathan Hall 2000

ISBN 0 75411 151 2

First Published 2000 by
MINERVA PRESS
315–317 Regent Street
London W1R 7YB

Printed in Great Britain for Minerva Press

NO END IN SIGHT

An autobiographical account of his early years

Foreword

My first impression of Jonathan Hall's Arnold Lodge School was that it must have been the best maintained in England: every windowsill newly painted, every flowerbed weed-free, every brick perfectly pointed.

This worried me rather. I thought our dreamy son, for whom tied-up laces and tucked-in shirts were a rarity, might be expected to be as neatly turned out as the tulips in the borders.

But when we met 'Mr Hall' we knew at once that this was no ordinary schoolmaster. His dedication to his school went a lot further than neatly mowed grass and polished windows. He had an entrepreneurial obsession I recognised. He strived for excellent academic results like I strived for Michelin stars. He cared about his pupils and parents as I cared about my restaurant customers. His enthusiasm for running a good business was encouraging and engaging.

But what really made us entrust our precious darlings to his care was an incident on the day Daniel went to do his entrance test for Arnold Lodge. With a crowd of other seven year olds, Daniel went off happily with a couple of teachers at 10.00 a.m. We parents were instructed to collect our darlings at noon.

At noon, Daniel was nowhere to be seen. Jonathan Hall, seeing my rising panic, walked with me towards the block in which they'd spent the morning, peering round corners on our way. We found Daniel almost at once – he had failed to follow the gang and had got lost – but not soon enough to prevent tears. Sniffling and miserable, but too much on his dignity to allow me to hug him or pick him up, he walked between Jonathan and me, fighting sobs.

Jonathan pulled a hanky out of his pocket and said 'Here, Daniel. What a horrible cold. Half the school is suffering from sniffles and sneezes.' Daniel, humiliation averted, blew his nose and cheered up in an instant.

After half a term, we moved our daughter to Arnold Lodge too. (Daniel's homework had progressed to fractions and geometry when his elder sister was still drawing pictures of groundsel and making trains out of loo-roll tubes.)

They both loved the school, and soon set up a clamour to be allowed to board. Reluctantly we agreed to weekly boarding.

On the Tuesday of their first week, my mother called me to the telephone. 'It's Daniel, telephoning from the matron's room.'

I rounded on my husband: 'There you are. He's unhappy. I told you he would be. He wants to come home.'

Not a bit of it, 'Mum, can we stay the weekend?'

One more insight into Jonathan Hall, and his school. When Daniel took his Common Entrance Exam, on which entry to Eton depended, he panicked. Sitting in the Arnold Lodge classroom, he stared at the paper without writing more than his name. After an hour the invigilator sent him up to the sickroom, and informed Jonathan.

Jonathan rang us 'Thought you should know that Daniel had a bit of a problem with the exam today, but we know he's up to it. So I've spoken to Eton, and they've agreed that if we keep him isolated until this afternoon, he can have another crack at it.' That little bit of tolerance and care meant, for one young lad, the difference between enormous success and abject failure.

No End in Sight is fascinating. For Jonathan to have turned out to be the sort of Headmaster he was, is remarkable. His own schooldays were miserable, and ill luck and tragedy have dogged him all his life. But he turned Arnold Lodge round, twice, against all the odds.

Anyone who has ever had a child at prep school, anyone who has ever run a struggling business, and anyone who cares about education, should read this book.

Prue Leith OBE
28 October 1999

Preface

Having compiled the account of my early years, I feel that the dichotomy of material might lead some readers to think I should have written two separate books. A history of Arnold Lodge School, with anecdotal references to staff, together with a chronicle of the most significant developments, would provide sufficient material for one book. The other, of a much deeper nature, would outline the case history of a man struggling to find and develop his own identity.

It was my choice to combine the two, which are, in any event, inescapably linked. It is, after all, my story. If the recollections of school and emotional conflicts were separated or excluded, an essential part of what makes up the whole and the real me would be missing.

Although I am able to recollect the content of conversations going back many years, the use of direct speech in certain instances is, of course, fictional. This is one of the reasons why *No End in Sight* cannot be described as an autobiography in the accepted sense. I have, however, taken pains to devise a dialogue that is in keeping with the spirit and atmosphere of the occasions in question.

I am indebted to my father, whose diaries I still have in my possession. He wrote these up on a daily basis with great thoroughness until two days before his death in September 1972. His jottings, and a number of school records, helped me piece together much fragmented information when in the process of carrying out my research.

Contents

Introduction

Apart from two notable exceptions, my ancestors were un-remarkable, hard-working people. Class origins are not easy to pinpoint accurately, although sufficient is known to suggest that both my parents came from middle-class backgrounds of varying poshness, with a preponderance of civil servants on my father's side. He shared his family antecedence between Northumberland and Guernsey. The bluntness inherited from his northern ancestors, who were tenant farmers, remained with him throughout life. The French flavour of the Channel Islands did not appear to have rubbed off on him, so inept were his attempts at even the simplest spoken French.

Mother hailed from the quiet Herefordshire market town of Leominster, where Grandfather Bradford owned an old coaching inn, The Royal Oak. He was a welcoming host, whose cheerful, engaging personality made the hotel a popular meeting place. Apart from dealing with the accounts and overseeing the hotel, he left most of the domestic running, including the catering, to his less jovial but extremely capable wife.

Grandfather possessed unusual musical gifts. Having studied singing under Professor John Bacon Welch of the Guildhall School of Music, he became bass soloist in the Temple Choir, under Dr E J Hopkins, and took part in the choirs for the Coronations of King Edward VII and King George V. When not committed to concert work, he indulged in the more frivolous pursuits of hunting, fishing and shooting as often as he was able. In the early part of this century, in addition to his eight horses, the many carriages and traps, Grandfather purchased a Rambler car, one of the first motor vehicles in Herefordshire. The family was driven about by a chauffeur for a while, but some years later he invested in a flashy American Buick convertible which he or his son, Norman, drove.

My father was proud to be able to claim to have been the great-nephew of Henry Philpott, formerly master of St Catharine's College, Cambridge. College masters in those times automatically became vice-chancellor of the university on a rotational basis. During his academic life he was for a while tutor to Prince Albert when chancellor of Cambridge University. Philpott once entertained Queen Victoria and other eminent people, including the duke of Wellington, for an evening meal at St Catharine's. Sir Robert Peel was way down the social pecking order on the glittering guest list. When Queen Victoria took her leave after what must have been a splendid occasion, she said that she had never before felt so at home in a commoner's house! Philpott was ultimately appointed bishop of Worcester; whilst holding this office he resided in the lovely Hartlebury Castle. His impressive monument in Worcester Cathedral symbolises the esteem felt for the man, bishop for twenty-nine years until 1890. He finally retired when he had reached the age of eighty-three.

My mother's great-uncle founded the East London Hospital for Children and Dispensary for Women at his own expense. The idea originated while Nathaniel Heckford, a brilliant young surgeon, was caring for the cholera victims of Wapping. In the epidemic of 1866 he worked with Sarah Goff, a nurse, whom he later married. Together they undertook the care of sick children. Heckford, dying at the young age of twenty-nine, did not live to see his ambitions fulfilled. The institution gained an international reputation for its 'ever open door' welcome to the sick children of east London. When Charles Dickens heard the hospital was experiencing financial difficulties and might close, he wrote articles and made an appeal in emotional prose so successful that it was possible for the work to continue and a new hospital to be built.

Death of a Dream

For as long as I can remember, I had harboured a dream. The dream was a quixotic vision of the perfect school I wanted ours to be. With ruthless savagery, this fantasy was shattered on a sultry August day.

Devitalised by a headache of horrifying ferocity, I clung for dear life to any object I could find as I attempted to move about the house. The problems of balance and sickness were so severe that I knew this was no common illness.

For two years I had felt unwell. I was aware my professional competence was declining and, though lapses in memory privately caused me to panic, I was too scared to consciously accept it was anything other than an aberration. Either the strain of fulfilling a headmaster's role for twenty years was finally proving too much or I was suffering from the early signs of senile dementia.

My GP put me in touch with an ENT specialist. Over a period of several months he must have seen me on at least ten occasions. I continued to drag myself to school, constant sensations of dizziness, nausea and imbalance convincing me that something was wrong. Becoming more irritable and disheartened, I urged my consultant to check me out again.

'I have, as you know, already ruled out an acoustic neuroma, a particularly nasty tumour which grows on the nerve to the ear,' he said. 'I'm sure nothing will show up, but I'll carry out the tests again to be doubly sure.'

The further test results proved negative. Registering impatience for the first time, the consultant suggested my problems were psychosomatic, that the stressful nature of my work had caused me to imagine I was ill.

A few weeks later I noticed a deterioration in my eyesight. Without bothering to examine me, my medical adviser was dismissive of my anxiety; he nonetheless referred me to an ophthalmologist. Chronic papilloedema was immediately diagnosed, suggesting raised pressure in the brain and necessitating a scan the following week.

The next day I stood at the lectern in our local church to read from St John's Gospel the ninth lesson at the school's Christmas carol service. To my horror, I realised all I could see on the sheet in front of me was a mass of blurs. I was incapable of deciphering any of the words. God's hand must have been guiding me because, despite familiarity with the text, I would have been incapable of remembering the words parrot-fashion without careful revision. A rare miracle took place during those agonising moments, enabling me to recollect the passage faultlessly.

The ENT specialist's clinical judgement proved patently wrong when the scan showed up a large acoustic neuroma. An appointment was speedily arranged with a neurosurgeon. After carrying out a thorough examination, the neurosurgeon addressed me solemnly.

'You are going to have to undergo two operations,' he said. 'The first will need to be carried out as soon as possible. It will involve the drainage of fluid from the brain by the insertion of a ventriculo-peritoneal shunt; this is a straightforward procedure and there is no reason why you should not be well enough to return home in time for Christmas. The second procedure, the removal of the tumour, is likely to be a lengthy and dangerous one that will be taxing in the extreme.'

'Must I really have two operations?' I asked.

'If you do not, you'll die,' he replied with ice-cold candour.

Incarcerated in the intensive care unit on the fifth floor of Coventry's Walsgrave Hospital, it was clear my recovery from the initial operation was going to be less routine than the surgeon's confident predictions had suggested. The muffled comments of white-coated strangers strengthened my belief that I would not be going home for Christmas after all. It was some while, however, before I was told I had suffered a surgical stroke, or of the determination and drive that would be needed to rehabilitate myself.

I was transferred by ambulance to the Warwickshire Private Hospital to convalesce. Spending the first few days in a state of moribund oblivion, I was vaguely conscious of a pain developing in my left calf. Little did I know this was a deep venous thrombosis or of the complications that might ensue in view of my inability to move about. When the blood clot later reached the region of my chest, a throbbing pain that was growing in intensity caused me to writhe in agony as I panted for breath.

No nurse arrived in answer to my summonses for help. Again I pressed the emergency button, but to no avail. Using the bedside telephone, in desperation I called my wife, Lesley, at home. It was a merciful relief that she was in the house and not at work or out shopping, as well she might have been.

'For Christ's sake, get one of the nurses to come to me at once,' I pleaded frantically. 'I keep ringing the bell and no one's taking any notice. I'm having a heart attack!'

Had it not been for Lesley's swift action, I am certain I would not have lived to see another day. Two nurses and a doctor rushed to my aid with an oxygen mask, conscience-stricken faces revealing their alarm at finding an abandoned patient about to die from a pulmonary embolism.

That same day our family cat, Lisa, was run over by a car. Lesley discovered her mangled remains as she was leaving the house to visit me at the hospital. Not one to give way to emotional outbursts, Lesley disguised her true feelings for my sake by remaining calm whilst in my presence. After leaving the ward, she buried her face in her hands and was no longer able to control the sobs that flowed relentlessly.

'In less than a week my husband's had a stroke and a blood clot that nearly killed him,' she lamented. 'What with all these disasters, including Lisa's accident, I shudder to think what could go wrong next!'

The paralysis increased my difficulty in mastering the anti-thrombotic stockings, which, together with warfarin tablets and regular blood tests, became part of the daily regimen. A physio-therapist bullied me first into learning how to crawl before I was ready to progress to the more challenging process of walking with a frame. I continued to work with determination to regain my mobility in readiness for the complex operation to remove the tumour itself. An unpleasant bout of sickness led to more tests being carried out, after which it was felt the operation should not be further delayed as the tumour had by now increased in size.

Early in February 1986, in a nine-hour operation, the neuro-surgeon and his team successfully removed an extremely large benign tumour, confirmed as an acoustic neuroma. I stress that it was a large tumour because surgeons can much more easily and safely remove the smaller ones, underlining the importance of early detection. Hearing in my left ear, the destruction of my left facial nerve and damage to my brain stem were sacrifices that had to be made in order to save my life. Subsequently I realised my visual acuity had been impaired and double vision in the left eye for several months made doctors anxious lest my sixth cranial nerve had been permanently damaged. This, fortunately, turned out not to be the case.

It seemed to me that neither the surgeon, a brilliant technician, nor the nursing staff were capable of giving the reassurance that is vital after a patient suffers the trauma of a tremendous upheaval inside his skull. This is an experience shared by many other patients with whom I have since been in touch, and who suffered similar ordeals.

On regaining consciousness in intensive care, one is hardly in a position to describe the desperation felt when the full implications of the body's battering become apparent. What is it like to have had a tumour on the brain, some ask? I once described it as having the sensation of a raging volcano in my head, about to erupt, and that was before it had even been diagnosed as a tumour!

After the operation, sensibility was numb. It was as if I was suffering from an ever-present hangover of unendurable intensity. For a period of years my head seemed not to belong to my body; clear thinking and undivided concentration are luxuries which still elude me.

Gradually it dawned on me that I had several disabilities to face, each demanding a special and individual attention, requiring of me the effort only to be expected of a fit and rational person, which at that time I certainly was not. To combat the balance problem and to improve mobility, I practised standing on one leg for long periods, paid regular visits to a gym and walked five miles each day until I was confident enough to discard the stick.

My mind worked slowly, with indistinct speech adding to the frustrations as I tackled the most basic daily hurdles. For many months and in my blackest moments I did not want to carry on. I would smash valuable possessions, uttering foul oaths as I did so, in a vain attempt to express the depths of the suffering with which I was weighed down.

My wife, herself a medical practitioner, and my teenage sons had difficulty in coping with the acceptance of the damage done to me. For a time family relationships were very strained. In the wider sense, I found it hard to relate to anyone on any level, emotionally, socially or professionally. These harsh realities emphasised my feeling of isolation and inner emptiness. Slowly the barriers were broken down; people around me began to realise, with some surprise, that I was not mentally unhinged and that my thinking processes were still intact.

In the acceptance of my new self, the mind wandered through a series of conflicting emotions, with anger, bitterness and depression most in evidence. Not having abused my body with large quantities of alcohol or cigarettes, I asked myself why, in my prime, I had been afflicted in this way. I could see around me the healthy majority, many of whom burn the candle at both ends and do all the wrong things without causing hardship to themselves.

Any bitterness has now vanished. This has been substituted by a quiet sadness, knowing as I do the heavy losses that can never be replaced or compensated for. My obsessive personality may have heightened the stress which is felt to exacerbate potential health problems. There is also no doubt in my mind that the pre-occupation with faultlessness was instrumental, too, in enabling my personally devised programme of physical and mental exercises to pay dividends. These efforts will need unyieldingly to continue as long as I expect to compete on equal terms with the able-bodied whose wholeness I envy.

The facial nerve loss was the most devastating of the disabilities. Vanity is a distinguishing feature of most of us and I am no exception. It was demoralising to discover my facial distortions frightened some of the pupils at my school; people with whom I had been friendly in the past would cross the road to avoid a face-to-face encounter. Eating and speech difficulties caused me acute embarrassment in almost every social situation. Rudest awakening of all was the discovery that I would never again be able to blow my clarinet. The playing of jazz had been the one sure means of enabling me to relax. Skills in musicianship acquired from years of dedicated practice were cruelly forfeited through the severance of my facial nerve.

Deciding to wage war on these frustrations, I opted for more treatment. A plastic surgeon performed a painful operation on my face, with the purpose of improving its function and appearance. The surgery was as successful as could have been expected, but still I was not satisfied.

One of the world's leading facial nerve experts carried out an anastomosis of my left facial and hypoglossal nerves at the University Hospital in Zürich. In an intricate procedure, he used a nerve removed from the tongue to work the muscles of the face which had lost their own nerve. There was the subsequent scare of post-operative haemorrhaging, needing some revision to the incision, but luckily the anastomosis did not have to be disturbed.

Apart from a slight improvement with facial symmetry, aided by hundreds of hours of rigorous daily tongue and facial exercises prescribed by the Swiss therapist, progress with the functioning of my mouth has been minimal. My left eye, despite earlier promises, will not close, requiring as it does frequent liquid tears to prevent ulceration.

Perceiving the recovery to be as complete as it would ever be, I assumed I would soon be back to normal, able to tackle my heavy work schedule as in past years. It was distressing to discover I was a shadow of my former self, lacking in stamina, no longer effective as a leader, and with a less precise memory for names and faces that highlighted a feeling of incompetence. No matter how hard I persevered, there was a sluggishness in my pace of work I was unable to accelerate. I began to look upon life with a completely new perspective. No longer wanting to be a high-profile boss, I preferred to labour behind the scenes as a back-room boy. Impairment of face and tongue caused a reluctance on my part to deliver speeches in public; on the few occasions I engaged myself in this activity, I became jittery and tense. But worst of all, I was incapable of coping with any kind of stress.

For many years I had run the school as an autocrat. In the earliest days, had I chosen to delegate to any extent, there was neither the income nor the quality of staffing for this to have been possible. As pupil numbers increased, my management techniques altered very little, apart from any tricks or secrets I acquired instinctively. Not to delegate had become a habit.

Resuming overall control following my illness, I adopted a different strategy. Administrative and pastoral duties were more widely distributed through the selection of a team of key staff members. In theory, this was the right way forward, the ideal approach to modern management. The weakness was the idea was felt by many to have created jealousy and divisiveness amongst the staff. Parents were confused by the apportionment of staff responsibilities. One was heard to comment: 'The trouble with the team arrangement is there are too many chiefs and not enough Indians. It's hard to know who is responsible for what!'

Scurrying about rabbit-like and getting nowhere fast is not how I would ever have wanted to evaluate my contribution in the workplace, yet this was how I was functioning. It was not dissimilar to attempting to drive an out-of-hand vehicle, with the disadvantage of sitting in the back seat, unable to apply my foot to the brake. At the young age of forty-eight, as a result of the extensive surgery, my career had all but ended.

I came under attack from staff and parents, some of whom inferred I was shirking in my output. Presuming I was restored to perfect health, they argued it was about time I began subscribing one hundred per cent effort. Taking into account my diminished energy and concentration, I was giving a level of commitment that was greatly in excess of that. To have admitted I was not coping would have been tantamount to saying the quality of the service I was offering to pupils and parents was deficient.

It was during this tempestuous period that I received a gigantic offer for the school site from a London property developer. Tempting though the offer was, particularly as I was keen to retire altogether from what had become an oppressive situation, it would have been morally unacceptable to have treated the proposition seriously. In a talk given to staff shortly afterwards, I appeased their worst fears by saying, 'To have sold the school would have made me feel like a Judas. It would have been an empty exercise to gain great wealth at the expense of destroying the institution my family and I have always cherished.'

The honourable solution was for me to appoint an experienced educationist in my place. Andrew Reekes, who had been director of studies at Cheltenham College, was given a three-year contract. To let go of the reins after thirty years of total absorption into the life of the school was a heartbreaking experience. With nothing to replace what had for me been a true love affair it was worse than a bereavement.

Had my sons at that time expressed an interest in carrying on the family tradition, I would have reconstructed the composition of the school to accommodate this possibility. Pleasing though it would have been to have had a third-generation Hall family member to succeed me, I never pressurised either of them into following in my footsteps, knowing the first move had to come from them. My elder son, Douglas, is a busy lawyer. His brother, David, works as a planner with a rapidly expanding advertising agency. Based in London and with good Oxbridge degrees, they both prefer the cut and thrust of the metropolis to the idea of functioning as pedagogues in the provinces.

Despite having decamped from the front line, ideological thoughts for the betterment of the school were always on my mind. As a young man, I had set out on an extensive journey. Certain of my ambitions had been achieved along the way, but I wanted to leave behind some legacies that constituted permanence. My vision, Utopian in essence, contained clearly defined aims, some of which I felt were still achievable. I made it known that my prime objective was for the school to become a charitable trust before I reached the age of sixty. My family's work would in this way continue in perpetuity under the trusteeship of a board of governors.

It is my passionate belief that opportunities enjoyed by the privileged few should be made available to children from a wider range of backgrounds. The best private schools by virtue of small classes and their pursuit of academic excellence provide the ideal learning environment for the gifted child. I offered scholarships to some talented boys and girls whose parents would not have been able to afford our fees. The results gained by many of these youngsters were so impressive that I wanted to extend the scope and number of these awards.

The most effective way of enabling the school to achieve charitable status would have been for me to give the business away outright. As landlord, I would then have received a rental income for the premises from the trust. In addition, I was determined to use some of the monies I had invested over the years to sponsor more scholarships. I was gullible enough to imagine that philanthropic well-wishers, including local businessmen, would come forward in large numbers, eager for their names to be associated with a scheme of so much worth.

A spate of unexpected circumstances, all of them causing financial nervousness, put paid to my well-intentioned plans.

After a marriage spanning twenty-one years, Lesley and I decided we wanted a divorce. It was my second matrimonial breakdown. Our relationship had not been one of constant bickering and recrimination; there was even so an emotional gulf that had widened so much that we both yearned for freedom and a new beginning. Some years earlier, we had accepted that separation would be the eventual outcome. For the sake of our sons, we stayed together until they had left school and were attending university.

Incompatible though Lesley and I were as partners, there were two basic beliefs about which we never differed. One was that the well-being of our sons took pride of place, no matter what; the other was that in our professional dealings we endeavoured to provide the highest standards possible. The least avaricious person I know, she was typically undemanding when we negotiated a monetary settlement prior to the divorce. Unpretentious and always dependable, Lesley gave me more loyalty and support than I could ever have deserved.

Cautious by nature, I had never been driven by a desire to gamble. Casinos, the horses, lotteries and all forms of wagering were anathemas to me. Apart from the occasional acquisition of high-risk shares, I had built up a portfolio of investments that concentrated on well-tried, blue-chip equities.

The insurance market was a realm of finance about which I knew nothing. Some of my friends were Lloyd's Names. 'By being a Name,' one of them said, 'my investments are made to work for me twice. As well as receiving share dividend entitlements, I pick up an annual cheque from each of the profitable syndicates in which I participate. I've not had a bad year yet!'

Market insiders were equally effusive in their commendations. I had meetings with three underwriting agents, all of whom used their powers of persuasion to maximum effect. Singing from the same hymn sheet, they worked hard to instil in my mind the conviction that membership of Lloyd's was a chance I would be foolish to resist. 'If you join our agency,' they all boasted as if in unison, 'we guarantee you'll be placed in the best performing syndicates. The risks are negligible, the rewards tremendous!'

In common with other unsuspecting investors, my application for membership of Lloyd's of London was eagerly approved. What I did not know was that I had joined what was later to become the world's most expensive club.

Financial disaster began to strike soon afterwards with a three-pronged attack that looked to be contagious. In October 1987, the stock market crash depleted the value of my equities by more than a third.

Two years later, spiralling losses in some of the badly managed Lloyd's syndicates wiped out what was left of my share portfolio; the situation worsened when a series of worldwide disasters placed pressures on the ill-fated insurance industry as never before. It was impossible to predict the extent of future calls on my resources, nor did I know how or where I was going to find the funds to meet the escalating bills.

Throughout this unnerving period almost every business in the United Kingdom was having to battle to survive the ravages of recession. Numbers in the school had declined since my illness. By the time the effects of the economic downturn were fully felt, the pupil roll stood at 330, a decrease of 70 in the space of seven years.

To retrieve a potentially disastrous situation, it was imperative to reduce outgoings in proportion to the loss of income. Distasteful though the decisions were, Andrew Reekes and I were left with no option other than to implement a cost-cutting exercise that included staff redundancies. With my own financial pressures mounting, it was becoming increasingly clear that the time had come for me to offload the burden of school ownership.

So much of what I had set out to do had been foiled by misadventure. Marking the end of an era, I finally succumbed to the inevitable. Far from being satisfied with my achievements, I regretted the wasted years, the failed intentions, the dreams destroyed. The best way of salvaging the hapless situation was for me to seek a successor who would love and nurture the school in the way my family and I had done.

A Close-Run Thing

On condition the vendor sets a realistic asking price, selling a house is relatively straightforward. To unearth prospective purchasers for a school business, however, is a convoluted process. Fee-paying parents are sensitive to rumours that might give rise to the disruption of their children's education. For this reason, negotiations involving the sale of the school had to be conducted in an atmosphere of total confidentiality.

Agents specialising in the disposal of privately-owned schools are few in number. School Transfer Consultants, a husband and wife team based in Southfleet, advertised their services in *Prep School*, the official journal of the preparatory school world. An initial consultation was arranged.

To attract as little attention as possible, Peers and Susan Carter chose to visit me on a Sunday. They said a number of clients on their books had the funds and expertise required to purchase and manage the school. 'It may take time before we find a suitable purchaser, but find one we shall,' they assured me.

The unfavourable economic climate caused me to sit tight and be patient, knowing the recession was gradually ending. During this period, Peers Carter provided details of possible buyers, none of whom were suitable.

In October 1993 he telephoned with the news that two highly experienced prep school heads were interested in acquiring the school. I met Bob Collinge and Graham Hill on four occasions before Christmas. Liking what they saw, both expressed a desire to take over the running of the school as soon as contracts could be signed.

My solicitor was asked to check out the financial authenticity of the would-be purchasers; nothing showed up that gave cause for concern. Peers Carter, who had arranged transactions for them in the past, had no hesitation in vouching for his clients' professional integrity.

Bob Collinge was to provide the finance. Graham Hill and his wife, Gillie, would look after the school's day-to-day management. Graham Hill appeared to possess the skills needed to bring the school forward in the challenging years ahead. He had been owner and headmaster for seventeen years of Danes Hill School, a large day-only preparatory school in Oxshott, Surrey. For two years he had served on the governing council of the Incorporated Association of Preparatory Schools. I was convinced the school we as a family had developed over a period of sixty years could not fail to thrive under his direction.

Terms for the sale of the goodwill, fixtures and fittings were quickly agreed. I granted Messrs Collinge and Hill a twenty year lease on the premises, which allowed the tenants the further protection of being able to exercise an opt-out clause after a period of five years.

Near to tears, I told my employees of the decision to transfer the ownership of our much-prized business. Seated next to me was my ninety-year-old mother. From the day many years ago when she'd stepped down from a horse-drawn carriage to enter the run-down school building that was to be our family home, Mother had done everything in her power to serve the needs of others. The thought of parting with the school, by now the very essence of her being, affected her deeply. Her sense of realism enabled her to accept I was no longer well enough to carry a burden of so much weight.

Putting a brave face on what was for us a profoundly sad and poignant situation, I gave my loyal staff an upbeat version of our future plans.

'My mother and I commend these changes to you,' I said. 'Under Graham and Gillie Hill the school will be in expert hands. It will be our pleasure to follow the school's progress in its continued upward path.'

I wrote to the new owners, wishing them success in their venture. I added I would be pleased to assist them in any way; all they had to do was let me know what help was needed. Failing to acknowledge my offer of friendship, Graham and Gillie Hill were unforthcoming and aloof. Apart from being invited to the school's speech day, contact with my former place of work was minimal. On the first occasion Gillie Hill greeted me like a long-lost brother with a flamboyant kiss; at the second prize-giving she ignored me completely. I could not understand what I'd done to cause her to behave so rudely.

The Hills were skilful at turning on the charm when it suited. Soon after settling in, he asked me to act as honest broker in a merger he was hoping to arrange with a rival preparatory school. Despite these discussions failing to bear fruit, Hill stunned me by saying he nevertheless intended to transfer the school to a site that would accommodate five hundred pupils. I had parted with my business at a knock-down price because I believed Hill would genuinely protect the long-term interests of the school. His next objective was to renegotiate the lease. As a result, the twenty-year lease agreement signed only months previously was already in danger of being broken.

There had been two significant developments by November 1996. Hill had parted company with his partner, Bob Collinge, who rightly expected the money he had invested in the business to be repaid. Notwithstanding this setback, Hill was hell-bent on relocating the school to an hotel building a mile from the existing site.

That same month I received a two-page missive from Hill implying his financial position was less secure than I imagined. In view of the non-existent relationship with my tenant, the brazenness of the opening paragraph, in which he referred to me as a friend, defied belief.

Alluding to the proposal to move the school to other premises, he came up with the outrageous suggestion that I should provide a cash sum of two hundred thousand pounds up front of the deal. He went on to say that the premium would help pay Bob Collinge off and also act as a contribution towards the project.

He made an alternative suggestion for me to gift him one of the school buildings with a market value of half a million pounds. When I reported these proposals to my accountant, he was struck dumb with astonishment.

I had taken the decision to sell the business and rent out the premises to reduce the stress and provide myself with a pension.

By relinquishing the lease I would be left with an empty school, no income and a lot of hassle. Hill was crazy to think I would be foolish enough to pay him a large premium to assist him in a scheme detrimental to my interests.

Unwilling to agree to the termination of the lease, I reminded him he must honour all obligations to me before I would accept back the premises for which he was legally responsible. Undeterred, he instructed architects to draw up plans for the extension of the out-of-town hotel that would provide quarters for the new establishment. I believed the scheme to be fraught with difficulties, particularly with regard to planning issues. But rather than be accused of sour grapes, I held my peace.

Hill came to see me to discuss his plans in greater depth. He told me the projected outgoings for the relocation project had doubled to the staggering total of four million pounds!

In shock, I pondered long and hard before venturing to ask, 'But where's the money coming from?'

'Two million will be raised through the bank; the balance will be provided by parental donations.'

I had heard some optimistic musings in my time, but this one took the biscuit. Parents would never be persuaded to subscribe absurd amounts towards a scheme in which the school owner was the beneficiary. Hill must have been incredibly blinkered to have imagined otherwise.

Convinced he was intent on moving the school, I had to consider alternative uses for the premises. Contrary to my tenant's assumptions, the last thing I wanted was to develop the site. My preferred option would be to arrange a lease with another school. Discreet approaches made to the governing body of a nearby independent school elicited no response.

Other than the unlikely acquisition of the buildings as an hotel or nursing home, the only practical solution was for me to sell for redevelopment. I quickly found the property world to be a minefield in which the unwary are cheated with alarming regularity. The more surveyors, architects and builders I met, the more confused and anxious I became. Not before planning permission had been granted would I have an accurate idea of the site's development potential. Hill seemed happy for me to sweat it out in a state of uncertainty, knowing my plans would remain undetermined until the lease had been rescinded.

A chance meeting with a friend led to my discovering by an amazing coincidence that a former pupil of mine named Adam was about to take legal action against Hill for the recovery of a debt. The claim resulted from an investment he made in 1990 when my tenant had been boss of ISM Schools Limited, a group that had managed three preparatory schools and operated an educational advisory and tutoring service in London and the south of England. My suspicions intensified because no mention had been made on Hill's CV of either ISM or several other companies in which he had held directorships.

Exasperated by Hill's unfulfilled promises and cat-and-mouse tactics, Adam's patience finally ran out. He decided the time had come to institute bankruptcy proceedings against his debtor. Backed into a corner, Hill was again bold enough to ask for my assistance in a situation that was no concern of mine.

'Could you, as his old head, possibly speak to Adam and bring him to his senses?' he entreated. 'I've got a solicitor involved, but think Adam might take more notice of you, were you to phone him.'

In view of our strained relationship, in no way was I prepared to attempt to do his dirty work. I told him it would be better for him or his solicitor to deal direct with Adam. Hill then asked if I would give my personal guarantee in the sum of £125,000 for six months to enable him to secure a short-term overdraft at Lloyds Bank. As an inducement, he offered me a twenty per cent cash interest payment on the guaranteed sum.

Before I was able to give a negative response to this dubious request, Hill advised me he had solved the problem. A reliable source informed me that the amount owed to Adam had been covered by a loan from a parent of the school.

Under the terms of the lease, the tenant was obliged to redecorate the interior and exterior of the school premises at least once every three years. After my surveyor had carried out his annual inspection in May 1997, he told me little work had been undertaken and that clearly there had been a breach of covenant.

Seeing that Hill was in no mood to cooperate, I contacted his erstwhile partner, Bob Collinge. As a signatory of the lease, he remained legally committed until such time as the break clause had been implemented. Bob gave me disturbing news about Hill's excessive borrowings. It had recently led to the bank's refusal to sanction any more cheque payments, a cataclysmic state of affairs that very nearly brought about the closure of the school. Bob reassured me the school's future had been safeguarded by the rescue efforts of a more tolerant bank. He gave me his word that the necessary property repairs would be dealt with as a matter of priority.

By August it had come to my attention that Hill was again in breach of the lease by trading through a limited company, a step he had taken without soliciting my approval. He was prepared to ride roughshod over any obstacle that crossed his path, providing it suited his own self-interested agenda.

I inspected the school premises with the bursar before the start of the new academic year, horrified at the state of neglect in evidence. Apart from minor decoration carried out in one building, the list of outstanding works had, for the most part, been disregarded. I could now see why, from the outset, Hill had kept himself well distanced from me. With so much to hide, it must have been an irritation that my home was situated a mere stone's throw from his office.

Hill's refusal to deal with the backlog of decorations and repairs led to my taking legal advice. Following a meeting with my solicitor, a Section 146 notice was served on my tenant, setting the wheels in motion for his ultimate eviction.

Looking more fully into the situation, I discovered the position less clear-cut than imagined. To persuade Hill to comply with the provisions of the lease, or for a court to dispossess him of the tenancy, would be a long-drawn-out process. Confident I would do nothing to bring about the destruction of the school, he opted to play a waiting game rather than take any action. The surveyor had sent Hill a full list of dilapidations, specifying 246 items requiring attention at an estimated cost of fifty thousand pounds. Angered that he was continuing to drag his feet, I asked what his plans were for the completion of the work.

'I'm sorry we're a little behind our targets, but I can assure you the maintenance team has been working flat out,' he ventured cheerfully. 'I'll let you have a timetable showing our proposals by the end of the week.'

Eight weeks went by, with still no contact from my tenant. I was furious to think he was again cocking a snook at his unduly patient landlord. When at last I issued an ultimatum, he hurled abuse at me, suggesting the only way to settle our differences was to have a punch-up!

Shortly after the altercation, Hill instigated the removal of family portraits from the building dedicated to my parents' lifelong efforts. The sole purpose of this gesture had been to hit me where it hurt most. As well as insulting the memory of my late father, he had maligned the reputation of my mother, without whose labours the school would have long since ceased to function. This ill-natured act symbolised Hill's severance of all links with my family.

Abandoning the relocation scheme, he found another site that caught his fancy. Hill must have rubbed his hands with relish at the thought of profits generated from yet another venture financed through the capital of others. Bad-mouthing me at every opportunity, he attributed his financial woes to the rent I charged. After the deduction of the rent, I knew the school was making a substantial profit out of which were taken Graham and Gillie Hill's drawings. Had pupil numbers reached capacity levels, profits would have been a great deal higher.

There was no excuse for Hill to have ignored the building maintenance requirements, or reduce to the bare bones expenditure on educational resources. Properly managed, the school was a first-rate business, rendering the owners a good living, with more than sufficient left over for the worthwhile reinvestment of surplus funds. What I wanted to know was where all the money had gone.

It came as no surprise that his second attempt to move the school failed to materialise. Dreaming up schemes that lacked all practical reasoning, he was a master in the art of subterfuge. Bank borrowings had escalated so much that the school's survival was again at risk. It was as well the staff were unaware it was touch and go whether they received their monthly salaries. Scrounging fifty thousand pounds from another trusting parent, Hill became more daring with his pleas for help.

Bob Collinge was meanwhile getting hot under the collar, alleging Hill had repeatedly reneged on his promise to repay one hundred and fifty thousand pounds still owed following the dissolution of the partnership. Bob was especially vulnerable. His co-signatory failing to pay the rent or be sued over the maintenance requirements, it would have fallen on him to stump up in Hill's place.

Frustrated by the deadlock, Bob decided to force Hill to invoke the break clause under the terms of the partnership agreement. In April 1998, four years after selling the business, I was given notice of the termination of the lease, to take effect one year later. Relieved though I was at the thought of being rid of an ungovernable tenant, my overriding concern was for the children's security and for the school to continue under more scrupulous management.

Until I received a telephone call from the chief executive, Peter Aughterson, I had not heard of Asquith Court Schools, an organisation established in 1989 which owns and manages over thirty independent schools throughout the south of England. Declaring he wanted to take over the lease from Graham Hill, he said he would be in touch again later.

Seven weeks went by before Peter Aughterson paid me a visit. There was an arrogance about his manner to which I immediately took exception. Behaving as if he was seeking to purchase a sausage factory, rather than secure the future of a prestigious school, he made no mention of his attitudes as prospective tenant or of the rent he was prepared to pay.

As soon as I discovered Hill had at one time worked with Asquith Court and was described as a friend by Peter Aughterson, I assumed I would not be the one to receive preferential treatment in any deal on offer. Knowing Asquith Court was going to have to pay over the odds to cover Hill's massive liabilities, the shock was less pronounced when my solicitor informed me I was being asked to accept a reduction in the rent.

An agreement in principle was eventually reached, after which I asked for two days to consider the proposals. Providing his company consented to making the five-yearly rental increases inflation-linked, I told Peter Aughterson I would be willing to proceed. He gave me a flat refusal, saying the deal was off. I at once advised Hill of the turn of events, asking him to refrain from making an announcement to staff and parents until such time as further talks had taken place.

Two days later, I gleaned some staggering news from a parent that set alarm bells ringing. Former professional wrestler Tony Walsh, who runs a thriving security company, lost no time in telling me a letter had been sent by Hill to all the parents. In this he stated he had transferred the business of the school into the ownership of Asquith Court Schools Limited. In the same envelope, a separate letter had been sent by Asquith Court, confirming the disclosure.

I faxed Asquith's solicitors to find out what was going on. Based on the instructions they received, the misrepresentation of the facts in their reply was so great that it bore no resemblance to the truth. It was going to need a miracle for me to be able to trust either Hill or Asquith Court in future dealings.

A long-standing friend, Tony Walsh was one of a small number of people in whom I felt able to confide. Remembering the way the school had been run prior to Hill's arrival, Tony expressed concern at the decline in confidence and a worsening of staff morale. He was well aware, as were certain other parents, that financial collapse was imminent. Deeply conscious of the seriousness of the situation, he knew it would not take much for my patience finally to snap.

In subsequent discussions, Peter Aughterson remained high-handed and remote. He endeavoured to bully and play games with my emotions, using every device imaginable to get me to agree to his rapacious terms. Indifferent to the love my family and I had invested in the school for two generations, he displayed a fish-cold frostiness throughout our dealings. Not once did he attempt to demonstrate the quality of the Asquith Court empire by inviting me to see one of their many schools at work. There was nothing to suggest under Asquith's amorphous ownership they would perform as managers and tenants any better than the artful Hill had done.

Grief-stricken in a way too painful to express, I made the most difficult decision of my lifetime. Three weeks before Christmas, I was in serious discussions with builders. The school site was up for grabs for redevelopment.

After the news was leaked to the press, it was panic stations. Unprepared to admit he was in any way at fault, Hill pointed the finger of blame in my direction. He formed a parents' action group whose purpose it was to prevent the school from closing. Giving an Oscar-like performance in a packed school hall, Hill revealed he had held talks with a backer over relocating the school to a new and better site. Hyping up his audience into a state of euphoria, he inveigled the parents into giving an overwhelming show of hands to support his action plans. To add credence to the genuineness of his presentation, the entire staff stood up as a demonstration of their loyalty to the school.

The occasion had been so brilliantly stage-managed that onlookers were in no mood to listen to dissenters. Tony Walsh, who had already done some homework, was not to be suppressed. He challenged Hill to confirm or deny if the school had an overdraft of more than five hundred thousand pounds with the Royal Bank of Scotland.

Hill replied, 'It isn't true that the school has an overdraft of half a million and we don't bank with the Royal Bank of Scotland.'

What Hill did not admit was that the bank to which the school was indebted for a similar sum was the Bank of Scotland. Annoyed to have lost round one on a slip-of-the-tongue technicality, Tony was more determined than ever that the truth should come out.

Parents' action group member Dr Robert Ashford also had suspicions. He and his wife, Sheena, carried out extensive research into Hill's business background, including the extraction of information from records at Companies House. Prior to acquiring the school from me, it was discovered Hill owned a number of prep schools easily accessible from London, where the group's extravagantly appointed offices were based. There had been Daneshill in Stratfield Turgis, Hampshire; Great Ballard in

Chichester; Park in Bournemouth and part-ownership somewhat later of Claremont in St Leonards. During the past decade, a string of companies he operated to run the schools collapsed after hitting serious financial problems. Monies owed to creditors for just two of the companies totalled £1,460,000 in 1991.

Hill had dishonoured his undertakings to me, putting me through four years of wretchedness. Hiding behind a façade of respectability, he systematically over a period of years inflicted great stress and worry on hundreds of families. I was unprepared to offer him, or anyone with whom he was connected, a new lease on my let-go properties. Nothing would have induced me to change my mind.

A few days before Christmas, I was contacted by Wynford Dore, the man who was soon to prove to be our good Samaritan. A successful entrepreneur, with a passion for education, he had recently established a new company, The Education Partnership, with the purpose of creating a select group of private schools devoted to the pursuit of excellence.

Wynford saw the school's imminent closure as a business opportunity. Given closer financial control and substantial reinvestment, he knew his group was well qualified to remedy the ills. So much was I in despair of human nature by this time that, were it not for his patent sincerity, and the courteousness of his approach, I would almost certainly have rejected his proposals out of hand. What Wynford had to say made fundamental good sense. I trusted him instinctively, warming to the idea of a possible alliance that would be fruitful to us both and to the school.

The following day I met Wynford's board of directors, referred to by him as 'the troops'. One of its key members, Gareth Newman, had recently been honoured by the Blair government with a CBE for his services to education. As principal of Brooke Weston City Technology College in Corby, he had created one of the most highly acclaimed and radical schools in Europe. Not only is Gareth an educational guru, he positively effervesces with a confident enthusiasm that is breathtakingly refreshing.

Discussions with the board focused on child-related issues, technological innovation and the world of academia. Not once were financial matters discussed or even thought about. Delighted to find our philosophies were aligned so closely, the most compelling recommendation, in my view, was that these were honourable people, who were more than adequately equipped to fortify and run our badly damaged school.

A letter of intent and heads of agreement were signed by Wynford Dore and myself, offering The Education Partnership the security of a long-term lease. After the company Hill had set up to run the school went into liquidation, he had no option other than to resign as principal. He and Gillie departed a few days later, leaving behind a trail of debts, masses of problems and some very angry parents. The arrival of Wynford's team in the nick of time can only be described as providential. With dynamic new management in place, the school's future was assured.

Gareth Newman made this pledge to all the parents: 'It is my responsibility to protect its values, vision and future by creating, with the principal and the staff, one of the finest preparatory schools in the country. I do not intend to betray the confidence bestowed in me.'

A tall order perhaps, but if anyone is capable of restoring the school to perfect health, Gareth possesses the skills needed to prescribe the treatment. In turn, I could at last step back, confident I had upheld with honour my parents' and my own association with the school, to see it remain a respected place of learning.

In the Beginning

Before my birth in October 1937 my mother, it seems, became partial to green apples. This desire having been satisfied, she experienced heaving pains in her stomach region and immediately went into labour. My arrival was by Caesarean section, requiring my mother to remain for several weeks in the Victorian nursing home where my life began.

We enter the world as fragile, hopeful beings. There is an optimism in childhood which assumes naively that people are honourable, reliable and that life's path, even if mildly tortuous, always leads to happiness. I have mixed feelings and memories of my earliest years. I cannot remember having been idyllically content, but equally I do not recollect any periods of protracted misery.

My parents owned and ran Arnold Lodge, a small preparatory school for boys in a Midland spa town. Because of her professional duties, it was necessary for my mother to hire a nanny to look after me until I was two and a half years old. My mother insisted always on bathing and putting me to bed each night. My memories of Nanny are naturally slim. I do, however, vaguely recall our being approached by a 'Stop me and buy one' ice cream salesman when she was wheeling me in my pushchair in a country lane on the edge of town.

We escaped most of the traumas of the Second World War. My father had served over twenty years previously as an officer in the Royal West Kent Regiment. He had witnessed the pointlessness, the unnecessary loss of life, the tragic waste of the ill-managed 1914–1918 encounter known as the Great War. He spent three Christmases, including his twenty-first birthday, in the trenches in France, an experience that developed within him the emotional resilience only to be found in those who have suffered greatly.

He was eventually invalided out, having twice been seriously wounded. Shot through a lung, he had to have a rib removed.

Told he might never walk again, a further warning was that he would almost certainly never play the many sports he loved so much. He worked on a farm for three years to regain his strength. A tribute to his determination and courage is that he recovered sufficiently to play cricket for Kent 2nd XI and lead a normal life. Despite volunteering for military service in 1939, he was considered to be too old and unfit to serve his country again as a soldier. To be responsible for running a school in wartime England nevertheless enabled him to perform a valuable role.

The school expanded rapidly when large numbers of evacuees, mainly from London, settled in Warwickshire with the purpose of avoiding enemy bombs. Overcrowding was a social responsibility, so much so that my parents' sitting room became a classroom during the day. An attic room, despite lack of fire escape facilities, was converted into an unsafe extra dormitory. A few male teachers, mostly of mature years, supported the female staff contingent whilst all did their share of duty as air raid wardens.

At the start of the war the authorities advised my father to provide a spacious air raid shelter for the protection of staff and pupils. Soon after its completion, following a period of heavy rain, the shelter collapsed, calling for building work to be re-commenced. I can remember only once using this long trench, later covered with attractive flower beds, for the purpose which it was intended. Illuminated by car headlight bulbs, there was a damp curtain across the entrance to prevent access of poisonous gas. It was later felt it was safer for us to seek refuge in the school basement, where the ground level windows had been specially reinforced.

I was three years old when five hundred German bombers flew over the town of Leamington on the night of 14 November 1940 to ravage nearby Coventry in a devastating blitz. The planes dropped five hundred tons of high explosive bombs and thirty thousand incendiaries. For eleven hours Coventry was pounded into ruins. It is thought over one thousand men, women and children perished. Thousands more were injured. That night my parents looked northwards from their sitting room window, and it was as if nine mile distant Coventry were surrounded by daylight. The entire city was ablaze. The droning of enemy aeroplane engines, the menacing air raid siren alerts, are nightmare sounds that linger even now in my muddled thoughts of those far-off days.

My parents struggled hard to make ends meet. Although dedicated to the welfare of their charges, there were often times when their many cares and pressures taxed them greatly. Even at a very tender age I was aware of the stresses and strains which consistently bore down on them; it pained me to see them working so hard, with seemingly little reward other than that of knowing they were doing their best. The overcrowding at the school increased their burden of responsibility, especially as some of the masters, either wartime conscientious objectors or elderly public school teacher rejects, were not up to the task for which they were employed.

Many of the boys attending the school were rough and unruly. My father did his best to maintain good discipline, achieved by shouting fiercely at the malefactors, of whom there were several. His face would go an ugly puce colour whenever he lost his temper and I became concerned for his health; a regular tension pain in the pit of my stomach was a daily occurrence. One of the masters with a French-sounding name was reputed to have used a cricket stump with a nail in it for the enforcement of law and order. I became increasingly upset to witness situations which were affecting my parents' well-being and over which I had no control. I would have liked to have had a brother or sister with whom to share my anxieties, but this was not to be.

In those days, infectious illnesses seemed to strike an entire community at one and the same time. I remember the occasion when most of the dormitories became sickrooms in order to accommodate the many boarders who had contracted chickenpox. I was one of the infected patients. Boys with varying degrees of itchiness scratched away at the spots, despite the attempts of the lady matron helpers to prevent this from happening.

Ted Edgar, destined in years to come to be a celebrated showjumper, occupied the bed opposite mine. He was without question the most troublesome boy in the school. His father came to enquire about Ted's behaviour, with seemingly little concern for the boy's state of health. When my father reported that Ted had yet again been an infernal nuisance, Mr Edgar, a large hot-tempered farmer with a florid complexion, boomed angrily, 'I'll take the bloody stick to him.' This he did there and then, much to the consternation of boy witnesses. Ted was eventually expelled from the school and other educational establishments. His wildness and aggression, for which he has often hit the headlines, may well have resulted from the violence he experienced as a youngster.

The war was coming to a close. To celebrate VE Day on 8 May 1945, as a defiant gesture late that evening, my parents switched on all the lights at the front of the school building, discarding the blackout blinds. The boarders were then treated, myself included, to a tour of the town where we witnessed glorious light in abundance, much jollity and our first glimpse of drunkenness.

Victory was also marked in another way. Boarders and staff were taken as a special treat on the back of a lorry provided by Mr Edgar to a gymkhana, held in the grounds of Stoneleigh Abbey. The boys were divided into small groups, each of which was the responsibility of one of the teachers. I was in Mr Shrewsbury's group. He disappeared into a tent that was serving free beer, leaving the boys he was supposed to be supervising, some of whom were very young, to fend for themselves. When the appointed hour arrived for us all to meet up at the lorry and return to school, Mr Shrewsbury was nowhere to be seen. The adults knew, of course, what he was up to, but the cat was put well and truly among the pigeons when I shrieked out at the top of my voice for all to hear, 'But we can't go without Mr Shrewsbury!' Attempts to depart discreetly were, in consequence, ruined.

The sequel to this incident was that it uncovered the fact Mr Shrewsbury had a reputation for heavy drinking. It was rumoured he had on occasion been conveyed back drunk to his lodgings in a wheelbarrow after pub closing time. My father's patience vanished altogether when Mr Shrewsbury, a young man with thick red hair, shouted at him one day at tea in front of both staff and boarders. A bitter and noisy argument then followed, culminating in Mr Shrewsbury's public sacking. I thought a fight would ensue. If it had done, I would not have rated father's chances against the bigger and younger man. If only the floor had opened up, enveloped me and I had been transported far away from the scene during those few dreadful moments! Instead, I sat dumbfounded and sick inside, incapable of coping with an exhibition of malevolence and anger so close to home. Finally Mr Shrewsbury stormed out, frothing, spluttering, threatening and swearing. We never saw him again.

Not having experienced anything different, I had been unaware of any wartime deprivations. My mother, who did most of the cooking at the school throughout the war, strove to see that we ate reasonably well, despite the shortages. A matron once literally forced me to eat burnt custard, telling me how lucky I was to have it. Apart from that injustice, I had no reason to complain about the food. Three cheers for the food were given at end-of-term assemblies, led by the head boy, as a tribute to my mother's conscientious efforts, a tradition which carried on for many years.

I had never before seen a banana until one night my father returned home from the Conservative Club with a look of triumph on his face. He produced from his pocket a sad-looking specimen, wrinkled, bruised, mushy, overripe, black with age and shrivelled not unlike a chipolata. 'This', he said, 'is for you, Jonathan!' He handed it over to me tenderly, as if parting with a family heirloom. With my mother's help, the skin was removed from the banana; its meagre contents were carefully cut into small pieces and placed in a bowl. Sugar was sprinkled liberally, with milk added. I sat at the kitchen table to devour the exotic delicacy. It was my most exciting meal ever.

Soon after the war ended, news filtered through that a shop in the backstreets of Leamington was selling ice cream. The information was investigated and verified. A representative from the school joined the long queue outside the suddenly popular shop, with instructions to buy sufficient ice cream for all the pupils. Far from being the gastronomic experience we had expected, although the ice cream had plenty of ice, there was seemingly no cream at all. If the tasteless dish was the ice cream we had heard so much about, we decided we would prefer to stick to the old faithfuls of spotted dick or rice pudding. At least they were edible.

There were two resident bachelor masters at the school, Dr Jones and Mr Walden. They were close friends and shared a bedroom, which was very unusual, even in those times. Dr Jones insisted that all the boys plastered down their hair smartly with Brylcreem or water, a bizarre habit that nevertheless made us feel very grown-up. My only other memory of the pair is that Mr Walden used to follow Dr Jones about like a devoted shadow. An objective observer would have been suspicious of their relationship.

The two men planned to set up their own school locally. In the middle of the night when my parents were asleep, they invaded Father's study in order to discover the names and addresses of all the parents, to whom they sent a circular letter. The school they were to open, the circular stated, would be better and cheaper than Arnold Lodge. Thus it was that Ardmore School set up in opposition, supported by a number of parents who immediately transferred their sons, entrusting them to the uncertainties of the new venture. This happening coincided with the anticipated departure of the evacuees from the Midlands now that the war was over. Pupil numbers at Arnold Lodge dropped sharply.

My father was sincere, high-principled and industrious but never a businessman. He chose to attempt to expand the school rather than to rationalise, which is what he should have done, in response to the lessening of demand for places. He rashly purchased a large house, Briarfield, in a neighbouring street as a separate junior department. Unfortunately planning permission precluded the garden from being used as a play area for the boys; furthermore, a busy road had to be crossed when junior pupils and staff returned to the main school for lunch each day. Numbers continued to drift downward and six years later Briarfield was forced to close. Some considerable time later, the property was sold at a substantial loss.

The political undercurrents of my parents' troubles and the reasons for their constant tenseness were not readily apparent to me. The school seemed to rush from one crisis situation to another with such speed and regularity that each day presented new problems, worries, let-downs, heartaches. Unknowingly, my parents' anxieties were transmitted to me with a poignant despair that seemed to be asking me, a mere child, to offer help. There was nothing I could do apart from observe with wretched frustration the gradual deterioration of their gritty spirit that had remained indomitable and for which they had been admired throughout the war. The school was capturing all their energy and more; they worked with such intensity that there was no time ever for them to take stock or to plan. Fun, humour, carefree pleasures and the joys of family life were to us unknown.

I was aware that my parents loved me, but the affection they bestowed upon me was insufficiently warm and physical for me to feel safe, of real value or to shut out the loneliness. Being an only child increased my sense of responsibility, knowing that all their hopes and aspirations were invested in me. One of the factors governing my insecurity may well have been that too much was expected of me. I was strictly reared, an example of which is that the red dressing gown, given to me one Christmas and enabling me to dress up as Santa Claus, disappeared whenever I was naughty.

Less than perfect behaviour thereafter became synonymous with deprivation, a guilt sensation that haunts me even now. My mother had two ways of getting me to behave in the desired manner. She would either spank me, using her hand or a slipper, or attempt the much more effective blackmail approach of bursting into tears if I argued or disobeyed. It was at this time that I began to masturbate, a supposedly sinful practice that, with increasing frequency, I carried out under the blankets when the lights were out.

My vivid imagination would often run riot. For some reason I was convinced that my father was about to leave home. There was a big sense of relief when he returned from a straightforward local errand. I also imagined he would soon be ill and would die. These and other hidden anxieties I bottled up in my mind, unable to communicate my concerns to anybody.

There had been talk about my being sent to boarding school. My parents were too busy to give me the time and attention I needed; they argued that I would benefit from the independence being away from home would be bound to give me. They gradually sowed the seeds in such a way that attempts were obviously being made to get me positively excited at the prospect of attending boarding school. I was taken to visit the school of their choice. It was decided that I would start there several months later.

Meanwhile the indoctrination and persuasion continued. 'It is a lovely school,' enthused my mother. 'They have a clock golf course, marvellous grounds and a marionette theatre. In the summer you wear sunhats and can go camping. You can even take your own tent!'

I was not interested in clock golf, marionette theatres, sunhats or tents. What I wanted was a secure home from which to proceed into the wider world. I was unready for the rigours of tough residential community living. Apprehension grew as the awful day approached. I expected optimistically to wake one day to find the plan was a bad dream.

My father was a cricket fanatic. It is not surprising that his passion for the game inspired me early on; there was a bat in my hand almost as soon as I could walk. I spent pleasurable times at the local cricket club where my father played. Batting was his speciality. With enormous enthusiasm he passed on his knowledge to the keenest boy players on a small patch of grass surrounded by a protective net at the rear of the school, adjacent to the redundant air raid shelter.

Because of the closeness of certain buildings, the hard balls used at net practice often inflicted damage to nearby windows. The greatest hazard was Mr Gordon Brown's greenhouse. He was the owner of the next-door property, Lillington Lodge. At the back of his garden was the large greenhouse of which he was particularly proud. Gordon Brown-baiting was not a sport in which we indulged consciously, even though a broken pane from a cricket ball in his greenhouse resulted in Mr Brown giving vent to a rage of gigantic proportions. We were fascinated and scared by his dramatic outbursts. For the second time that particular summer a ball hit over the wall had shattered the glass in his fragile edifice. Mr Brown, an elderly man well covered from good eating, turned up at the school's front door as quickly as he was able, demanding at once to see the offending child.

'Where is the boy who wrecked my greenhouse?' he thundered. 'When I catch him I'm going to skin him like a rabbit!'

One day I persuaded one of my father's cricketing friends, who happened to be a bowler, to play with some of us in the school playground. The game itself was uneventful, except that it was thrilling to play with one of my childhood heroes, whom we nicknamed Robbo. A few days later Robbo presented me with a new cricket bat. I could not believe my luck. The drawback was that because the bat was full size it was as much as I could do to lift it, let alone use it effectively for scoring runs.

I was due to captain the school under IX cricket team in a match against my future boarding school. The visiting team arrived punctually at the cricket field. They were smart, toffee-nosed and wore crimson caps with a black palm tree badge. I did not like the look of them at all. Having won the toss, I elected for Arnold Lodge to bat. Ignoring my father's advice that a smaller bat was essential, I went out to the crease proudly wielding Robbo's treasured gift. I was clean bowled first ball, much to the amusement of our superior visitors, who sniggered as I returned embarrassed to the pavilion.

After the tea interval thick black clouds overshadowed the ground, to be followed by flashing lightning, thunderclaps and torrential rain of such magnitude that the match had to be abandoned. If the afternoon's events were to be interpreted as auguries, it was clear to me I was going to hate my boarding school.

Prep School Days

It showed wisdom on the part of my parents to send me to a boarding preparatory school when I was eight. It would have been difficult for them and for me had I remained a pupil at their own school, but I bitterly resented being packed off to an unfamiliar environment at a time when I badly needed the reassurance of the routine of a normal home.

In those days it was fashionable for middle-class children to be educated at preparatory schools on the south coast. The school selected for me was in the heart of England, outside the small town of Henley-in-Arden, only ten miles from my home. Because of its rural setting, I immediately felt isolated and disorientated. Being the product of a town, I have always been more at ease in a busy city, in preference to a sleepy backwater.

I woke on my first morning at boarding school and looked out on cedar trees dominating the large lawn close to the dormitory. I felt trapped and resolved there and then to run away. After breakfast, I separated myself from the orderly line of pupils as we left the dining hall, making for the long drive which led to the main Birmingham–Stratford road. Running breathlessly, I was determined to get home as soon as humanly possible. Conflicting thoughts raced through my mind as I listed quite logically the numerous reasons why I already assumed I was going to dislike my new school.

I must have looked a strange sight that bright September morning in my smart grey suit. Because of the removal of all signposts, a wartime precaution to confuse potential enemy invaders, a mile or so out of Henley I had to ask a village shop-keeper the way to Warwick. She viewed me with great suspicion and asked me why I was all alone on the road with so far to walk on foot.

'My father's car is parked round the corner. He wants to know if we are on the right road for Warwick.'

When I was seen to continue running, with no motor vehicle in sight, the shopkeeper must have alerted the police. As I approached the outskirts of Warwick, a car screeched to a halt beside me. I jumped into the ditch to hide. The headmaster sprang out of his car, grabbed me and returned me to his school, a prisoner.

Homesickness is not easy to describe or explain. Some psychiatrists say it is brought about by a mother or father's subconscious unwillingness to part with a child. Parental sorrow of this kind can be sensed quickly by those who are absent from their homes, not unlike a guilt reaction. I was quite certain my mother and father would miss me desperately now that I was away from them. I never for one moment doubted my parents' sincerity or the depth of their love for me. Life at home had been so tense, so confused, so formal and so undemonstrative from the point of view of our being able to express our feelings and affections openly that I had no calm picture in my mind of the protected haven that I wanted home to be.

I again found myself burdened with a sense of impending doom, wondering whether the flimsy base would still be intact after a twelve-week term away. The fact we were only allowed home for two nights in the middle of the term, with no weekend exeats, increased the agony and sense of despair. Three months seemed like an eternity.

The headmaster's wife looked after me in the private part of the house once I was back at the school, releasing me from all lessons for the remainder of the first day of term. She was assisted in her efforts by one of her two daughters, Victoria. They were kind and consoling. They attempted to bribe me with sweets and used every trick in the book to win my confidence. I remained apathetic, intransigent, sullen. They could have offered me the entire world to no useful purpose. Any efforts they made to quell my depression were met with negative responses. It was as if I was paralysed by an inertia that was nullifying any will I might have had to see reason. I sobbed my heart out until I was devoid of all sense of what was going on around me. This helpless sensation must have been endured for at least two days. I became weak, listless, with gripping pains all over through lack of food and sheer mental anguish. My whole body began to ache. The ability to offer anything at all of myself was numbed, shrunken, with what little personality there might have been hidden by the depth of the hurting. I was unable to identify with a living soul, nor did I wish to try to do so.

Some of the boys made praiseworthy attempts to get me to see matters in proportion by explaining that the school was not as bad as it must have appeared to me. 'You'll soon settle down and will enjoy it here in time,' they encouraged.

'Oh no, I won't. I am going to run away again and again until my parents have me back home for keeps.'

It is said homesickness is generally overcome after a period of about three weeks, providing there is little or no parental contact during that time. My mother and father visited me briefly one Saturday early in the term; apart from that I was left to my own devices. Very gradually, I settled down to the routines of the school, making the best of it, bearing in mind the rigid restrictions placed on all of us. To be surrounded by fields, far away from the noisier town life with which I was familiar, exaggerated the sense of loneliness. Even at the end of five years at the school, I had not properly adjusted to the rural setting.

My first year at boarding school coincided with one of the coldest winters on record. There were coal fires in some of the classrooms; elsewhere there was no form of heating whatsoever. We were exceedingly cold. I suffered from the most unpleasant chilblains and on one occasion the discomfort was so great that it was impossible for me to write.

I showed red swollen fingers to the matron, who proffered little encouragement when she barked, 'What do you expect me to do about it?' My chilblains rapidly disappeared whenever I returned home for the mid-term break or at the end of term. Since those grim days I have rarely bothered with gloves, nor have I in adult life been plagued with a repeat dose of sores, resulting from extreme cold or circulatory problems.

My second half-term holiday was mercifully extended. Mother went down with mumps, which prevented me from returning to boarding school on account of my being in quarantine. I was delighted to attend lessons at my parents' school for the next few weeks, wishing I had been able to continue my education there.

I was very insecure at the time, needful of physical reassurance. The temporary matron, who was taking my mother's place, was a dark-haired beauty, Miss Russell-Wilkes. Aged in her early twenties, she had at one time been an hotel secretary. Despite my being only nine, her magnetic attractiveness riveted me with a suddenness that quite took my breath away. In the middle of the night I would tiptoe from the sickroom where I slept to seek refuge in Miss Russell-Wilkes' bed. Here, much to my surprise and delight, I was rewarded with the generous cuddles I must have felt I had missed in babyhood.

I was soon to become possessive of Miss Russell-Wilkes' affections in a way that was most unhealthy. I became jealous of her boyfriend, Frank, a local farmer. My nightly visits came abruptly to an end when she began to use some noxious-smelling cream on her person that would have discouraged the most eager of lovers. I suspect she was endeavouring to let me down gently, viewing me sympathetically as an oversensitive little boy who would have found outright rejection difficult to take. She felt sorry for me and was sufficiently caring to risk upsetting her employers by giving fleeting warmth and solace to their only son.

I had become an expert on film stars and the cinema. I took the trouble to write to all the big names in England and America, asking for their autographed photographs. I built up an impressive collection, which supplemented the many books I had purchased on the subject. I held a special admiration for James Mason, whose acting skills I placed top of my list. I would not settle down happily in the school dormitory after bath time unless I had with me my film reference books and biographical encyclopaedia of the stars, which I would study avidly. My knowledge of the subject became considerable.

It was my ambition to be a film star. I wrote to various film directors asking if I might be given a screen test. In the absence of a response, I turned to more dramatic methods to demonstrate my potential star quality. When out shopping with my mother during the holidays, I threw myself down on the pavement, pretending to be dead to the astonishment of passers-by.

'Get up, you stupid little boy,' shouted my mother.

'No, I won't,' I replied. 'I'm only trying to prove what a good actor I am!'

I told school friends that my mother was Anna Neagle, the film star, and that my father was her director husband, Herbert Wilcox. It was sad that I felt the need to lie about my parentage. I was ashamed of their ordinariness, of their honest conventionality, not realising that my tales were making me a laughing-stock among contemporaries.

Some time later, when practising hockey skills in the Quarry in Shrewsbury with some childhood acquaintances, I pretended to be boy film actor John Howard Davies, whom I resembled strikingly. He had starred in *The Rocking-Horse Winner* and *Oliver Twist*. Queues of children pursued me for my autograph. I obliged them gleefully, imagination obscuring my real identity so that I was beginning to mistake fiction for fact.

The staff at my prep school were a miscellaneous bunch. The headmaster, Jack Nelson, known by us as Jacko, had inherited Acton House from his father. He was a tall, thin, aesthetic man with protruding and distinctly grey false teeth. Devout and dedicated, he was not a person whom I could have approached had I needed his help. In a distant way most of us respected him. He was, sad to say, a depressive and had to take one term off because of a nervous breakdown. This sudden and temporary departure mystified us all, but the more discerning recognised the nature of his illness. He retired relatively early to Chipping Campden, where he tragically put an end to his life by hanging himself.

Some of the staff were chronologically very ancient. Miss Cowden, privately known as Cowpat, had taught the headmaster mathematics many years previously; a conservative guess would have made her no less than seventy. She ruled her department with a rod of iron and terrorised us with her loud, rasping voice. She had the reputation for being a fine teacher. My impression was that she had little patience with anybody other than the quick learner, which mathematically speaking ruled me out. She had certain pet phrases, one of which she often spat out if displeased. 'If I had my way, I would have you thrashed till you couldn't even move. I would *really*.' It is hardly surprising that I always suffered from tummy pains, in anticipation of a double period with her on a Tuesday morning.

There was an elderly master by the name of Potts, who also possessed a raucous voice. On one occasion I was sharpening a pencil during a lesson and was misbehaving, trying to attract the attention of the class by pulling silly faces. Unknown to me, this foolishness had been spotted by Mr Potts. He crept up behind me stealthily and gave my rear quarters an almighty kick, sending me reeling several yards, causing substantial and immediate pain. I wonder what would happen today if a teacher were seen to be guilty of such brutality?

I was no angel. The kick up the backside was undeserved; a later sin, however, did merit strict measures. Our Latin master, Mr Robinson, could not control his classes. There were never riots in his lessons, although our behaviour was once quite scandalous. The classroom in which we were working was equipped with old-fashioned long desks, where half a dozen or so boys sat on the same bench side by side. As Mr Robinson was marking the work of the boys in front of us, we flicked the ink from our pens onto the back of his jacket and trousers. The incident resulted in an inquisition, presided over by Jacko, who was also an experienced magistrate. He was so nonplussed by our naughtiness that he seemed incapable of dealing with the offenders, none of whom owned up. The entire class was confined to the Big School Room for the remaining four weeks of the term. I dread to think what the outcome would have been had we confessed.

I am not certain that it involved the same ineffective master, but very probably it did. When we wanted to go to the lavatory, we were expected to ask: 'Please may I leave the room?' During a lesson I recall once making this particular request only to be told that I would have to wait until break. I was not aware of having a weak bladder at the time, which made my peeing on the floor all the more villainous. Mr Robinson (if it was he) dared not to punish me, having refused my initial request to 'leave the room'.

Talking of going to the loo, a strange rule existed at the school, whereby the eighty or so boarders were supposed to cross their names off a list displayed daily in the Big School Room, signifying that we had had our bowels opened. Lack of lavatory success resulted in Matron doling out some foul medicine. What seemed extraordinary to us was that failure to cross off our name was met with the kind of reprimand that forced us to regard the process of erasing the name as a much more important priority than that of recording the state of our bowels.

We were given the unproductive task of writing lines as a punishment for minor transgressions. A star and stripe system operated to reward good work and to draw to Jacko's attention those of us who had behaved badly in the classroom. Recipients of stripes waited meekly in a corner outside Jacko's study after breakfast, in fear and trembling of what consequences might ensue.

Canings were relatively rare, though a form of extra drill was a popular alternative. The half-hour's physical torture began with the criminals hanging from the wall bars in the gymnasium, after which we were made to run round gym or field with hands above our heads, until the pain was excruciating. Two dozen press-ups were thrown in for good measure to complete the sadistic punishment, a watered-down version of the milder chastisements that had been endured by members of the armed forces in prisoner-of-war camps in Japan and Germany.

By no means everything at Acton House was negative and discouraging. I was a sensitive boy and think that I experienced more difficulty in adapting to the life there than most of the others, who appeared to take things in their stride. Some of my experiences at the school were valuable and I remember with pleasure the influence of Mr Charles Stuart-Jervis, an able and dynamic teacher of English. He had at one time been an actor and he impressed us all with his well-tailored suits and impeccable appearance, which singled him out as a much more sophisticated man than his drab colleagues. He initiated a duplicated termly magazine, known as the *Acton House Echo*. I derived much pleasure from writing stories for this publication.

Prep school days for me highlighted my tendency to pursue certain specialised interests with a fanaticism that was almost paranoid in intensity; these bouts of totally consuming devotion to the current fad gave me time for little else while the mania lasted. I developed an exceptional ability as a table tennis player, winning the school trophy four years running. My father's dearest wish was for me to play cricket for England. With this in mind, he was planning after the preparatory school stage of my education to send me on to Repton School because its reputation for cricket was among the best in the country.

I suppose that most of us tend to remember facts and statistics which are of greatest interest to us. I was beginning to develop a memory of photographic accuracy, which has served me well throughout my life. Doubtless aided by the mechanical learning methods of the early post-war years, my memory stored up vast quantities of knowledge, not only of films and their stars, but also of county cricketers, match results and averages. When I was prompter for the school's marionette theatre production of *A Christmas Carol* I could recite the entire play by heart, repeating the words in my mind before finally going to sleep each night.

I spent much of my time during school holidays on my own. Not being sufficiently confident or extrovert to be able to make friends easily, I had to find ways of filling the empty hours. Most of my school friends lived in other areas, although the few I did see occasionally were often put off by my bossy manner. I was capable, too, of bullying if my companion was weak enough to allow himself to be intimated in this way. Being an only child had prevented me so far from knowing how to share. There was little to recommend me as a potential friend.

My continued interest in films led me often to visit a cinema, providing there was nothing better for me to do. Invariably I would go to the cinema unaccompanied. There was no difficulty in attending a U category film, but I had to ask to join an unsuspecting member of the public, usually some middle-aged female, whenever I wished to see a film that was suitable for adults only. One afternoon at the Clifton Cinema in Leamington, a man next to me began gently to brush his knee against my leg. At first I took no notice, but when he put his hand up my shorts and gave my penis a little squeeze, I was left in no doubt as to his intentions. I rushed out of the cinema, covering the mile or so journey home in record time. A trembling lip and pale face indicated my distress.

My parents quizzed me, of course, but I knew full well that had I related to them what had happened I would never again have been allowed to visit the cinema without a responsible adult escort.

Briarfield, the new junior school building purchased by my father, was large enough to provide us with separate family quarters in the holidays. I actually had my own bedroom, which was a vast improvement on having to occupy the school sickroom. One of the most welcome milestones in my entire childhood was the accomplishment at long last of having a proper base and a room that belonged to me. The substantial Victorian house possessed a spacious bathroom in which we kept my budgerigars, Jimmy and Jane. These birds and other personal items were transported in my father's Morris Ten car from Briarfield to Arnold Lodge and vice versa according to whether it was the beginning or end of a term. Though it was not ideal for our home to occupy five rooms, spread over four floors, we found it preferable to the cramped accommodation we had previously occupied during the frantic war years.

Much of my time was spent listening to the antiquated wireless set I had been given, capable only of tuning in to the Home Service and the Third Programme. I did not seem to mind that the content of many of the programmes was far too highbrow for someone of my age. Prolonged periods of isolation, with only the background noise of a voice or music to keep me company, helped to increase my sensitive awareness, as well as developing an imagination that would frequently lose touch with the realities around me. A special treat was for me to retire to my bedroom with beans on toast and an egg on top and listen to *Saturday Night Theatre*.

There was one friend with whom I had an affinity. Anthony Kaye, a boy of much the same age as me, joined me in a number of escapades. We were wicked enough to attempt to shoot birds with air rifles, but our initiation as private detectives was much more exciting. Donning trilby hats we would follow suspicious-looking characters we spied in the town. We made copious notes about them, drawing the most fantastic conclusions from our primitive observations. One poor man with the bulging Adam's apple and piercing eyes of a sufferer with thyroid problems was found by us to be guilty on sight because of his frightening appearance. He was subsequently referred to by us as 'the man with the staring eyes'. Night-times were more eventful still when we would, from a discreet distance, shine powerful torches into the faces of our suspects. Anthony was good fun to be with; there was rarely a dull moment when we were together.

Holidays at home were often colourless and dull. My parents arranged, however, on a couple of occasions for us to visit London. We stayed at the Regent Palace Hotel on the edge of Soho, just off Piccadilly Circus. The hotel was the most luxurious place I had ever seen in my life, although by London standards it was and still is a mediocre establishment. We had to wait for at least half an hour before the head waiter was able to find us a table at breakfast, so long were the queues of residents, all awaiting their turn. Anthony Kaye was able to outdo me by saying that when he visited London with his parents he had stayed at the Piccadilly Hotel, which was a cut above the more down-at-heel Regent Palace.

We did the usual sightseeing and attended some shows as well. After seeing *Treasure Island* one Christmas, my father treated us to a meal at the Trocadero restaurant. A fine band, with smartly jacketed musicians, provided music for dancing. An Egyptian waiter wearing a turban served us his special brand of coffee. I was learning there was a different world out there. Perhaps one day I was going to discover more about it.

The most poisonous feature of my childhood experiences is yet to be unveiled. When aged ten I came under the influence of a man who took advantage of the fact that I was a vulnerable and insecure child. It was some time before I appreciated his interest in me was rather odd, and in consequence the shock I felt when he finally exposed himself to me was like a thunderclap. His homosexual perversions were cleverly and deviously conducted. He had spent some years in Malaysia, where he informed me he had acquired certain black magic gifts which could, if necessary, be used to his advantage.

He wanted me to participate in the most appalling of rituals, saying that if I told anyone of his behaviour he would commit suicide by throwing himself in front of an oncoming train. I determined not to allow him to touch me again and would not cooperate with his disgusting demands.

There was, however, one later occasion when he inveigled me to a wood, where he stripped himself and forced me to urinate over him. This vile act left me in a state of stupefaction and utter revulsion, worsened by the realisation he had received sexual gratification at my expense, albeit that my understanding of such things at that time was virtually non-existent.

It was clever of him to suggest that his supernatural powers would at once indicate to him if his trust had been betrayed. I was petrified at his evil threats to end his own life, if reported. My disgust for all that had happened developed into a hatred of the man. Nevertheless I did not dare to divulge my tragic story, even to my parents, my only protection being the decision to avoid him in future and to have nothing whatever to do with him. This was not easy, but I succeeded in ignoring him and resolved to inform an adult should he attempt to interfere with me again.

The emotional damage done to me, as a result of this abuse, can never be quantified. There is little doubt I was scarred in a way that for a long time hampered my ability to form stable relationships in adult life.

Who knows what had made my abuser into the man he was? My estimate now is that he must have been aged about forty. He was square-jawed and had a swarthy, weather-beaten look about him, portraying himself as a person one associates with motor-bikes and tatty cars. With greasy fingernails, through constant tinkering with engines, he never looked clean somehow, wearing as one might expect grubby overalls and oil-stained garments. I shudder at the very thought of him even after all this time. I shall never forget his gruesome attempts to contaminate my development.

The highlight of summer terms back at Acton House for me was the cricket. By prep school standards I was a goodish medium pace bowler. I played regularly for the school 1st XI from the age of ten and was fortunate enough to capture lots of wickets in matches against other schools. I shaped well as a batsman in the nets, but was less successful when it came to the real thing. My delight at being awarded my cricket colours at the young age of eleven was unimaginable; no other achievement could possibly have produced greater joy.

When the weather was fine, we spent many spare moments in the evenings and weekends on the cricket field. Some boys pitched tents around the field's perimeter, pretending to be scouts or campers. Cricket fanatics such as myself had little space left in which to practise. One day when having a knockabout with friends, a hard ball from a neighbouring game smacked into my left temple with such force that I collapsed unconscious. I was dazed and badly shaken; when sufficiently recovered to be able to stagger up, anxious boys led me to Matron for attention. The callous spinster was no less dismissive than she had been when I had complained about my chilblains in the February of my second term at Acton House. She again sent me packing with a flea in my ear, ignoring totally the bruise on the side of my head and the possible dangers.

Neither of my parents liked the water; in fact, I do not think my father had ever swum. It was unknown for my mother and father to be seen in bathing costumes, even when on holiday. The fear I had developed for aquatic activity was quite out of proportion, bearing in mind any apprehension I might unwittingly have inherited. It was compulsory to spend half an hour each day in the unheated Acton House outdoor swimming pool throughout the second half of each summer term, irrespective of weather conditions.

I dreaded these sessions to such an extent that no day was pleasurable until the ghastly experience was over. I cannot be precise as to the root cause of my phobia. It is true I disliked parading my slender, uncovered frame before an audience, with the irrational imagining I was being ridiculed by other boys. The helpless, suffocating sensation of being submerged in cold water, with eyes, ears, mouth and nostrils sufficiently drenched, disabled, to panic me into gasping for the breath of life, was real enough. I was convinced that one day I would die from drowning.

Bitter Aloes was the nickname we gave to the PT master, Mr Allen. He was, we gathered, unqualified, but had served in the Royal Navy during the war. As a major part of our programme of physical exercise, he would instruct us to march in step round the gymnasium, whose shutters rather than windows opened out on to the cricket field. Many of us were highly amused by this formal procedure. After tense minutes of silent marching, some of us could no longer control our giggles, which signalled our nervous protest at the crazy drill. Mr Allen would then order us back to the changing room, where he lectured us ponderously for the remainder of the lesson on the evils of unwarranted mirth.

As well as being responsible for the PT, Mr Allen attended to certain groundsman's duties. On scorching hot days, wearing shorts and no shirt, his brown muscular body was a familiar sight as he used his scythe to good effect in the orchard paddock or at the edge of the cricket field. He increased his status in our eyes when, mounted on the sizeable motor-mower like a proud Indian prince, he saw to it that the grass of the field was manicured to suitable shortness. After the machine had been out of action for several weeks, in every available spare moment we were made to pick the stiff stalks of grass known as bents which had grown too long for the mower to remove. PT lessons were temporarily given over to this pastime, a consequence we much welcomed.

Mr Allen tried in vain to teach me how to swim, with the aid of a pole and other devices. The provision of a rubber ring, an obvious confidence booster, might have helped to translate failure into success. Had a prize been awarded at the school for the non-swimmer who showed the least courage, promise or inclination, I would have won hands down.

My final year at Acton House promised to open up new doors for me. I became one of the school's monitors, the equivalent to being a prefect. After a simple religious initiation ceremony, alongside the other new monitors, I was presented with the purple badge of authority that carried with it so much prestige in the school community. Jacko encouraged our best efforts by arranging regular meetings with his team of boy lieutenants. It is true that we operated more as policemen than as welfare officers; we were not shrewd enough to realise that we were, in fact, Jacko's personal spies. A doubtful monitor's privilege was the invitation we received to attend supper in Mr and Mrs Nelson's private dining room with the staff on certain Sunday evenings.

Conversation was always stiff and artificial on these occasions, at the end of which we would escape from the ordeal to our dormitories with some relief.

I took my monitor's duties most seriously. I was beginning to recognise that I preferred order to chaos and that satisfaction was to be gained from fastidious organisation. My strength as a leader was that I did not mind too much if I was unpopular with the other boys, providing I felt able to justify my actions. I tried to be scrupulously fair in all my dealings and in the use of the power with which I had been entrusted. A strong character was developing. A sense of pride made me intent upon proving myself to be one of the best monitors in the school.

It had been more or less assumed I would captain the Acton House 1st XI cricket team the following summer. When my future Repton housemaster informed my parents that he wanted me to take up my place there one term early, by which stage I would have reached the age of thirteen and a half, it meant that the opportunity for me to become the school's cricketing hero had been removed. I visited Repton to meet Mr Barnard, housemaster of the Orchard. I was astonished when he called me Jonathan, as up until then schoolmasters had only ever addressed me by my surname. Mr Barnard was eager to hear about my hobbies and he tried to elicit from me something about my academic strengths and of my intelligence, if any. I must have forgotten I had read most of the works of Dickens and much more besides by the age of eleven, because in answer to his question 'Do you read much?' I replied to his bewilderment that I spent more of my time writing than reading. 'If that's the case, you must do very little reading,' he commented drily.

I was the school's only Common Entrance examination candidate that February. I worked through the various papers in the headmaster's private dining room, in the presence of the vicar of Henley who acted as invigilator. I thought I had done reasonably well. A week later I was summoned to Jacko's study to be told condescendingly that I had been accepted by Repton, but no mention was made of my having actually passed the Common Entrance.

The results were variable. I had obtained high marks in French and English subjects, whereas mathematics and Latin marks were poor by comparison. Mr Bennett, head of French and Jacko's partner, was delighted with my performance in his subject. Miss Cowden, on the other hand, never forgave me for achieving less than fifty per cent in one of the three mathematics papers. She vowed never to speak to me again. She maintained her silence and ignored me for the remaining few weeks of my last term at Acton House. I was mistaken in thinking she had been pulling my leg; she was, it so happened, absolutely in earnest. Miss Cowden's unforgiving virulence of feeling was impossible for me to comprehend.

An unpleasant incident that same term marred what might have been a happier conclusion to my Acton House career. Mr Allen one day took a group of us on a ramble, allowing us to paddle in the stream bordering the school grounds, with the explicit instructions that we were not to permit water to get inside our wellington boots. I had to borrow someone else's boots because mine were missing, only to discover later that Jacko was on the warpath, tracking down the owners of boots with water stains inside. My boots, miraculously now back in place, bore the telltale marks of the heinous crime, requiring immediate retribution. Try as I did to explain that my boots had been removed from my locker, my excuse was not believed by Jacko, despite my being a monitor. It all seemed so trivial.

Disgruntled and miserable because of the lack of trust shown in me, I resigned from my position of responsibility. Jacko was taken aback, finding it hard to believe that I had dared to return to him the purple monitor's badge that meant so much to me. He endeavoured to persuade me to change my mind. I have never failed to react strongly to injustice, choosing to isolate myself from the common herd in preference to allowing fair play to be sacrificed. Jacko thus lost the services of a loyal monitor. Outwardly I exhibited no signs of emotion; deep down, however, I seethed with anger at the thought of the unreasonableness of the treatment that had been meted out.

Although sworn to secrecy not to report what had been said to them by Jacko in his very private talks, past leavers had given me advance warning of what was in store for me. The appointed hour arrived and I entered Jacko's sitting room, intrigued to know what lurid truths I was to hear. He did not beat about the bush and commenced, with not a moment's delay, by asking me a candid question that made me blush like a beetroot.

'Do you have any hairs growing near your cock?'

'Well, sir, a few, I think, sir.'

Other equally outrageous questions followed, with similar stilted responses on my part.

'What I want you to realise, Hall,' he went on to say, 'is that these changes in your body are a perfectly natural process in your physical development and are nothing to worry about.'

He stumbled on to talk about the birth of babies and the mysteries of sex. By this time he appeared so uncomfortable that I began to feel quite sorry for him. With mouth open wide, I listened incredulously to Jacko's ramblings about the birds and the bees. It was obvious he had delivered these same carefully chosen words on countless occasions in the past. By the time the soliloquy was over, my understanding of the unmentionable was more confused than ever.

Jacko's attributes were many. He was sincere, devoted to his school, punctilious and diligent to a fault. Unwilling to delegate, he gathered round him men and women staff with little or no initiative. He was a talented artist, as well as being a keen mountaineer and Outward Bound devotee. These qualifications, on top of his Clare College, Cambridge degree, made him impressive enough. But he lacked the most essential quality of all. He did not understand boys, nor did he relate to them at all.

Acton House was well thought of in those days, even though I am unable to look back upon my time there with any pleasure. The bad food and unnecessary regimentation will not easily be forgotten; it was the frequent unjustness that proved to be the worst aspect of all. My original premonition that I was going to dislike my first boarding school was spot on.

Repton (1)

The first boy I met at my Repton boarding house was a scholarly individual, who boasted to the matron that he had read over thirty books during the short Easter holiday. This put my meagre record to shame, by comparison, and I was hugely relieved when I discovered that this boy, the son of Professor Brogan of BBC fame, was not a typical Reptonian.

I had been placed in the bottom form with the 'dimwits', a rude awakening that confirmed I had not performed as well in the Common Entrance examination as I had imagined. I was very much in awe of the more quick-witted of my peers. To have found myself near to being last academically in the entire school did nothing to improve my already shaky confidence. In my life so far I had rarely been patted on the back in an attempt to encourage concealed talents to emerge. There had been plenty of stick; with the exception of prep school cricket colours, the carrot was conspicuous by its absence. An inferiority complex of gigantic proportions was developing, so ashamed was I of my intellectual deficiencies.

Len Cattley, my crusty, well into middle age form master, whose reputation for being the strict Priory housemaster went before him, did little to strengthen our belief in ourselves. He was capable of sarcasm, with mild bullying tactics thrown in. A skilled and caring schoolmaster would have been able to inspire the weaker brethren into producing their best efforts; Len Cattley, too intellectually bright to be able to adapt to the needs of the less able, stifled our will to succeed, unwittingly banishing eager enthusiasms from his classroom.

The Reverend Douglas Argyle, Dougie Argyle to us, taught the lowest Latin set; he was known to be a poor teacher. It did not take us long to realise we had already been dismissed as Latin duffers. By this time I was regretting I had not taken my Latin studies at Acton House more seriously. The folly of playing up

Mr Robinson for so many years had finally caught me out. Latin was an essential qualifying subject for entry to major universities. Doors were closed in consequence when, comparatively early on, I gave the subject up.

I also found I was out of my depth socially at Repton. Fathers with large, expensive cars and pinstripe suits, accompanied by glamorous ladies, exuding the self-assurance that tends to accompany affluence, was my perception of the parents of most of the other boys. My view of myself, and that was what mattered, was that I came from a lowly background, which compounded my feelings of inadequacy. Some time later, when imagining I was being fashionable by wearing a white silk scarf with a smart dark overcoat, a boy called Sieff, one of the heirs to the Marks & Spencer empire, destroyed my buoyancy in one sentence, taunting me with the words: 'That's how the miners dress when they go to the pits!' No matter what I did, I always seemed to be one step behind the rest.

Thirty years on, when I was father of two sensitive, intelligent boys, I intended that all their strengths should be applauded and encouraged; it was important for them to taste a measure of success early on. I was reluctant, even unwilling, to reprimand or criticise them. I wanted them to avoid the mass of complexes that had sprung up in my formative years and for them not to be imprisoned by guilt.

The first fortnight at Repton was taken up with committing to memory as much as could be assimilated about the place, including the learning by heart of the two school songs, one of which was in Latin. It was necessary also to master the special terminology, which for generations had become part of Reptonians' daily vocabulary. New pupils were given a test, known as a 'new youths' bumf', to verify that all relevant facts about the school had been properly digested. We were scared into doing the necessary preparation conscientiously, having been misled into believing that failure of the test would reward us with corporal punishment.

In the 1950s Repton was beginning to soften a little after a period of extreme toughness that has doubtless been magnified with the telling. The general atmosphere had become quite civilised, despite the strange and archaic customs that remained. I heard appalling tales of the goings-on at certain other public schools, where sadistic beatings and cruel initiation ceremonies took place. Had I been subjected to this kind of treatment, I am sure it would have broken me; it was, therefore, a relief to me that my parents had the good judgement to send me to Repton.

Introduction to life at public school reinforced the fact I must have been very protected hitherto; in consequence the boisterousness and bad language of the other boys shocked me more than was reasonable. I was unused to the lively and carefree banter of my teenage companions, most of whom behaved less sedately than my prep school friends. To a mild extent I blame my mother, who had been reluctant to encourage me to take risks or seek physical adventure in my earlier years. Emotionally I must have seemed a spineless thirteen year old, with many edges urgently needing to be knocked off, or at least smoothed. So began the slow, painful process of attempting to grow up.

I was dismayed when I discovered there were no doors to the lavatory cubicles in our house toilet block, immediately adjacent to the yard, which was outside the main building. To be seated for all to see was an undignified embarrassment, and until I felt sufficiently uninhibited to conform to this prehistoric routine, I used to slink away to the privacy of an upstairs loo, even though the dormitory or 'bedder' areas were out of bounds during the day. In extremes of winter the uninviting 'rears', as we crudely called them, were heated by a brazier, whose toxic fumes effectively eradicated the pongs made by the temporary inhabitants.

Swimming was an activity that I still detested, a legacy from my prep school, where we had shared the pool with tadpoles and frogs. I had developed an even greater pathological fear and dislike of the water, but discovered that once I could swim my length and had passed Test A, I would never again be bullied by Mr Mawer, the swimming master, to enter the pool. The goal was quickly achieved during my first term at Repton and, truth to tell, I have never swum another stroke since. I still blush recalling that this achievement would not have been possible at all had some kind boy not propped me up under water whilst the test was in progress. Without his assistance, I might still have been struggling to pass Test A.

I became skilful at cleaning the boots and corps kit of my prefect study holder, but was nervous when as a fag I was allocated to sweep the long passage outside the line of studies in the evenings. Traditionally the duty prefect would shine his torch under the heating pipes to see whether a speck of dust had been missed. Rumour had it that failure to achieve perfection would lead to the luckless fag being beaten, although the threat was never actually implemented. Flapping or beating with a shoe or slipper by senior boys was a punishment few of us escaped. Talking after lights out and arriving in the washroom one second late were two instances which brought about this particular treatment in my case.

We were burdened with unwelcome fagging duties for our first two years at Repton. We ran errands for seniors and attended to a number of domestic duties in the house. For the most part our prefect bosses did not take advantage of their boy 'slaves'. Rebelliousness was far from our thoughts, as we accepted the system for what it was. We would, hopefully, in time have fags to do our chores.

The historic village of Repton would have possessed interesting features, even if the school had not been established there. The executors of Sir John Port purchased in 1557 a monastery building which had been established by the Austin canons in the twelfth century; it was here that the life of the great school began. Repton was, however, the capital of Mercia in Saxon times. Appropriately, the spire of the village church stands out as a landmark from afar, and can be seen long before any of the school buildings are visible.

It pleased me that the eight boarding houses were spread about the village, rather than being contained within a campus, as is the case at schools like Stowe and Malvern. We were in touch with the wider world and were able to be on nodding terms with members of the village community as we moved about to sports fields, squash court or gymnasium, which was a welcome change after the isolation of Acton House.

The countryside on the way to nearby Ashby is rugged and picturesque, but for really breathtaking scenery one needed to travel further north to the Peak District. I remember a Combined Cadet Force night operation on the moorland outside Buxton, when the eerie darkness intensified the marvels of that beautiful area. Less thrilling was the town of Burton upon Trent, four miles from Repton. Here we occasionally travelled on the bus to do our shopping; we were almost infected by the smell of brewing that pervaded the place. All in all, Repton and district was an ideal setting for a school.

A trauma occurred early on. Having left the abuse saga behind me, for the first time I felt ready to confide in others about what had happened. Quite clearly some of the listeners misinterpreted the facts. With a stupidly boastful air, I told some of the boys in the house about the homosexual perversions I had witnessed. I must have appeared to them as a very forward 'new youth', who had seemingly derived pleasure from the melodramatic events. The camouflaging of my true feelings by bravado was my method of offloading an enormous burden and of bringing it to the surface. News of the scandal spread around the school like wildfire; my reputation had been ruined in one breath.

The head of house informed Mr Barnard, housemaster of the Orchard. John Barnard was a kindly man whom we suspected was more progressive than the school's policy at that time would have permitted. Had he been given carte blanche he would, we were sure, have banned fagging and would have introduced to Repton a more humanitarian regime of which most former pupils and traditionalists on the staff would have strongly disapproved. Bullseye Barnard, as we called him, because of his glass eye, was always approachable, if a little reticent. He wanted to believe my account of what had happened, but I could judge from his face that he did not trust me.

'I want you to understand, Jonathan,' he informed me, 'that you can always come and see me if there is anything else that you wish to add about what happened during your childhood. It would be very serious indeed if you were to behave immorally at Repton. I hope you understand that. Do you?'

'Of course, sir,' I answered in amazement, baffled by the insinuation I had been the culprit rather than the victim.

The seriousness of the situation was increased when he added, 'The headmaster now wants to see you. I must warn you that he will be less sympathetic than I have been.'

I could not believe the speed with which events had developed. The injustice of it all was incredible, although I had myself to blame for allowing the bottled-up secrets to be disclosed to my critical boy audience, without any thought having been given to the emphasis or accuracy of my graphic descriptions. In spite of his doubts, I felt Mr Barnard was supporting me in my dark hour. The interview with the headmaster, who was reputed to be capable of ruthless and uncompromising treatment, was a different matter, an ordeal best concluded as quickly as possible.

Turning left a few yards after the parish church and under the school arch past the marshal's lodge, across the yard where the masters assembled between lessons, I walked briskly towards the headmaster's house. Theodore Lynam Thomas and his family occupied an imposing section of the Hall; the less impressive but much larger adjoining brick-faced wing accommodated one hundred boarders in Spartan, cramped conditions. TLT, referred to respectfully as the Boss by boys and masters, was waiting for me in his study. A man in his early fifties, he was broad, physically powerful, with distinguished silver hair and yellowish teeth. He had been appointed by the governors of Repton to lick the school into shape, after a successful period as a Rugby housemaster. As usual, he was wearing a dark blue double-breasted suit; apart from the time when I unexpectedly caught sight of him in more casual dress on the Bretby golf course, on no other occasion did I see him less formally attired.

Fluency of speech was not one of TLT's strengths. Ums and ers were the most common words in his no-nonsense repertoire. He clumsily waded in by asking me for a detailed account of the happenings. I told him everything I could remember, sparing him none of the details. TLT sat expressionless, unmoved and unimpressed. After a brief silence, he looked me straight in the eye before castigating me roundly, avoiding any frills and expletives.

'I trust that you are, um, thoroughly ashamed of the trouble you have, er, already caused here, Hall. Repton, um, does not, er, want boys of your ilk, and if you are ever involved with dating boys or decide to take part in dubious, er, sexual experiments, you will be asked to leave Repton right away. Let's hope that, er, we shall see no more of this nonsense and that you have learnt that behaviour of this sort does not pay.'

What he meant by 'behaviour of this sort' I did not know. With tail between my legs, I departed from TLT's study like some tortured dumb animal in shock, shamed into thinking I had committed an act that might have warranted expulsion. I had been made to feel I had been let off lightly. God help me if I tangled with the Repton authorities again.

I had come to expect schoolmasters to judge harshly and for punishments to be doled out as a matter of impulse; I had at least been given a suspended sentence. To have been disapproved of and ignored by virtually the entire Repton boy population was almost more than I could take. The only boys who paid any attention to me at all were those with questionable morals. No matter what I did or said from now on, I had been condemned to the life of an outcast. I was *persona non grata* to all bar the ones who liked 'smoothies', the term used to describe younger boys with girlish looks.

My father was sent for. He arrived looking anxious and harassed, his tired eyes exposing the depth of his agony. Parking his car a mile or so out of the village, away from the prying stares of potential gossips, as best he could he tried to give me support and wise counsel. I needed his understanding so much; he gave it to me in full measure. A private, discerning and deeply proud person, he managed in precious moments of fatherly affection to identify with my sense of isolation and to shoulder some of the bitterness. He could not forgive himself for having failed to recognise the pernicious signs of the ill-fated previous events.

Although short in stature, my father was a giant of a man. He helped me to wipe away the tears that flowed undisturbed at long last. I had always idolised him, but until then barriers brought about by his shyness had made him a distant figure, greatly revered though he was. He refused to allow my mother to be worried by the Repton developments. We both decided to keep the secret to ourselves as our manly pact.

The two unattractive options open to me were either to leave the school at the start of my Repton career or to battle on with head held high. The idea of opting out had some appeal; be that as it may, my parents would have been broken-hearted, ashamed to see me surrender to the pressures. Thankfully I was made of sterner stuff; a stubborn character, already in evidence at Acton House, enabled me without too much loss of dignity to resist the cruel taunts and antagonistic glances. I was friendless, isolated from the rest of the boys, as if living in a vacuum. The façade I exhibited was impenetrable; personal pride would not allow me to let anyone know how upset I really was. It was my hell on earth.

It is not easy to detach oneself from others in a noisy boarding house. I turned into myself, preferring the world of make-believe, where long periods of escape with the aid of books were punctuated by pauses for reflection aimed to retain a personal identity and to protect my sanity. I devoured numerous gripping fiction books with an avidity previously unknown. As a therapeutic exercise it was valuable, but my work in no way benefited, as progress at school had ground to a halt.

Severely depressed for several weeks, I became increasingly nervous and highly strung. Despair began to manifest itself in a number of ways. One day, whilst viewing myself in a mirror, I discovered that I was losing my hair. The parting had widened so markedly that I was sent to be examined by the school doctor in the sanatorium. He informed the house matron I was run down and was to drink plenty of milk. Soon after, I noticed that tufts of hair and flakes of scurf were obscuring the words on the page of a book I was reading. Only then did it dawn on me that I had for some time been scratching my scalp and pulling out large quantities of hair, a subconscious attempt to punish myself.

The only redeeming feature during my first term at Repton was that I achieved modest success as a cricketer. I played for the junior house team, cherishing the secret ambition one day to represent the school at 1st XI level. Senior boys with cricket 'teamers' or colours wore a yellow braid on their blazers, an eye-catching recognition of their achievements. If I were later to earn such an honour, I assumed that the contempt levelled so meanly in my direction would turn into admiration and respect. This optimistic notion offered me nothing more than a glimmer of hope when all else was negative.

On my end of term report, Mr Barnard glossed over the initial difficulties. He did not forget to offer some encouragement when he wrote: 'His first term at Repton has presented problems, but with goodwill and common sense he should win through. A keen cricketer.'

To be home for the summer holidays after a gruelling term was a great relief. I envied many of the Repton boys, whose parents were able to take them on exotic holidays. If we went away at all, we tended to spend a few unexciting days in Criccieth, Minehead or Worthing, but never abroad. My father had once planned to take us for a fortnight to Switzerland; the trip, however, had to be cancelled because chimney stack and roof repairs at the school had to be paid for instead.

Having lost a lot of hair, I was becoming critical of my appearance. Anthony Kaye made fun of me when I told him I had set my heart on developing a suntan. I made up my mind to emulate the sophisticated people I knew by looking as if I had returned from a tropical island, even though there was no possibility of our being able to afford a holiday at all that year. With the absence of much real sun or even a sun lamp, I devised my own way of getting brown. This was simply to sprinkle permanganate of potash into my bath. The result was not as anticipated, for the much hoped-for tan soon departed from my skin, leaving a speckled effect, whilst the bath was permanently stained, much to my mother's anguish.

Anthony, still my best friend and now well established as a boarder at Bloxham School in Oxfordshire, was derisive of my foolhardy suntan experiment. He had grown up appreciably since our last meeting, whereas the disastrous experiences of my first term at Repton had stultified my advancement as a person in many ways. I was fearful lest Anthony would soon be seeking a more mature holiday companion.

There was one Repton boy who came to visit me that same holiday. Malcolm Sowdon, the son of a retired brigadier, had family connections with Leamington; although not especially a friend, he and I shared certain interests. What it was that prompted us to try our hands as amateur schoolmasters I do not know. Wearing gowns belonging to two Arnold Lodge masters, we each in turn took on the role of teacher in one of the school's empty classrooms. Malcolm pontificated using his powerful, nasal voice before an imaginary pupil audience. I followed him with my own teaching attempts, adopting a much more authoritative air than I would have thought possible. The harmless mimicry appealed to both of us, although it would have confounded us then to have been told that we were later destined to become schoolmasters, which is exactly what was to happen.

I was most concerned about my father; he had become withdrawn and troubled. The atmosphere at home was such that my parents were unable to conceal the fact that Arnold Lodge was in a financial mess. It was only a matter of time before Briarfield, the recently purchased junior school building that was also used as our holiday retreat, would have to be closed down. I was made to feel that it was a financial struggle for me to be educated privately; this knowledge greatly added to my own burden of responsibility, especially as I saw myself as not being worth the sacrifice. Staff problems at the school were continuing to cause serious headaches, so much so that my parents wondered whether the agonies of running a preparatory school were not slowly driving them mad and that there would be merit in giving up before their lives had been wrecked through financial ruin and the destruction of their health.

I did not hold passionate views on the subject of the school's future until the day I overheard a rude remark shouted out by a teenage youth to his friend as they cycled past Arnold Lodge. Pointing mockingly at the shabby school building he yelled, 'There's that dump, Arnold Lodge, the worst school in Leamington. It's nothing like as good as the council schools, and yet they have to pay to go there. Mad, isn't it?'

He may well have been right, but the insult cut me to the quick. Knowing my parents had already devoted seventeen of their best years to the school, I was damned if I was going to allow their earlier plans, endeavours and honest achievements to come to nothing. The memory of the thoughtless remark was embedded in my heart until much later when I became aware that my inevitable mission in life, irrespective of the personal price paid, was to try to make Arnold Lodge into one of the best prep schools in England.

My father announced casually one day that he had developed sores on various parts of his anatomy. My mother rightly took his observations seriously, knowing he was never one to complain or fuss unnecessarily about his health. She examined him and was shocked to see that his body was covered with dozens of ugly-looking rashes. My mother's alarm increased when it was apparent that the blisters were spreading rapidly to his face which soon became a confusion of blotches. The general practitioner was consulted. He suggested that it might have be an allergy, dermatitis or eczema. Unable to make a positive diagnosis or to prescribe suitable treatment, an appointment with a skin specialist was arranged.

The specialist visited my father at home. At first he suspected skin cancer, which was later ruled out. He too was in a quandary as to the root cause of the problem and of a suitable remedy. Trial and error experiments, using a multitude of ointments and pills, all failed. Meanwhile my father's condition worsened. By the time I was due to return to Repton, my father was so unwell that it was out of the question for him to be able to resume his headmaster's duties when in such a state. The parents of a friend kindly offered to drive me back to school. My father stood in his dressing gown by the window to wave goodbye. His unshaven, ulcerated face made him look a pathetic figure. My heart cried out for him at that moment, but there was nothing I could usefully do to help.

Back at school I could not dismiss from my thoughts the image of my father's woeful appearance. I knew he was intensely worried about the future of Arnold Lodge. The dream that he and my mother had shared when they purchased the run-down school in 1934 had become a nightmare, a disillusionment, brought about by their having been too trustful of others. My father's troubles I knew instinctively had deepened because of my abysmal first term at Repton, the secrets of which my mother still knew nothing. I was convinced the distressing skin condition was all my fault. I prayed for my father's recovery; I prayed for the welfare of the family school; I prayed for tolerance and for the miracle of my acceptance at Repton. I became preoccupied by the home problems, wishing for the power to make amends for what I considered to be my past sins and for my father's hurt to be assuaged. The second term at Repton was, therefore, littered with obstacles. Head still held high, with nobody aware of the personal agonies causing the distress, I tried as best I could to continue to battle on.

My father's skin slowly responded to treatment; at last he was well enough to resume his normal working duties. There was little means of release for him, as his self-disciplined exterior cleverly hid from those around him the extreme sensitivity of his character. In later years, no matter how well he disguised his cares, when pressures became acute the skin rashes would return in modified form, as nature's way of speaking words he could not himself utter.

Musical activity at Acton House had been limited to an abundance of boy pianists, mostly of elementary achievement, and an inferior choir. I had taken a liking to dance music, contenting myself initially to listening to *Music While You Work* and other programmes on the school radio. I had for some time wanted to play an instrument. When it appeared I was gifted with a good sense of rhythm, in next to no time I was tapping out the beat with a hairbrush on a biscuit tin, and a pair of rhythm brushes was soon purchased instead. The innocent pursuit satisfied me for a while, but the wider scope offered by Repton made me more ambitious. I dismissed the dull option of becoming a drummer in the corps band, as my interest had focused firmly on the dance band.

Without any drums I was at a distinct disadvantage, so I worked hard on my father to try to persuade him to buy me a snare drum. Despite there being little spare cash available for anything other than essentials, the drum was acquired, after much cajoling.

A drummer bandleader, who was a family friend, gave me lessons during the Christmas holidays. My obsessive practice schedule, sometimes involving as many as six hours a day, quickly taught me that there was much more to drumming than random tapping and banging. I eventually mastered the roll and various techniques. As with any musical instrument, percussion skills develop only after years of concentrated effort.

My next task was to find a bass drum to add to my collection. While staying with relatives in Purley, I discovered an old-fashioned, cumbersome bass drum in a second-hand shop in Croydon. Once again my father dipped his hand into his pocket and for the princely sum of five pounds the drum, much to my delight, became my property. I transported the strange object back home on the train. I felt at long last I was well on the way to achieving something concrete and that membership of the school dance band was within my reach.

Repton (2)

On a bleak February day in 1952, as we made our way to the next lesson, the school's Union Jack above Pears School building was drooping ominously at half-mast. We were informed that King George VI had died. One reason why I remember this as a particular milestone is that it led to our being allowed the bonus of spending a couple of nights at home in term-time the following year, in honour of Queen Elizabeth II's coronation. The celebration coincided with a major disappointment for me.

I had been much looking forward to seeing Anthony Kaye again. He lived with his parents and two younger brothers in a spacious ground floor flat a few doors away from us. Assuming that he, too, would be home from school I went to the flat, hoping to find him in. I rang the bell. He came to the door in person, rapidly changing his expression to one of ungracious sullenness the moment he set eyes on me.

'My parents will not allow me to have anything more to do with you. Don't bother to come again!' he said in a cold, dismissive manner that seemed unreal.

Without giving me the chance to respond or react, he slammed the door in my face. I found it hard to believe that a person I had for some time regarded with so much respect and admiration was capable in two short sentences, without any explanation, of drawing a line under the friendship I thought we both valued. The peremptory rejection had a deep impact on my later emotional attitudes, leaving me bitterly hurt. This was by no means my first or last real taste of inconceivable loneliness, a feature that has beleaguered my life in short and longer bursts ever since.

I tried to work out what had led Anthony to snub me in this way. Imagination ran riot. I found no satisfactory answers to the many questions I continually asked myself. Had a distorted account of my disastrous first term at Repton finally filtered through to Anthony and his parents? If so, was it taken for granted that I was morally unsuitable to be Anthony's or anybody else's friend? Had Anthony outgrown my childish tastes or was he merely bored with my company?

I would have preferred to have known the truth, no matter how much it might have hurt. Anthony's middle brother, Michael, an academic high-flyer, was in his final year at Arnold Lodge. There had been some problems over Michael's public school scholarship preparation. My parents were uncommunicative on the subject, although they did infer that a disloyal member of the Arnold Lodge teaching staff had criticised the school in sufficiently disparaging terms to cause a rift between themselves and Mr and Mrs Kaye. These circumstances could well have explained why I was no longer welcome at Anthony's home. Any small amounts of confidence that up until then I had managed to cling on to had been quashed by the unaccountable rebuff.

My way of dealing with the troubles of home and school, as well as Anthony's rejection, was to plunge my energies into solitary pursuits that enabled me to develop skills that required no help from others. I gave the impression of seeming to participate as a cheerful member of the Repton community when in actual fact I had opted out. The barriers with which I surrounded myself offered protection and camouflage as I sought to achieve my principal goal with self-disciplined, stubborn, egotistical determination.

Holiday drumming took priority over all else. Choosing for this noisy occupation the most distant room at my parents' school, there was practice, more practice and still more practice. I wanted to become sufficiently adept to prove myself to be better than any Repton competitor. It was vital for me to succeed at something. Every penny I could muster was spent on improving or extending my drum kit. Tom-toms, cymbals, bongoes and a smaller bass drum were purchased. Hours of daily practice continued. I was at last ready for my musical inauguration.

Although I had become more established at Repton, beneath the misleading veneer I remained an insecure, lonesome fifteen year old. Having shown little academic promise until then, I had begun to assume I was intellectually stupid, especially when I compared my powers of reasoning and ability to absorb ideas with other boys of my age. It would have been easy to offer emotional disturbances and lack of motivation as excuses for my scholastic shortcomings. The fact was, however, that my interest in work was nil, with concentration and incentive to succeed no better, which made it impossible to deduce how well I might have performed had I treated the work with as much dedication as the drumming.

I was so muddled by erratic feelings that an inner turmoil increased the ambivalence as I agonised over key issues. I wanted to be capable of expressing feelings of warmth to family and friends but had never been shown how to do this. The restraints of an undemonstrative family and attendance at two formal boarding schools had forced me to conceal spontaneous inclinations. The stiff upper lip English reserve had always been expected of me, unnatural though it was. I had developed the characteristics of a repressed extrovert, whose exhibitionist tendencies were being held back by constant pressures to conform.

TLT announced that he would be addressing members of our year in the Old Priory. We assembled in one of the upstairs classrooms. He began straightforwardly enough until he moved on to the controversial topic of masturbation.

'I hope, um, that none of you feel the, er, need to masturbate,' he said with emphasis. 'If masturbation is, um, a problem for you, it is most important, er, for you to seek help. Your housemaster is well qualified to give advice and you should, er, if necessary, see him as soon as possible. I must, er, impress upon you that failure to control this bad habit could prove very damaging to you later on.'

I do not recall what else TLT said in his talk, but the references to masturbation, about which he spoke at length, remain lodged in my memory. Like most Repton boys, I masturbated regularly. Nothing, however, would have induced me to raise the very delicate and personal subject with Mr Barnard, who was probably the most approachable of the Repton housemasters. We had all heard the nonsensical tales about losing a pint of blood each time we ejaculated or that it caused insanity, blindness or other disorders. These misconceived ideas made no difference to our surreptitious nocturnal dormitory habits.

From the beds of randy, wide-awake teenage boys would come rhythmical rustles of the sheets and muffled sighs of pleasure, following frantic breathing, as we masturbated in the darkness. The secret practices, in which many of us indulged, allowed our individual sexual fantasies to be satisfied. TLT should have known better than to have us think that what came naturally to most young men was a criminal offence, but he was a product of his age.

The Repton dance band, not so far recognised as a legal school activity, was in need of change. Some of the original members had left or were about to leave the school. I soon took over responsibility for the band. This was harder than might have been imagined; because our sessions were 'unofficial' we had nowhere to practise. In addition, there was no pianist in the school with sufficient skill to fulfil our needs. I blossomed when presented with these challenges. It gave me pleasure to arrange rehearsals in the most unlikely places, with the excitement of never knowing whether the director of music, Mervyn Williams, a volatile Welshman, would suddenly appear to banish us from what he regarded as his territory.

I grew to appreciate Mervyn Williams's musical and other qualities, as time went by. He was a genius of a kind, and although a love-hate relationship existed between us, we both detected in the other a single-mindedness of purpose, which we respected. Some years later, quite by chance, I met Mervyn in a bar in Nice; despite his being somewhat the worse for wear, we finally buried the hatchet and developed an uncanny rapport. This was shortly before his death. I was greatly saddened when I read his obituary.

We managed to unearth a suitable pianist by the name of David Matthews. He was not a pupil at Repton, but was articled to a firm of accountants in Burton. As his participation with the Repton band was never authorised, he was required to present himself at rehearsals dressed as if he were a boy at the school. For the period of at least two years, members of staff did not tumble to the fact that he was a trespasser. He was an outstanding keyboard player, who gave up accountancy in favour of a musical career.

Some years later, one of his compositions sung by Matt Munro topped the hit parade.

The other band members were genuine Reptonians, although we did occasionally smuggle in musicians with tenuous connections. Richard Proctor-Pearson was the alto saxophone player; his style of playing was quite unusual. He could have become a professional had he chosen to do so, but instead, against his will, qualified as a solicitor. Years later, changing direction completely, he opened an art gallery in Manchester. We were joined on string bass by Roger Clarke, whose talents were in due course to be appreciated by the Cambridge University Modern Jazz Quartet, of which he became a member.

The band's early days were full of activity. I recollect the occasion when several of us carried bodily a very heavy piano from one end of the village of Repton to the other, then up very awkward steps to the army lecture room, in preparation for a concert we were giving one Sunday morning. The hazardous journey caused the bearers much hilarity as masters on their way to chapel watched in amazement the ridiculous passing convoy. It was fortuitous rather than good management that the instrument, borrowed without permission, did not smash into smithereens when it was dropped halfway up the slippery iron steps. Apart from a minor scratch the piano, by this time badly out of tune, was safely in place in time for the performance.

I was studying for my O levels, but not with any enthusiasm. Our history master that year, a former county cricketer, was Johnny Eggar, the Draconian housemaster of Brook House. His teaching technique was merely to dictate notes, which we, in turn, attempted to write down legibly. There was no explanation, discussion or stimulation, nor was it intended that there was to be any alternative to laborious learning by rote.

You can imagine our disbelief and shock when Mr Eggar admitted to us a few weeks before the examination that we had been covering the wrong syllabus. Hurried dictation of the barest of notes completed our preparation as far as he was concerned. I cloistered myself in solitude to learn the fragmentary facts we had been provided. Being blessed with a good memory, I was able to regurgitate the information at the right time and was one of the few in the set to pass.

Characters on the staff there were many. H H Davidson epitomised the English gentleman. He was a benevolent house-master, whose teaching of modern languages was enlivened by a contrived childish wit to which he expected us to react with groans of derision. It was rare for him not to be seen wearing his mortarboard, without which he would have looked somehow incomplete. His unflattering nickname of Pee Hard could be explained by the directions he gave us in French lessons to pronounce the consonant P hard. We preferred, however, the far-fetched myth that, after he had been seen to leave the toilets under the cloisters, it was noticed that an enormous crack had developed in the porcelain urinals.

In addition to Johnny Eggar, two other masters who taught me later became headmasters. Guy Willatt, who had a sabbatical term in order to captain the England cricket team, left Repton in 1955 to be head of Yorkshire's Pocklington School. Dick Sale, another former county cricketer, put us through our paces with Chaucer's Prologue. He insisted on our absolute cooperation, without which there were threats of the dire consequence of having to learn the entire fourteenth-century English Prologue parrot-fashion. It was difficult to assess whether or not his whimsical and sometimes cynical humour was to be taken seriously, but we did not dare to take the risk.

I was never taught by Frank Fisher, whose father, Archbishop Fisher, had been Headmaster of Repton for eighteen years until 1932. Frank Fisher was the officer in charge of the CCF; we all came into contact with him in this connection. He was a brilliant organiser, one of his greatest achievements being the master-minding of a special parade and drill display in which I took part in honour of an inspection by Field Marshal Montgomery one speech day. Mr Fisher was appointed warden of St Edward's, Oxford, and later became master of Wellington College, during which period he served for one year as chairman of the head-masters' conference.

Once my O level resits had resulted in passes, I impulsively decided that the time had come for me to leave school, a strong influence being a friend at another public school with similar plans, coupled with my desire to be liberated from the fetters of public school life. Possessing the required qualifications, it was arranged for me to become articled to a firm of estate agents in Leamington, which would, I hoped, pave the way to my becoming a property magnate in time. Notice to leave Repton was duly given, so I left the school, complete with old boys' tie, presenting leaving presents to favoured staff and delivering a speech at the last house supper.

When my future boss told me that I would, as a junior, need to cycle about the town delivering messages, I was greatly perturbed because I could not ride, and had never ridden, a bike. This put a different complexion on my career plans. Without further ado I decided that I wanted to go back to Repton for a period of further study, which would enable me also to expand the scope of the dance band.

I wrote to my housemaster, requesting my return to school, explaining that, on reflection, I had concluded that the estate agency profession was a dishonourable one and was not for me. Another letter was sent to the firm briefly saying I had changed my mind, having decided not to take up their kind offer after all. The irony was that I placed both these letters in the wrong envelope, and it took me several years before I was able to look Mr Griffiths, the firm's boss, in the eye whenever our paths met.

Whether I would have made a success of the opportunity I had turned down will never be known. It has often been said that I have an instinct for business, as well as being a born salesman. There is every chance, therefore, that, apart from my inability to balance myself on a push-bike, I would have made a fortune in the cut-throat field of land and buildings. Mr Griffiths, who followed the advancement of my finally chosen career, told me some years later that he would have expected me to go far, had I not turned tail and left him in the lurch.

News of my return to Repton caused little comment. It seemed that I had at last been accepted by the majority of the boys, who by now looked upon me as something of an eccentric. The dance band musicians, relieved they no longer had to seek a drummer or leader replacement, greeted my reappearance with enthusiasm. Mr Barnard was more reserved with his welcome. I knew he quite liked me, but I sensed, too, he thought my quiet depths would one day erupt into irksome antics that would spell trouble for him. He still did not trust me.

It had never occurred to me to be academically ambitious. The possibility of Oxford or Cambridge had already been ruled out because I had not taken O level Latin. With no specific career in mind, I could not find one good reason for pushing myself intellectually, apart from which I found study for its own sake exceedingly dull. Content to allow my brain to remain inactive, I was relegated to the general sixth, a polite term used to describe the comfortable refuge I shared with other rudderless souls.

My parents came to visit me at Repton at least twice a term on a Sunday. Attending the morning service, they sat with other parents, visitors and masters' wives in a separate section of the chapel, referred to by us as the 'hen pen'. One day my mother arrived wearing an outmoded, multicoloured hat with a long floppy ostrich feather thrusting upwards like a fractured aerial. To my acute embarrassment, in the middle of the service she made a spectacle of herself by standing up, feather twirling, when she should have been kneeling. I was convinced the eyes of every boy and master were fixed on the hat and its owner during those critical moments, so ashamed was I of my mother's obtrusiveness. The final insult was when she proceeded to sing with great gusto an octave higher and a great deal louder than other females in the congregation, thus drawing attention to herself even more. I took the derisive comments that inevitably followed very much to heart.

It is a reflection of the vulnerability of the young and of my own insecurity that I allowed myself to be ashamed of my mother's mode of dress and singing performance. It is only when we accept our parents' defects, perversities and eccentricities for what they are that we can achieve maturity ourselves. The unreal pretentiousness of life in a boarding community delayed this process for many of us; of this I am convinced.

In the privacy of my own thoughts I set myself three goals that I determined to try to achieve during my final terms at Repton. The first one, more easily attainable than the other two, was to increase my musical proficiency and for the dance band to be accepted by the authorities as a legitimate school activity. Less realistic were my ambitions to play for the cricket 1st XI and to become a house prefect; the fulfilment of either of these latter aims would, I knew, greatly strengthen my self-esteem.

The top cricket at Repton was of minor county standard. I gained my house cricket colours, mainly for my bowling. By this time my batting had developed a more aggressive style; on a good day I would knock up a reasonable score with risky, hard hitting. Quickness in the field and the accuracy and power of my throw were remarked upon. I was selected to play in one or two trial games; there was justification for mild optimism. Just as I was beginning to gain recognition, I developed a back injury, brought on, it was thought, by my extraordinary, contorted bowling action. Bowling round the wicket, I would approach the crease from a ninety-degree angle, turning suddenly at the time of delivery. The weird manoeuvre confounded the batsman, as well as immobilising my back. Each time the sharp pain returned, I was ordered to rest for a week or more.

The problem repeated itself many times, so that future prospects were blighted. My father was as upset as I was when I was forced to channel my physical energies into other pursuits. In consequence, he never did see me play on the hallowed square where the debut of so many cricketing heroes had taken place. One of my three possible accomplishments had been quickly removed. Of the two that remained, for me to be appointed a prefect it was essential for Mr Barnard to view me as a reformed character.

I had watched prefects, with varying degrees of commitment, as they carried out their duties. My observations convinced me that I was capable of performing as well as most. I knew an effective prefect needed above all to set a good example, but it was necessary also for him to be conscientious, a competent organiser, a genuine carer. These qualities, hidden but there nevertheless, I possessed. What was needed was for me to convince Mr Barnard of my worth. At Acton House I had carried out my monitor's tasks in exemplary fashion, until the fateful day I had thrown in the sponge in a fit of anger.

I made no attempt to behave obsequiously to gain favour. I wanted genuinely to contribute to the well-being of the house by exerting for the first time in my Repton career a positive influence. I led the Orchard choir to victory in the house singing competition, which surprised my critics, who had assumed that my musical talents were limited to the light-hearted variety. I gained pleasure from participating in the Repton Music Society's presentations of Fauré's *Requiem* and Handel's *Messiah*. I was ready to be given a role and some status, eager for the opportunity to prove how misjudged I had been in the past.

Some time before the prefectorial appointments for the following year were due to be considered, Mr Barnard asked to see me. He began talking about the subject that had occupied a prominent place in my thoughts since I had unexpectedly returned to Repton.

'I don't want you to be misled into thinking that you will be a prefect next year,' he said.

The introduction might have been taken to sound quite promising. I eagerly awaited what was to follow.

'You must realise, of course,' he continued 'that, because of your past record here, it is only fair that you should know that you will never ever be made a house prefect. The news will not surprise or disappoint you, I am sure, knowing that responsibility does not appeal to you.'

My whole world had caved in all at once. I felt utterly deflated. Mr Barnard, whom I had always respected, had shattered my hopes with a few glib words. He obviously had not the slightest idea of my secret designs or of the mental preparations I had been undergoing to make me fit for leadership. To have been told categorically I had been written off as a non-starter was insensitive and wounding in the extreme. The fresh blow to morale and pride increased my determination to express the developing bitterness much more openly. Apart from musical endeavours, I had been forced to abandon the other challenges.

So slighted did I feel that I became increasingly depressed by my dismal record of successive failures and rejections. Developing the brittle exterior of an angry young man, I was able, for the most part, to conceal the complexes and the yearnings. A giant chip on my shoulder led me to indulge in immature behaviour that quickly proved to Mr Barnard how right he had been not to give me the opportunity on which so many hopes had been pinned. I ceased to conform; I became noted for unconventional absurdities; the more threatened I became, the more outrageous was my behaviour.

The animosity, fury and frustration I felt, blaming the school environment and life in general for my condition, came flooding out in a critical paper that I wrote about the public school system. The essay had a limited circulation within the Repton community. One or two of the more liberal masters sympathised with some of the contents, but it was patently clear even to them that the censorious ramblings reflected my own inadequacies, the anguish, the bruised pride, the loss of dignity.

The road of advancement towards manhood for me was a long and arduous one. I needed, as do most of us, recognition, encouragement and for a subtle belief in myself to be drawn out. My form master in the sixth form was Tim Slack, an energetic young bachelor, who related well to me and my peers. He could understand as well as anybody the difficulties I was experiencing in the growing up process. In economics he instructed us in the mysteries of the Stock Exchange. He encouraged us to invest theoretically in blue-chip and more speculative companies, with interesting results. In one economics examination I gained the top mark by such a wide margin that I was puzzled I had achieved the distinction with so little effort. Old Wykehamist Mr Slack, soon to be appointed headmaster of Bedales, was the only Repton master to harness my interest in the classroom. It was through his inspired teaching that I first became interested in financial matters.

Music had become my passion. The syncopated noises produced by the Repton dance band were beginning to sound more and more like jazz. Jazz music or not, the familiar tunes were made to swing in a way that made people want to tap their feet or to dance. A master had been asked to vet our efforts to see whether we were good enough to provide the music for staff and prefects' dances. Our timing and versatility impressed him. We were appointed as the school's resident band, which spared the bursar from having to pay Musicians' Union rates. Girls from nearby Abbots Bromley School were imported for the prefects' dances. The presence of the girls' teacher guardians, the unduly bright lights and lack of alcohol turned the anticipated rave-ups into damp squibs; it was all too formal.

Having at last been given official school status, the band was allotted a regular practice venue. What began as a clandestine activity gained favour with all but the most conservative Reptonians, especially when we succeeded in raising money for charity. The concerts after Sunday morning chapel attracted vast numbers of boys and a handful of masters, who quickly transferred their allegiance from God to a new-found idol. My drum solos had become almost legendary, winning me approval that for so long had eluded me. In my dreams I saw myself as a theatrical impresario. On stage, however, the old shyness and lack of confidence returned so that the personality and star quality of my imaginings froze into insignificance. I lacked the electric magnetism required in a showbiz celebrity.

I had been teaching myself the clarinet since the age of fifteen. Harry Hole, who directed the Repton military band, had given me some lessons, but he despaired of my unwillingness to master the reading. A good ear enabled me soon to play most of the well known tunes in almost any key. Instinctively knowing the correct harmonies, I stole an advantage over most of the other budding jazz musicians. Harry Hole made an exception by allowing me to play in the military band without any sheet music, knowing I could be relied upon always to hit the right notes. The diversion of another musical skill led to my becoming a front-line clarinet soloist in the dance band when the opportunity arose.

Musical pursuits were not confined to school. I had been introduced to teenage pianist, Brian Hazelby, who worked in Leamington's town hall. In his lunch hour he would play the grand piano on the stage in the main hall with such rare skill that employees working in the building came to listen to him. Our first gig together, for which we were paid a pittance, was in a trio at an RAF base. To prevent a repeat of the exploitation from which we had already suffered, we swiftly joined the union.

I formed my own band in Leamington. As manager and agent it was necessary in term-time for me to coordinate the various engagements, some of which took place in my absence. Testing both initiative and organisation skills to the full, I staged concerts, advertised dances, liaised with clubs and committees. I was asked to provide the music for teenage parties. The Jonathan Hall Band became a familiar feature on the social circuit that catered for the sons and daughters of the better off. 'Yes, of course we shall include the veleta in your programme. No, no, we would not dream of playing too loud,' I would assure the indulgent, anxious parents.

During the Christmas period one year, I was appointed musical director at an hotel in Warwick. The pianist let me down at the last minute, which meant that I had the nightmare situation of having to hunt for a replacement at a time of year when most competent musicians were already booked. I consulted my Musicians' Union address list, only to discover that many of the possibles were not even on the telephone. Unable to drive a car or ride a bike, I tramped endlessly along the highways and byways of Leamington and district, eventually tracking down a lady pianist, who deputised well.

Apart from one or two minor successes, my time at Repton can be dismissed as a failure. TLT wrote on my final report, with his characteristic green ink: 'I am glad he has been able to complete the full course and although his interests and standards are not always conventional, he has made his mark in his own way – I wish him well in the future.'

These comments aptly sum up my undistinguished Repton years.

I was surprised that departure from the Repton scene, with vivid memories of introspective self-analysis and substantial torment, had left me with a sense of bereavement. I had loved, in particular, the chapel services, where I had been inspired by the feeling of oneness that the all-male community generated. There was much that I was going to miss.

Repton had begun to influence my destiny.

A Career in the Making

I arranged to meet some Repton friends in London on New Year's Eve. We celebrated the incoming year with the flamboyancy of youth, joining the thousands of revellers who had gathered in and around Trafalgar Square. After we had made our farewells the following day, I suffered an exaggerated version of the sense of loss that had been troubling me since my final days at Repton the previous month. The separation from Repton had dejected me more than I would have expected, with the brief reunion producing a disturbing sentimental yearning. I have never found it easy to let go of the past.

I wanted to retain my links with members of the Repton band. Returning to the school one Sunday with my drum kit and clarinet, I was guest musician at one of the jazz concerts. Glad to be back at Repton in many ways, it was with some sadness that I recognised I no longer felt at home there; this was my last visit to the school for several years.

Before doing my national service I was given the choice by my father either to work for him or to seek temporary employment elsewhere. I took what I considered to be the easier of the two options, agreeing to work for him.

I had developed a very strong sense of loyalty to my parents' endeavours. For a long time it had been apparent that the school to which they devoted so much energy and effort was ailing. The anxieties I bore on their behalf were out of all proportion. Whilst away at boarding school, I concluded weekly letters home with a lengthy questionnaire that made exhaustive enquiries about the school's progress. I longed for my parents and for the school to experience success. Unexpected good news would make me jubilant; spirits plummeted whenever negative happenings cancelled out any modest progress that had been made. My prayers repeatedly contained requests to God for His help in encouraging those in any way involved with Arnold Lodge to be loyal and to support its ideals with sincerity. Years of fanatical preoccupation with circumstances beyond my control had made me serious, intense and introverted. I lacked the sparkle and optimism that most young men of eighteen have in abundance. With no desire to sow any wild oats just yet, I began to find out what it was like to be a student teacher.

Arnold Lodge was at a particularly low ebb at this time. Pupil numbers were small; teachers came and went because salaries and conditions were poor. The small income that was generated meant that my parents struggled hard to cover basic costs.

After a period of inertia, the school was to be fated with a stroke of good fortune. Noel Carmen, the deputy headmaster of a large grammar school in his native Australia, had come to teach in England for two years, in order to get over a broken marriage. My father was fortunate enough to be able to secure his services for this period. Disabled through having been a polio victim, Mr Carmen was a man of great courage, who made light of his physical difficulties. The contributions he made to the life of the school were sufficient for my father to try to induce him to extend his contract permanently by offering him a partnership. Tempted by the unexpected opportunity, especially as he had by this time fallen in love with Jennifer Hermes, a member of the junior school staff, Mr Carmen returned to Adelaide with some reluctance to resume his duties as second in command at a school with over one thousand boys. The gap he left at Arnold Lodge was incalculable. It was at this juncture that I became professionally immersed for the first time in the prep school world.

My mother was a tower of strength. She was utterly devoted to the needs of the school, being prepared to cook, clean, teach or act as matron, undertaking, if necessary, all these functions with little or no thought for herself. The strain was written all over her face and she became very thin.

My father was dedicated in his own way. He needed to get away once in a while from the school to preserve his rationality. He smoked a great deal, his only other vice being a daily visit in the early evening before supper to a local pub, where he would meet some of his friends. I could see he was not a fit man. There was a feeling of unease about the future, which rang ominous bells in my imagination. I was in constant dread that he would soon be struck down by illness.

Preconceived ideas of what I would have to do as a teacher in a prep school were wide of the mark. I had previously only inherited from my parents the tensions, the frustrations. I was used to identifying with their distress as tantalising dramas upset the equilibrium of us all with a regularity that had become monotonous. I took to the duties like a duck to water. I discovered for the first time that I had a value because I was needed by others. Whether chasing up and down a football pitch with a whistle, supervising the boarders before bedtime or demonstrating how to bisect a line in a geometry lesson, I knew that my prime function was to help the boys in my care in the best ways possible. I found the work fulfilling and absorbing, determining it was the immense variety of occupation that appealed to me most.

Any ambitions I might have had to become a professional jazz musician were slipping from my mind. I knew in an uncanny way after only two or three weeks of involvement that I had a gift for teaching. Administrative tasks, vital to the successful running of a school, were also right up my street. My father, realising the extent of the workload carried by Noel Carmen, was beginning to rely on me heavily as a general factotum and troubleshooter. The month before I had no career plans. Now hesitancy and lack of an objective had been replaced by the certainty that my sole aim was to see the school thrive under my leadership one day. Nothing was to allow me to deviate from the task.

Working in an independent school has put me in touch with people from all walks of life. As well as the many humble parents with mundane jobs and modest incomes, I have been involved with the education of the sons of peers of the realm, landed gentry, judges, industrial tycoons, pop stars, a government minister, diplomats, sporting personalities, professional men and women in their droves.

My first encounter with a well known personality was one cold February afternoon during my first term on the staff. As I returned to the school with a group of footballers, we were excited to see parked in the drive a gold-plated Daimler limousine, the like of which was only to be found on a film set. Lady Docker, who was paying for the education of one of the boarders, had called unexpectedly to inspect the school's facilities and to visit her protégé. She was at that time preparing to attend two months later the wedding of film actress Grace Kelly to Prince Rainier in Monaco's Cathedral of St Nicholas. My parents were fascinated to hear of the presents she and her husband were planning to give to the royal couple. Escorted by my father, Lady Docker was treated as if she herself were a blue-blooded aristocrat. She stopped with regal splendour in the boarders' prep room, where I was in charge. She addressed me personally.

'Do come and visit us on our yacht in Monte Carlo, if you are ever in the south of France. We should love to see you,' she cooed invitingly.

It was during the wedding festivities that the notorious wife of Daimler's chairman disgraced herself by insulting the principality's royal family in a much publicised incident. Sir Bernard Docker, Daimler's chairman, was formerly a pupil of Beech Lawn and Greyfriars School in Leamington, whose goodwill was coincidentally purchased by Arnold Lodge in 1935. Our knowledge of Lady Docker was limited, but we happened to know that, despite her ostentatious outbursts, in a quiet way she was responsible for many unselfish and generous deeds.

The days were numbered before I was to be called up to do my national service. I presented myself for a medical examination, as a result of which I was pronounced fully fit. Flat feet and a dicky back did not exempt me from the obligations in store for me. Opting for an army infantry regiment, I was surprised when papers finally arrived instructing me to report to Hadrian's Wall Camp, Carlisle. I was to become a trooper in the Royal Armoured Corps.

Carrying a bag containing basic toiletries, I mounted the Carlisle train at Rugby Station. The family school to which I had been obsessively wedded since my birth was going to have to survive without me for a while. The overriding fear that occupied my mind as the train sped northwards was that Arnold Lodge might not still exist after I had completed the two years' national service, a thought too horrifying to contemplate.

Wearing a herringbone tweed jacket, Repton old boys' tie and cavalry twill trousers, I stepped down on to the station platform at Carlisle. With expectant faces that disguised the apprehension we must have felt, other young men joined me in the queue at the barrier, travel vouchers in our hands. A kindly looking soldier with distinctive sergeant's stripes on his arms approached me genially.

'Have you come to join the army, laddie?' he asked with a gentleness that seemed too good to be true.

Encouraged by his reassuring manner, I showed him my call-up papers. The sergeant's expression immediately changed to one of ugly malevolence.

'Get on that bloody lorry and look lively, lad,' he bellowed. 'From now on I'm going to make your life a fuckin' misery. And I don't mean maybe!'

I must have looked to him like the proverbial wally. I had been singled out already. My spell in the army had begun.

At the camp I was greeted by another recruit, who recognised my Repton tie. Old Etonian Dominic Barrington-Browne seemed to have settled in comfortably already. Because he had joined up as a regular, he had been instructed to report twenty-four hours earlier than the rest of us. There was no question of his being taken advantage of by any non-commissioned officer, not him. He informed me that the evening before he had told one of the sergeants to get stuffed, knowing full well that the army's authority over him did not officially commence until the following day. The sergeant's response is unprintable. Dominic Barrington-Browne's devil-may-care attitude was to keep us well entertained. I had little doubt he would succeed in his ambition to become an officer in the stylish 11th Hussars Regiment, otherwise known as 'The Cherry Pickers'.

We were fitted out with our uniforms. The intake was divided into three squads, selection being based on our height. I was tall enough to be included in Squad A, which contained a number of huge individuals of well over six foot. The first four weeks were taken up with cleaning kit and the acquisition of marching and pistol drill skills. The training was intensive and rigorous, with no time to think or socialise.

The squad to which I was allocated was under a sadistic bully, Sergeant Woods, the same sergeant who had met me at the station. He had, we were told, beaten up recruits in the past. Frequently threatening to do us an injury with his pace stick, he intimidated us verbally without actually laying hands on anyone. One afternoon he took me to task over the cleaning of my boots. With pace stick raised, he advanced towards me menacingly. 'Son of a filthy pig!' he shouted accusingly. Afraid for my safety, but seething with anger nevertheless at his coarse insult, I made for the nearest lavatory, locking myself in. 'Come out, you fuckin' coward,' he yelled. I remained installed in my refuge until the coast was clear.

Sergeant Woods's one and only ambition was for our squad to win the drill competition at the end of the four-week training period. His coercive tactics brought about the desired result. As usual, his squad came first. Contemptuous of the other drill instructors in their moment of defeat, Sergeant Woods strutted away from the parade ground like a vain peacock, eager to persecute the next batch of raw recruits.

Every conceivable background was represented in our intake. For the majority of the time we all got along well together. Dominic Barrington-Browne, always relaxed and full of confidence, showed no sensitivity to those around him. Making little effort to mix, he regarded the others as his inferiors. The tongue-in-cheek arrogance, displayed for the benefit of his audience, provided us with something to think about other than the dull routine. I suspect I may have been alone in being quietly envious of his nonchalant conceit. Many of the men found him most objectionable, a view which hardened when Barrington-Browne claimed to be connected with the commanding officer, with whom he used sometimes to go fishing at weekends. It was said that some of his fellow troopers had to clean his kit during these weekend sprees, a malicious rumour that could not possibly be substantiated.

We were preparing for a camp dance, with the obvious conjecture about how many women there would be and what they would be like. After derogatory comments concerning the 'scrubbers' likely to attend, Barrington-Browne puffed out his chest and announced, 'I'm a deb's delight and can have any woman I choose!' Whether said in jest or not, this was the final straw as far as tough Glaswegian, Bruce, was concerned. He and several others set upon Barrington-Browne, intending to teach him a lesson. Fighting for his honour and proving himself to be as strong as an ox, despite his flabby bulk, he gave his aggressors no easy task. After a fierce struggle, they were eventually able to remove some of Barrington-Browne's clothing and to black his arse with boot polish. Seemingly undeterred by the degrading assault on his previously snow-white bottom, the Etonian's boastful utterances continued as before.

We had to take our turn in doing guard duty. When I was selected by the inspecting officer as being the smartest turned out soldier (stick man) in the guard parade, I was rewarded by being released from the duty. Confounded and yet elated at the news, I placed my pistol on my bed in the billet before going to the guardroom to take NAAFI orders from the men whose entire night was to be taken up in guarding the camp from we knew not what.

I was arrested and charged for failing to return the pistol to the armoury, with the accusation that my irresponsible action was inviting others to steal the weapon. The result was that I was given seven days' jankers, a most disagreeable, inconvenient and regular reporting system, requiring different uniforms to be worn in spotless condition and at unsociable hours, commencing early in the morning.

Having been placed on jankers, I found it impossible to be released from the commitment. There was always a good reason why I should be forced to continue to report, such as my inability to shave my acned and spotty face, or the state of my denims after a wet and muddy assault course attempt.

It would have been fair enough for me to have been given some short, sharp punishment for the pistol blunder. I could see I was going to remain on jankers indefinitely. Some of the officers and most of the NCO's delighted in the fact they had found a mug that could be made to squirm. 'We can break this trooper,' remarked one.

'I see that Sonny Jim can't shave over his spots. Better to let them bleed next time. Another seven days' jankers!'

'How come you fell in the river? Is that why your denims are so wet? Another seven days' jankers!'

As days became weeks, the odious taunts intensified. There was no relief to my predicament in sight.

Examination results at school had qualified me to apply for a commission. I had been moved to the potential officers' wing, along with Barrington-Browne and several others. So mature and cocksure were the short-term national service officers that I could not imagine myself being able to emulate them, even assuming I succeeded in accomplishing the preliminary selection hurdles. Officers in the Royal Armoured Corps regiments came mainly from upper or upper-middle-class backgrounds, with products of Eton and Harrow monopolising the exclusive mess halls. Grammar school boys, not many of whom achieved national service commissions in the superior cavalry regiments, were looked upon as social lightweights. The Repton advantages with which I had been endowed were insufficient to improve my low self-esteem. As a potential officer I was useless. Disastrous attempts to lead were soon to highlight my incompetence before an audience made up of men whose unconcealed abilities further deflated my spirits.

Much more strenuous demands were made of us than during the basic training. A fear of heights and of the water militated against me on the tough assault courses, with poor stamina causing me to be quickly out of breath. There were lessons in map-reading; we indulged in rifle practice; we made speeches and gave talks. Leadership and initiative skills were tested in practical ways out of doors. On one such exercise I was responsible for leading a small group whose purpose it was to attack an imaginary enemy base. I thought I had accomplished the mission adequately. The officer in charge had opposite views.

'You'll never make an officer, you daft shit, unless you can learn to be much more forceful,' he said. 'Never say please! You're not a wet nanny running a Sunday school. Shout, get nasty and show them who's the fucking boss!'

Try as I might, it was not in my nature at that time to bully and swear in the way required of me. If aggressive bawling at the men was a characteristic feature of a good officer, the wet nanny role appealed to me more.

Foolishly impractical, I panicked when given the task of or-ganising the pitching of tents on a stretch of moorland. Chances of advancement to the next rung of the leadership ladder were scuppered altogether by my decision to choose for our campsite an unsuitable piece of ground on a steepish incline. The clamorous laughter of the men and some choice words from another exasperated officer reduced me to the status of idiot in the eyes of all.

It was with diffidence and a heavy heart that I presented myself for interview with the officer whose job it was to decide whether or not I was to be recommended to attend a full course of officer training. With not a flicker of optimism remaining, I marched into the office, stamping to a halt, eager still to manifest a willingness that had never been lacking. Saluting with too much brio, I overbalanced, falling flat on my face on the well-polished floor.

'Get up, you bloody twerp!' screamed the officer with biting scorn.

It had become clear I was suffering from depression. The valuable time being wasted by my army interlude had increased the feeling of hopelessness. It was obvious that my father's health was declining and Arnold Lodge was struggling to survive; these factors increased the sense of frustration that having to play toy soldiers produced in me. It was not as if there was a war to fight, whereas a war of a different kind needed to be fought, and urgently, on the home front.

I must have been mentally very unstable at that time. My thinking was muddled, ideas wild, with irrational reactions and thought processes overruling everything. I was in a complete emotional turmoil. I spent some days in the camp sickbay, where I recovered sufficiently to be made to feel really guilty by another failure to notch up one single positive achievement in my unimpressive personal diary of self-doubt.

Whilst I was in the sickbay I met up with Etonian Andrew Watson, a young baronet who, shortly after arriving at Hadrian's

Wall Camp to commence his national service in an intake subsequent to mine, had been brutally kicked and punched by some fellow recruits. When I first saw him I assumed he had been involved in a motor accident. His face was black and blue with bruises that covered his forehead, cheeks and chin. Body aching and eyes bloodshot and sore, he proceeded, with surprisingly little bitterness, to explain to me that the unprovoked attack had been made on him simply because he had a title. A real live baronet was beyond the range of experience of most of the men with whom Andrew was now mixing. The response to his presence of a despicable few was to clobber him when he was unsuspecting and on his own.

I asked Andrew whether he had come into contact with Barrington-Browne at Eton. Nodding wryly, he was diplomatic enough not to commit himself to expressing an opinion. Unlike Barrington-Browne, Andrew was a vulnerable, sensitive person. He told me he had inherited the family title at a very young age after his father had been killed in the Second World War. He was unable to understand why a gang of resentful thugs would have wanted to pound him with their fists because of his privileged background over which he had no control. Andrew, a sympathetic listener, could see I was hating the army. I unburdened to him, in condensed form, the unhappy events of the previous few weeks, without disclosing the root of my concerns, the troubled school in Leamington.

Andrew and I shared some basic philosophies. It was a strange coincidence that his family home, Talton House, near Shipston on Stour, was less than twenty miles from where I lived. On discovering that I, too, was Warwickshire born and bred, he promised to invite me for a game of tennis when our army days were over.

Prior to my release from sickbay I was informed that, because I had been downgraded medically, it was necessary for me to transfer to a camp at Crookham in Berkshire, which would be better suited to my meagre talents. The doctors who had been treating me had convinced themselves that it was the harsh regime that had caused me to cave in emotionally. I knew differently.

Changing stations in London, holding tightly on to the kitbag that contained any worldly goods I would be needing in the foreseeable future, I arrived at the headquarters of the Royal Army Medical Corps near Crookham. I received the news with consternation that I was to return at once to Carlisle as my papers were not in order.

'No, you cannot be admitted until you are in possession of the appropriate documentation,' I was told.

Seeing my distress, the duty officer put matters right with a quick telephone call. I was relieved to be safely installed in my new billet.

Nobody knew what to do with me at Crookham. I was an inconvenient nuisance. Lacking the stimulation of responsibilities to help pass away the time that could have been spent more profitably at home, boredom began to set in. The long days marched on drearily. Occasionally I was asked to assist in the cookhouse, a role that was an end in itself, with no avenue that might lead to more interesting employment even remotely in sight. The relegation to Crookham had made not a scrap of difference to my state of mind. The problems lay within my tangled self. Irrespective of what was to happen next, I was heading for a nervous breakdown, behaving senselessly and feeling the need to do myself an injury.

After a spell in the camp sickbay, where my odd behaviour was able to be observed, I was moved for reasons of my safety to Cambridge Military Hospital in Aldershot. Here I shared a locked ward with men described as dangerous, most of whom were army prisoners. Two male nurses whispered that it was planned for me to be transferred to Netley army mental hospital in Southampton. The final decision rested with a panel of three colonels, all of them psychiatrists. I had visions of being committed to a lunatic asylum for the rest of my life. I was beginning to think that I really was mad, wondering how on earth my parents would react to the revelation of their only son's insanity. The psychiatrists pondered over my fate with furrowed brows.

'When you leave the army, what kind of work do you have in mind to do?' asked one.

'I want to teach.'

On hearing of my plans, all three of them shook their heads.

'That would be one of the worst possible careers for you. You would never cope. The pressures of teaching would prove far too much for your sensitive nature. You will need to do something that involves a lot less stress,' advised the group's chairman.

Instead of going to Netley, therefore, I was given an honourable medical discharge from the army. I was soon on my way home.

Before leaving the hospital I had been able to take a quick glance at my medical records, which described me as a psychopathic personality. Using a medical dictionary, I discovered that a psychopath is someone with a personality disorder in which behaviour is antisocial and, in the extreme, may be criminal. To have been bracketed together with gangsters, hoodlums and unhinged desperadoes was a devastating shock that has haunted me ever since. I convinced myself that the army problems were brought about by my insecurity and rawness, although the unconventional ways in which I have handled the many emergencies and crises in later years might well give cause for my normality to be questioned.

It was acutely awkward for me to find reasons for my reappearance after my short stay in the army. It had been assumed I would return home with glittering medals and a commission, but to have been thrown out on account of emotional failings was a difficult truth to hide. Any attempts, no matter how plausible, to gloss over the events of the previous few weeks were met with a disdainful raising of eyebrows and scornful indifference on the part of onlookers.

I was embarking on a long, arduous journey, with the impossible hope of building an unflourishing preparatory school into something special. At this point it was doubtful whether I would have the ability to do the simplest of jobs, let alone inspire anyone's confidence in my ability even to make a stab at a giant-sized challenge.

Where does one begin when there are no redeeming features? To care desperately is a starting point, I am sure. Many of the ablest people I know have come a cropper at the first fence because they did not possess tenacity or grit. What I lacked in qualifications, experience or intellectual ability was compensated for by my total devotion to the needs of Arnold Lodge, to the exclusion of all else.

For the next two years my father paid me twenty-five shillings a week, in return for which I would often put in an eighteen-hour day, with duties covering all aspects of the business. As the self-appointed anchorman, I began to view myself as an indispensable assistant to my father. My function was varied, carrying with it responsibility for teaching, games coaching and overseeing the boys in their leisure moments. There was a feeling of satisfaction when tasks were successfully carried out. I enjoyed, too, helping some of the slow learners to overcome their difficulties, not minding how many hours were devoted to the challenging pastime.

The school had a poor reputation when we opened for the autumn term. The staff was small. My father, who had been denied the opportunity to go to Oxford because of his wartime service, had no qualifications whatsoever. In addition to myself, there were only two other masters and four lady teachers. Apart from the senior master, John Bridge, and a retired state school teacher, Mrs Mabel Lloyd, who was over seventy, all were unqualified. Any success achieved was due to the efforts expended by the teaching staff, rather than there being in evidence any real professionalism. Miss Fairbrother, despite her lack of paper qualifications, was an outstanding teacher, who made her lessons come to life in a way which aroused the interest of every boy with whom she came into contact.

Social life was halted for many months, during which time my clarinet remained firmly in its case and the drums were stored away in boxes in the attic. Unwilling to be disturbed by inter-ruptions or diversions, the school received my undivided attention.

Matron Bassam, 'Bashem' to the boys, was quite a character. When on duty she was very noisy. One of her favourite occu-pations was the supervision of the boys' bathing arrangements. After games all the boarders had to queue up outside one of the school's two small bathrooms for the long-winded process of getting clean. Day boys, on the other hand, returned home with muddy knees. When showers were eventually installed, Bashem turned the showering ritual into a veritable pantomime. Protecting her person with hat, wellingtons, raincoat and rubber gloves, she exercised control with the aid of a whistle. Her bark was worse than her bite. She went well and truly to town, however, when a boy was caught swearing, so incensed was she by any bad language that she would wash out his mouth with soap.

I cannot imagine why the morning lavatory ritual caused the kerfuffle it did. My mother had introduced a system that required each boarder to report after breakfast to the teacher on duty to confirm that he had had his bowels opened. If any boy was truthful enough to say he had been unsuccessful, the letter D was marked alongside his name in the dose book. To deal with the emergency, Bashem would force down the throat of the unhappy wretch a large spoonful of syrup of figs. The boys, quickly cottoning on to the imperfections of the system, rarely returned for a second dose, no matter how constipated they were.

Another of my mother's foibles was the cleanliness of the boys' teeth. Impressing upon them the need for teeth to be sparkling white at all times, she organised daily inspections and regular tooth competitions for which she gave marks out of ten, with prizes awarded to those with the whitest dazzles. To ensure that the highest standards of dental hygiene were achieved, she insisted that boys applied salt instead of toothpaste to their brushes whenever a competition was imminent.

Residential staff in third-rate boarding schools in those times frequently came from the ranks of social misfits. We knew little of the personal circumstances of the senior master, John Bridge, an overwrought man in his mid-thirties, who taught Latin. He took his duties so seriously that he was invariably tense and nervous. His agitation reached breaking point one evening. At staff supper, with seemingly no provocation, he got up, lifted a wheelback chair above his head and smashed it to pieces on the floor.

'I have had all I can take of Miss Fairbrother's supercilious attitude,' he yelled, his whole body quivering as he threatened speechless colleagues with a broken chair leg.

We had no idea what peaceable Miss Fairbrother had done to deserve his wrath. The outburst demonstrated how easily petty jealousies can shatter the stability of a close-knit community. Mr Bridge packed his bags and walked out there and then, slamming the front door so violently that the building shook. With only one qualified teacher now in his employment, my father urgently sought a substitute.

In November 1956 large numbers of Hungarian refugees fled from Budapest when Russian troops seized the city. Many settled in Britain. My father's motive in offering to educate free of charge a boy from one of these unfortunate families was not entirely altruistic. He was conscious pupil numbers had declined so much that an extra name on the school list might lift morale a little. He wrote to the refugee headquarters in London. In the absence of a reply, and on hearing a refugee camp had been set up near Stratford-upon-Avon, my father and I dispensed with protocol and visited the camp unannounced. Here we met nine-year-old Szabolcs Losy. Negotiations were speedily concluded. Szabolcs's parents were delighted at the prospect of having their son educated in a residential school, with no expenses to meet.

Shortly afterwards, Szabolcs became a boarder at the school. Quickly mastering the English language, he proved himself to be an alert student. He contributed usefully to various aspects of school life, both academically and on the sports field.

Some weeks after Szabolcs's arrival, my father received a telegram from the Hungarian refugee headquarters, which read:

JANOS SOPRONYI AGED TEN TO ARRIVE ARNOLD LODGE SCHOOL TODAY FROM LONDON WITH FATHER DR SOPRONYI 20.00 HOURS.

We were taken aback. Although not in a financial position to be able to give a free education to yet another boy, there could be no question of turning the second one away.

Eight o'clock came and went. By midnight we had retired to bed, assuming that Janos would not be coming after all. We were woken by the constant ringing of the doorbell in the early hours. Outside on the front drive was Dr Sopronyi, cold and bewildered, accompanied by Janos, a scrap of a boy, who was clearly petrified.

Despite his stilted English, Dr Sopronyi would have happily talked non-stop until breakfast time. It was with great difficulty that we finally persuaded him to retire for the night. Janos possessed no overnight things, so we found him a pair of pyjamas and a comfortable bed in which to sleep. Before departing for London next morning, Dr Sopronyi broke down in floods of tears when the time came for him to part with his son.

'My wife and daughter were killed in the uprising. Janos is all I have left. Love him, look after him, teach him the meaning of forgiveness. That is what I beg you to do for him.'

'Dr Sopronyi,' said my mother, 'I will treat Janos as my own child. That I promise you. Try not to worry about him. He will be in good, loving hands. We shall help him all we can to settle happily and will look after him until you are in a position to take care of him yourself.'

It was exceptionally trustful of Dr Sopronyi to leave Janos in the guardianship of complete strangers. He needed to find a job, however, and it was essential for him to have time on his own to begin a new life after having lost everything in Hungary.

My mother became very attached to Janos. With great patience she helped him to learn the words of our complex language. He was slower to settle than Szabolcs, his disposition being a great deal more excitable. He had witnessed horrendous atrocities in the Budapest revolution, events about which he was incapable of speaking. My mother's steadying influence encouraged Janos to display his enchanting smile with less frequent sullen intervals. Each day he gained the self-assurance that would in time enable his talents to emerge.

After some months we received a cable from Dr Sopronyi saying that Janos would be going to live with him in Canada. My mother was upset at the thought of the sudden separation, so much so that she wept when he left the school. Several weeks later a postcard arrived from Canada addressed to my mother, carrying the simple message:

Dear Mrs Hall,
  Thank you for the lovely.
  With love from Janos.

This spontaneous note was more treasured by my mother than any number of names on the honours board.

Widening Horizons

My parents, Douglas and Eileen, met in 1933. That September my father took up an appointment as teacher of mathematics and games at Harrow View House Preparatory School in Ealing, London. My mother had already been the school matron for two years. From the outset my father was fascinated by the tall, slim, attractive, dark-haired matron, who had declined his invitations to take her out so many times that he was losing heart. She had on each of these occasions already planned to meet relations or friends, arrangements from which she was unable to extricate herself. Little did my father know that his developing feelings for the alluring Eileen were beginning to be reciprocated.

Their first outing together early in the November was to the Popular Café in Piccadilly. Six weeks later, after a whirlwind courtship, they became engaged to be married. From his paltry salary of £125 per annum my father had to pay for his digs and help to support his widowed mother. After having worked in prep schools for over ten years, he had accumulated debts which totalled seven hundred pounds. Unable to provide anything better, he purchased from Woolworths a sixpenny engagement ring, with the promise that a real diamond one would be bought when times were better. My mother wore the sparkling imitation ring with a joy and pride that signified the helplessness of the love she felt for the man with whom she was to spend thirty-eight happy years.

Alongside a background of financial hardship, my father's ambition to own and run his own school was an illusory pipe dream. A dramatic turn of events made the vain hope into more than just a possibility. A young, unmarried master at Harrow View House, David Hardy, the elder son of Hardy of the Freeman, Hardy and Willis chain of shoe shops, had designs also on being his own boss. As well as having been a classical scholar of The Queen's College, Oxford, he had at his disposal a certain amount of capital. He and my parents planned to go into partnership together, but first they needed to find a suitable school.

With the help of scholastic agents, they considered various establishments. Arnold Lodge in Leamington Spa was finally selected, mainly because it was the least expensive of the three that had been shortlisted. A figure of £3,750, to include the freehold buildings, goodwill, fixtures and fittings, was agreed upon. David was to hold a two-thirds share, whereas my parents needed to find the balance. My mother had some savings, which she spent on paying off my father's debts. The sum of £1,250 still had to be found. My mother's father provided some of the cash whilst the West Bromwich Building Society offered a long-term mortgage. Contracts were exchanged and the deal was struck; the show was soon to be on the road.

My parents were married in Leominster parish church in August 1934. In view of her father's ill health, my mother insisted on having a quiet wedding, with the minimum of guests. My father, unable to afford a new outfit of clothes, presented himself at the church in a shabby, ill-fitting, shiny suit. Minutes after the ceremony, his exasperated mother-in-law, outraged by his seeming lack of decorum, commented cuttingly to my mother, 'You have just married the most casual man I've ever met!'

Frantic improvements were made to the down-at-heel Arnold Lodge premises in preparation for the new term. The outgoing proprietor, Mr E C Moir, whose delicate wife was a constant source of worry to him, had allowed the responsibilities to get on top of him. The school was in need of a facelift. Most of the tattered furniture was thrown out and replaced with less worn items; damaged ceilings were repaired; brighter colours obliterated the dowdy liquorice-black paintwork that was everywhere; electricity was partially installed.

The joint principals, David Hardy and my father, plunged themselves into the untested waters of a business that was theirs. The third member of the partnership, my mother, added her expertise and support as teacher, domestic supervisor and matron. With an air of freshness, amidst much animated excitement, the term began with forty boys, six of whom were boarders. The modest termly fees of eight guineas for day boys aged over ten guaranteed that no fortune was likely to be made by the three proprietors.

The school prospectus reflected my mother's dedication to the health and physical well-being of the boys in her care. 'To guard against infection all the classrooms are disinfected twice daily and the boarders gargle every day throughout the year,' began one of its paragraphs. Whether or not fastidiousness of this kind was going to attract more fee-paying parents remained to be seen.

David Hardy was a gifted teacher, especially with able boys. As the younger of the two teaching partners, he relied heavily on my father's experience and familiarity with the preparatory school ethos. The two men complemented each other by virtue of their widely differing talents. Arnold Lodge, noted for its happy atmosphere, expanded and flourished under them during the next four years.

The bombshell came when David announced that he wanted to take up an appointment in a public school, in order to be able to teach older boys. He was disappointed with the academic scope provided at Arnold Lodge, saying that most of the boys there were of limited intelligence only. An intellectual of the highest order, he wanted the challenge of brighter students at a more senior level.

My parents could see David's point of view. When, however, he decided unilaterally to remove the capital he had invested as a partner all at once, the school's survival prospects looked bleak. Fate mercifully intervened through my mother's timely inheritance of a thousand pound legacy from an aunt. In view of the financial progress the business had been making, the building society provided the extra funds needed by increasing the amount of the loan. The school's future was once again secure.

David's appointment to the staff at Campbell College, Belfast, was cut short when war broke out one year later. Serving as an army officer mainly in Italy, he was awarded the Military Cross for gallantry. Returning home after demobilisation, the fearful experiences of his active service had left him with shattered nerves.

David became a close friend of our family in subsequent years. He came to stay with us frequently during school holidays; and we made him vice-president of the old boys' association. In fact, he had begun to regard Arnold Lodge as a second home. He openly stated how much he regretted his impulsive selfishness in withdrawing his money in such haste, a decision that could so easily have brought about the school's closure.

A man of fluctuating moods, David's eccentric humour and behaviour, evident whenever he was in a manic state of mind, encouraged us to identify with his exuberance and respond to his calls for spontaneous fun. I shall not forget the party games we used to play at Christmas times, with David, dressing up preposterously, performing the silliest of parts in charades. The tears would dribble down our faces as we laughed uncontrollably at his hilarious acting attempts. The inconsolable depressions, brought on by the horrors of war, necessitated his having electroconvulsive therapy quite often. Adopting David as an uncle, I always looked forward to his fleeting visits. I loved him dearly.

David came to see us soon after I had been discharged from the army. By this time he was on the staff at Colet Court, the junior school of St Paul's in London. Although interested to learn of my career aspirations, he was unkind enough to reaffirm his view that Arnold Lodge would never hit the headlines, so certain was he that his original misgivings of the school's prospects were well founded. The cynical comments, though hardening my resolve still more, offered not one crumb of comfort. In the school's struggle for survival I had begun to regard myself as a vital element, a guardian angel. Bearing in mind the broken confidence and faltering emotions, this perception of my worth was an illogical contradiction. Lacking a detailed plan, I performed my duties as well as I was able, identifying certain needs.

The boys at Arnold Lodge knew exactly how to irritate ineffective teachers. Many weak disciplinarians had left as failures in the recent past. Most of the pupils assumed that, as the youngest master on the staff, I too would be completely at their mercy. After some initial battles, to the surprise of all, I quickly established my authority. I persuaded my father to introduce a star and stripe competition and a more meaningful detention system, together with other sanctions, in an attempt to raise standards of behaviour, courtesy and dress. I was convinced then and always will be that children feel more secure and are happier in a structured, ordered environment, providing direction is exercised calmly, fairly and with consistency.

I undertook the task of reviving the school magazine, *The Arnoldian*, abandoned after a one and only edition towards the end of the war. Gathering together every available scrap of news for the old pupils' section, which detailed the achievements of the most successful old boys, I sent copies of the publication to prominent Warwickshire families. This was my first public relations attempt.

Becoming more venturesome, I decided to arrange an old boys' dance at Leamington's Spa Ballroom. Thanks to my musical contacts, the booking of suitable bands was an easy task. In a virtually single-handed operation, announcement letters were posted and press releases issued; hundreds of posters were displayed in shops, hotels and pubs in Leamington, Warwick, Kenilworth and Stratford. I was determined to make the dance Leamington's social event of the year. Through newspaper and word-of-mouth publicity, the name of Arnold Lodge came to be recognised for the first time by people who had no professional connections with the place.

I became involved with most departments of school life. With so few teachers, each of us needed to be a jack of all trades. I taught French, history and mathematics to varying age levels. I took charge of the shooting club, coached the cricket 1st XI and arranged sports day along the lines recommended by Noel Carmen, whose meticulous organisation I attempted to match. In the few spare moments that remained, I assisted my father in dealing with the many forms, papers and letters that landed daily on his desk. Outings were confined to an occasional afternoon tea at a local café or a rare visit to the cinema, hardly stimulating pleasures for a young man of nineteen. I eagerly sought something, but I knew not what, the unattainable always managing to elude me.

I had been invited to an afternoon tennis party by a friend at his family's farm near Stratford. Derrick, the son of Charles Turriff, the millionaire builder, played tennis to a high standard. So he should have done, because his father had built two superb tennis courts, one of which was floodlit, in the grounds of his luxurious Leamington and Stratford homes. Derrick enjoyed the advantage, therefore, of being able to play as often as he wished in ideal conditions.

Following some lively sets, during the tea interval we went into the house for refreshments. Having already demonstrated my indifferent playing skills, I found a quiet spot in the sitting room, hopeful that I would slip unnoticed into the background. Mr Turriff, known for his Scottish bluntness, attracted everyone's attention as he shouted in my direction, 'Don't sit there expecting to be waited on! Can't you see there are young ladies present? Why do you think your parents paid for you to be sent to public school? Stand up, pass the tea things round and show us you have the manners of a gentleman!'

Seeing my extreme discomfort, one of the girls in the group came to my rescue; I badly needed friendly encouragement at that moment. Sixteen-year-old Gill seemed to possess all the essential ingredients of good looks, poise and self-assurance. She gave the impression of being genuinely interested in me, an unexpected compliment that flattered and excited me immeasurably. Never before had a girl made me feel so special and important, let alone one as attractive as Gill. Perceiving myself to be out of my depth socially with the classy creature, I was prepared all the same to risk emotional injury by attempting to meet her again.

Gill lived way out of town in a nearby village. Her father, a well-to-do gentleman farmer, was married to a snob. Unable to drive, the only way I was able to take Gill out was by asking Derrick to act as chauffeur. I cannot remember whether he actually sat in the cinema with the two of us, but I do recollect I was too nervous so much as to hold Gill's hand. The presence of a third party and the infra dig transport arrangement would have cramped the style of the most forward of suitors.

I was convinced it was love at first sight, a positive *coup de foudre*, as far as my feelings for Gill were concerned. To be able to win her over, it was essential for me to become more marketable and independent, by first of all learning to drive and to dance. Meanwhile thoughts of the lovely Gill were daily in my head to the point that the aching never ceased to hurt and the emotional longing intensified most alarmingly.

Alastair McCann, a man of twice my age, had at short notice replaced the chair-smashing John Bridge as teacher of Latin and history at the school. With the background of a good Cambridge classics degree he was an academic asset. Having no previous teaching experience, he at once realised that, when confronted with a class of disorderly and often cruel youngsters, technique mattered more than scholastic competence. His diffidence and apprehension made the poor fellow a sitting duck; he was played up mercilessly.

Alastair's conscientious willingness to play a full part in the life of the school was outweighed by the depth of his frustration because of his inability to cope as he would have liked. I respected his keenness, his good intentions; without wishing to interfere or to seem to be patronising, I encouraged him all I could. He was a self-critical perfectionist who took immense trouble over all aspects of his work. He would have made a first-class schoolmaster, given time, patience, some training and a belief in himself.

Shortly before taking his leave of us, having decided to discard the unfortunate teaching experiment in favour of less stressful employment, Alastair, with whom I had always been on the best of terms, stopped me in the passageway outside the dining hall. Looking at me with more than his usual earnestness, sincere as always, he made a short parting speech, the astonishing contents of which have remained indelibly in my memory.

'I would do anything to have half your ability. It is quite amazing how well the boys respond when you are in charge. You are a natural leader and I envy you so much. I can see that one of these days your ambitions for Arnold Lodge will be fulfilled. Try not to lose heart!'

It mattered to me that Alastair felt able to praise me for my strengths; nobody else had ever done so. I wondered what the three army psychiatrists would have made of his remarks!

My father insisted that it was essential for me to qualify as a teacher if I was to be properly groomed to take over the school at a later date. At a time when the survival prospects of Arnold Lodge were at best uncertain, my own preference would have been to have remained there as an unqualified master. To have taken the short-sighted step of allowing myself and the school to vegetate through negative action would, I am sure, have been a grave mistake.

A university degree of itself would not have qualified me to teach. Pessimism concerning my father's health led me to believe I could not afford to devote four years to study in order to obtain a degree and teaching diploma. I went for an interview at St Luke's College, Exeter, one of the best teacher training colleges. The principal, impressed with my sense of commitment, offered me a place on the two-year Certificate of Education course, to commence in September 1958. I readily accepted.

Before studying at Exeter, I was to spend one more year as a trainee teacher at Arnold Lodge, a year in which the pressures and tribulations of school turned out to be as unexpected as they were potentially disastrous. To revitalise me in preparation for the ordeals ahead, I agreed to go on a walking holiday in Germany that August with a friend, Paul, for my first ever taste of foreign adventure.

We had decided to begin at Heidelberg and were to use as our route the valley of the Neckar River. It rained for most of the time, so we amended our plans and made for Bavaria. Endowed with more than my share in the gullibility stakes, it is hardly surprising that self-inflicted disaster struck soon after we arrived at the village of Oberstdorf.

Paul was unenthusiastic when I suggested we might have a drink and listen to the live music at one of the hotels. I repeated to him my father's words: '"On the continent even the children drink wine like lemonade." So why don't we experiment?' I suggested.

'Wine taken in anything other than small measures can be as intoxicating as spirits. If you want to stay here to get pie-eyed, you can count me out!'

Leaving me to my own devices, Paul stalked off to explore the sights. Feeling very grown-up, I ordered a bottle of the local plonk. Before many minutes had elapsed, the sickly sweet substance had been drunk, with the bottle empty. I was beginning to enjoy the stuff; it was indeed no different from drinking lemonade. The music played on, rekindling for me memories of the Repton dance band. Already in a muzzy state, I ordered another bottle of wine. This one, too, I emptied.

Eventually I staggered back to the guest house where we had booked a room. Making for the nearest basin, I was unable to contain a moment longer the vomit that brought up with it much of the food and drink I had so recently sampled.

Paul was already in bed. 'You've woken me up with your revolting noises,' he exploded. 'You'll make *me* sick if you heave and retch about like that any longer. I warned you what would happen if you drank too much!'

Too ill for lengthy argument, I bad-mouthed him under my breath. 'Miserable, priggish, uncharitable sod!'

I was exceptionally ill with alcoholic poisoning for the ensuing forty-eight hours. The day after the night before I cared not whether I lived or died, a plight in no way aided by Paul's unpitying pose.

Returning to England, with at least one important lesson learned, sporting a healthy tan, I got stuck in once more to my teaching duties. I was hopeful my efforts during the new academic year would help to prevent the school's downward slide from continuing.

Staff changes were frequent, two new masters having joined Arnold Lodge in September. John Wightman, a bachelor in his mid-sixties and a former D'Oyly Carte Opera Company singer, was to teach English, art and singing. He had been housemaster of the boarders at Victoria College in Cairo until the school was commandeered by the police under the Nasser regime during the Suez Canal crisis.

An experienced younger master, Herbert Wright, who had previously worked for some years at a preparatory school in Yorkshire, impressed me greatly. Energetic and ambitious, he brought to the school a dynamism that had hitherto been absent. He quickly gained the respect of the pupils, and it was pleasingly obvious that here was a teacher with rare talents.

It was a relief to discover at long last a fellow spirit; it was going to be much easier to build up the school as a team effort than for me to attempt to do it single-handed. Mr Wright and I soon became firm friends. My father, encouraged by the good influence exerted by Mr Wright, promoted him to the position of senior master after his first half-term with us. All looked set for a more stable period in which we could expect to see a gradual improvement in the school's standards.

Herbert Wright was divorced; he used to visit his children in Staffordshire on a Monday afternoon, which was his half day. On one occasion he returned early in a state of agitation, sobbing uncontrollably. The separation from his children, together with their antagonistic attitude, had crushed his resolve; it was impossible to console him.

From that day on, the optimistic hopes of the past few weeks seemed to disintegrate. Herbert Wright went steadily downhill. He started to drink heavily; furthermore, pupils and parents were complaining that he actually went to sleep during lessons. The situation degenerated further when it became known he had taken up with a local barmaid, returning to his school accommodation in the small hours, always the worse for wear. It was little wonder that he was incapable of doing his job.

Problems were compounded when my father was rushed to hospital with excruciating stomach pains. He had looked unwell for some time, but preferred to suffer stoically than make a fuss. The school was in disarray. The headmaster was ill; the senior master was an alcoholic; in addition to myself, the only other master, John Wightman, was sufficiently near to retirement age not to want to take on additional burdens. Despite his impeccable credentials, John's private life was by no means straightforward. He did not attempt to hide his partiality for a particular adult male, which led us to conclude they were having a homosexual relationship. Arnold Lodge's position would have been irredeemable had we not instinctively known that John, a thorough gentleman, would never abuse his professional trust; nonetheless, I did not feel able to discuss with him the school's worsening situation.

I could once again sense the nervous tensions growing within me as I assumed the overall responsibility, an absurd undertaking for one so young. I became demented with anxiety and stress in a way which vividly revived the memories of those calamitous army days. My melancholy frame of mind affected the pupils I was teaching by causing them to fear me because of my fluctuating, unpredictable moods.

I was in need of psychiatric help. Dr Clifford Tetlow came to visit me. He recognised that, for the second time in less than two years, I was having a nervous breakdown. His immediate recommendation was a period of treatment as an in-patient at a nearby mental hospital. I was convinced it would have been fatal for me to consent to his advice, bearing in mind the school's defenceless position.

'By refusing to accept treatment you are taking a big risk,' said Dr Tetlow. 'I can see you would prefer to be in the thick of things, believing as you do that the school's outlook is grave, that your enforced absence would leave a significant gap. Do not forget if you allow your illness to affect the well-being of those in any way connected with the school, you would, in fact, be contributing to its undoing.'

My only option was to try to overcome the effects of the illness, to be able to cope rationally with the onerous workload. Determination and prayer jointly were responsible for averting the crisis. Erratic outbursts and emotional problems have occurred in later years, but thank God the ultimate loss of control has not needed treatment and never will. From that time on Dr Tetlow became a valued friend. He believed in me with an undaunted confidence; until his death in 1990 he helped me overcome a number of complex problems.

A few days before Christmas my father underwent an operation to remove his gall bladder. Complications set in, which caused him to be on the danger list for what seemed an eternity. His absence from the old boys' dance cast a cloud of gloom over the occasion. My father's indisposition failed to bring the best out of Herbert Wright, who, true to form, turned up drunk at the dance with his floozie.

During the second part of that term my mother had to combine the duties of cook and matron, the latter having also been admitted to hospital for a major operation. Because things could not have been more serious, it was all the more important for me to keep my head.

Throughout the following term Wright's behaviour became so disgraceful that his inefficiency, indolence and surliness were being openly criticised by disaffected parents. As acting head and the highest paid member of staff, he made not the slightest effort to fulfil his obligations. I was not the only one saddened to witness the self-destruction of a potentially able schoolmaster. In due course the disappointment developed into an anguish. We had all been let down by Wright, but for him to have failed to support my father, who was still unwell, was inexcusable. By Easter this wreck of a man had left us.

I had offered the hand of friendship to Wright from the moment he arrived in Leamington. Following his family's indifference to his weekly visits, I never once failed to stand loyally by him when he was lonesome, distracted and at odds with himself. I was happy to be a willing listener, a sounding board, a comforter. I had high hopes that, once he was more settled in his domestic life, the contributions he was capable of making towards the growth and improvement of the school, from which he would himself clearly benefit, would prove to be inestimable. My youthful innocence had prevented me from seeing through his selfish use of me as a stopgap ally. Wright's thoughtless abandonment of earlier promises, his total disregard for those who had no option but to depend on him, caused a bitterness to well up inside me, a bitterness that lingered and took some while to dissipate.

Despite the traumas that overwhelmed me throughout the gruelling winter, Gill's image remained firmly fixed in my thoughts. Perpetual imaginings of her had provided me with the strength to be able to endure hardship when all seemed lost. My longing for Gill's friendship and an affectionate response from her was developing into a fetish.

It is amazing what can be achieved when there is strong incentive. Interspersed between laborious efforts at the school, I strove to acquire two of the social skills that were lacking in my life, without which the Gill of my dreams would remain unconquered in her country seat. I attended a number of private dancing lessons. Having previously only provided music at dances as a musician on the rostrum, I was now poised to launch myself as a dance partner at a hunt ball, no less. Before becoming the newly serviced specimen that was necessary for the fruition of my plans, I needed next to learn to drive.

I almost had to bludgeon my father into attaching L-plates to his precious Wolseley car, whose gears were operated from the steering wheel. To supplement what I was being taught by the driving school instructor, my father sat in silent agony whilst I drove him about. Gritting his teeth nervously, the reluctant passenger survived the jerkings and emergency halts without undue incident; not once did he complain or lose his cool.

My parents decided to spend a few days of the summer half-term holiday with my father's sister and her husband at their Sussex home in Worthing. I was keen to join them for two reasons. For me to chauffeur them there and back would aid my preparations for the forthcoming driving test, but more important was the fact that Gill was a residential student at an exclusive finishing school at Cuckfield, which was within easy reach of where we would be staying.

The outward journey almost over, a signpost indicated that Cuckfield was a mere two miles away. My heart thumped as I burnt inside with impatient excitement. I insisted on driving past Gill's college, which stood well back from the road, surrounded by spacious well tended gardens. The grand building looked empty and impersonal. I parked the car and sat in silent contemplation. I was convinced a glorious miracle would suddenly produce Gill out of thin air, that she would come running towards the car, arms outstretched. Nothing stirred; nobody emerged; only the leaves rustled in the wind. The dearth of activity haunted my mood with the sensation that I had been blessed with supernatural powers that would cause Gill to appear at my beckoning. Still nothing stirred, not even an hallucinatory spectre brushed past.

I spent the entire Saturday in Brighton on my own. It was not unreasonable to assume that, in her weekend leisure moments, Gill would travel the seventeen miles to participate in Brighton's amusements with her college friends. I was counting on seeing her there; it was as if it was meant to be. Fate's way of sealing its approval on our union would be for the two of us to meet by chance in a charming seaside setting. Each teenage girl from afar became Gill's replica, until the brief recognition soured with tormenting disillusionment as they one and all became strangers unknown. Forlorn and unrewarded, I left behind me the pebbled beach, the candy floss, the sunlit Regency buildings.

One month later I took and passed my driving test. I was ready to ask Gill out again, this time without the need of a chaperone. I dialled her number as soon as I had parked the car. The distant ringing buzzed with a rhythmical boldness that expressed the intensity of my arousing passions. There was no answer. The suspense was intolerable; so much depended on the outcome of this call. At last a familiar voice answered. It was Gill's condescending mother.

'Claverdon 445,' she opened with high-pitched sweetness, as if butter would have been incapable of melting in her mouth.

'Please may I speak to Gill?'

'Who is that speaking?'

'Jonathan Hall.'

'Oh!' she sighed. Then after a long pause came the curt, staccato words, 'She's out.'

'Can you please tell me when Gill is likely to be in?'

'I've no idea of her movements. She's hardly ever here!'

She rang off, making it clear she had no intention of prolonging the conversation or of being in any way helpful.

After numerous telephone call attempts, each bringing about the same response, I was forced to take the hint. Gill's family behaved towards me in a frosty manner that left no doubt they considered me unfit so much as to enter via their tradesman's door.

There must have been an inadequacy in my emotional chemistry that caused Anthony Kaye to reject me, the army to relegate me to a prison hospital and Herbert Wright to treat with contempt my attempts to befriend him at his time of need. The vulnerability of youth was tested no less when Gill dismissed me too. Having been encouraged and misled by Gill's seductive attitudes at Derrick's party, it was of modest consolation to learn when last I heard of her that she had never married and was on the shelf.

Before embarking upon my college course at Exeter, I arranged to meet up with a former school friend in Paris. Peter had recently come down from Oxford, where he had been reading history.

It gave Peter pleasure to show me the sights of that well planned city. Having exhausted his not inconsiderable knowledge on me in a way which would have tested the stamina of the most saintly of men, he excitedly announced the next stop would be Avignon in Provence. With time to spare before catching the midnight train that was to transport us to a warmer climate, we slipped inside a tiny backstreet cinema to while away a couple of hours before making for the station.

It was not until I was on the train, sandwiched tightly between two voluminous ladies who reeked of garlic, that I began to itch. The lack of ventilation and sweltering temperature aggravated the itching so much that I scratched in silent agony for the entire journey. At least one active flea had affixed itself to my person in the Paris cinema. Alighting from the train at Avignon early in the morning, the sun already burning hot, my urgent need was for a bath. To locate a moderately priced hotel with this facility in the bustling month of August was easier said than done. We booked ourselves a dingy room. The hotel proprietor was happy to unlock the one and only bathroom for an extra charge. In preparation for a change of clothes, I gratefully submerged my badly bitten body in the soapy water. The flea was thereby drowned.

With limitless enthusiasm inappropriate in such humid conditions, Peter hurried me along the narrow streets of the medieval city that is ringed with four thousand metres of fourteenth-century walls. The whistle-stop tour brought us past the pedestrianised Place du Palais and up the steps to the eight-towered Palace of the Popes, the magnificent building to which the papacy transferred from Rome.

Bubbling over with excitement and eagerness, my guide led me out of Avignon across the suspension bridge, high above the treacherous River Rhône. To our right we spied the famous truncated Pont Saint-Bénézet about which we had sung as children. '*On y danse tous en rond,*' proclaims the old nursery rhyme. We marched uphill to another town that is steeped in history, Villeneuve-lès-Avignon. Peter was in his element. Treating the imposing six-hundred-year-old Fort Saint-André as if it were his own creation, he expounded the virtues of its towers, the twelfth-century Romanesque-style chapel, the remains of a former Benedictine abbey, the tumbledown ruins of a village.

But the exertions of our action-packed pilgrimage caused Peter to collapse with a frightening attack of asthma. Producing a portable inhaler, he slumped into a sitting position at the roadside. The anxious eyes that were sunken into a pale, emaciated face registered his alarm at his predicament. He had always looked a feeble, scrawny specimen. I had been unaware up until then of the extreme delicacy of his health and of the responsibility I was taking on by going away with him. I managed to persuade a French schoolmaster whom we had just met to drive us back to our hotel. A doctor was sent for. I was convinced that Peter was going to suffocate. He wheezed, puffed, heaved and choked, struggling for the breath of life. For an extortionate fee, the doctor injected Peter and issued him with a prescription. Partially recovered, Peter stubbornly refused to abandon the holiday, protesting that the sightseeing had barely started. Our purses lighter, obtusely thinking that Peter's nasty ailment would be blown away by the sea air of the Mediterranean, we caught a bus for Nice.

Contrary to my advice, Peter was unwilling to put his feet up and relax in our Riviera base. I reminded him we were on holiday and that there was something to be said in favour of having at least one restful day. He wanted to explore the marvels of the Grande Corniche, the spectacular mountain route that leads with awe-inspiring splendour from Nice to the Italian border. Inseparable from Monaco is Monte Carlo, which grew around the casino at the end of the last century. Descriptions of the glitzy Monte Carlo had never seized me with a desire to pay a visit there, although I would have been intrigued to catch a glimpse of Sir Bernard and Lady Docker's yacht, *Shemara*, which was still moored in the harbour. Peter had an alternative expedition in mind. He dragged me to the top of the rock that dominates Monaco, to view the exterior of Prince Rainier's stately palace.

Autocratic policemen controlled the principality's traffic with a fierceness that offended the most easygoing of the pleasure-seeking visitors. Monaco's catchpenny superficialities did not appeal to me one bit; the inhabitants' hostility was plain enough. Depending in large measure on the tourist trade, they offered no more than a frigid welcome. Considering the purchase of some small gifts to take back with us to our families in England, we entered a souvenir shop to have a look around. Back outside on the street, our hands empty, we continued to scrutinise the objects in the same shop's window from the narrow pavement.

To our surprise, the shopkeeper, a dumpy middle-aged woman with a gigantic bosom, waddled towards us, her face flushed with intolerant fury. My French was stronger than Peter's, so I became the duo's spokesman in the exchange that followed.

'If you are not going to buy something, move on!' she ordered.

'Surely we are entitled to look before we decide whether or not we wish to buy from your shop.'

'You've been here long enough. You are blocking the view of others. Go away!'

'We have no intention of moving until we've finished seeing what you have for sale. Is this not a public pavement?'

Greatly embarrassed, Peter proceeded to safer regions. I stood my ground. The shopkeeper began to push me from the pavement on to the street itself. The passers-by, unwilling to offer help, hoped from a discreet distance for the pleasure of witnessing my instant demise under some lethal motor vehicle. It was going to be fun to watch what would ensue. From the point of view of sheer bulk and weight the female of the species must have been the favourite. I had the advantage of my youth, agility and speed; the odds were even. The throng of spectators multiplied as a battle royal commenced. We prodded, heaved, shoved, pulled, elbowed, mangled, tangled, jostled, grasped, clasped, edged and nudged. A policeman appeared on the scene. Unwilling to intervene in the savage shemozzle, he contented himself with blowing his whistle continuously. The street was in an uproar. Some supported the lady wrestler; others cheered me on. Feelings were running high.

The noise was tumultuous. With partisan bias the audience whooped, yelled, jeered, sneered, scoffed, coughed, hissed and booed, each offering invaluable advice with pontificating bluster.

The slapstick comedy of a contest over, the shopkeeper began to swoon, although she was sufficiently in command of herself to give a distorted account of the events to those still present. The policeman ambled over to the scene of the disturbance; treating me as a vexatious foreigner, he ordered me to leave Monaco without delay. It was little wonder that Peter's asthma was troubling him again. The bus journey back to Nice was expedient as well as timely.

Peter's condition was deteriorating. Rather than risk the terrors of a French hospital, we decided it would be prudent to travel home to England as soon as possible. A day's rest was necessary to prepare Peter for the bus ride back to Avignon, whence we would catch the Paris train. Peter languished in the airless Nice hotel room, desiring only peace and quiet.

The fifth largest city in France, Nice offers a comfortable charm that is unique. My appetite was whetted as I viewed the spacious squares and gardens, the old town sheltered to the east, the glamour and the want. I enviously eyed some of Europe's millionaires as they wined, dined and danced on the terrace of the sumptuous Hotel Negresco on the Promenade des Anglais. One day I would be back.

When we arrived at Avignon, Peter was so ill that further medical help was sought. There were more injections for which we parted with our few remaining francs. The doctor spelt out the urgency of the need for a swift return to England. The train journey home was precarious. Peter, in a state of near collapse, was like a zombie for the entire excursion. Having negotiated Paris and the Channel crossing unscathed, the relief was ecstatic when I finally handed Peter over to the safety of a hospital in Paddington.

A Taste of Freedom

The authorities of St Luke's, a Church of England college that catered only for male students, subjected us to more rigid rules than was customary at most teacher training colleges. Doors were locked at 11 p.m. and we all had to wear suits on Sundays; girls were under no circumstances permitted to visit us in our rooms at any time. Attendance at lectures was more or less obligatory, irrespective of whether or not we were to gain any value from them. Some of the lecturers treated us with an anachronistic formality unfitting and demeaning for men of our age. The wind of change that was to liberalise St Luke's and educational establishments at every level was as yet a mere whiff in the air.

The qualifications needed to become a teacher during this era were so basic that many students with only a handful of O levels and none of the social graces were offered places. The course involved academic study, educational theory and practical teaching experience, on successful completion of which we were to be let loose on the country's young, with inadequate knowledge and immature techniques.

It was obvious that the principal, Mr J L Smeall, was proud of St Luke's. He was a commanding orator, with a tongue that could be persuasive when the spirit moved him. He had a deep-seated distrust of preparatory schools. On at least three occasions I heard him address students publicly with comments such as these: 'I would advise you to avoid teaching in a preparatory school. If you do take up a post in one, you will probably find that your salary increments will not be honoured after the first two or three years. Most of these schools do not stick to the accepted salary scales, even though headmasters at interviews can be misleadingly plausible.'

There was truth in these remarks as far as Arnold Lodge was concerned. I was not aware my father had ever paid increments to any of his teachers. Heads of the better established preparatory schools, however, would have been justified in reacting indignantly to what Mr Smeall had said.

St Luke's enviable reputation for prowess at rugby football was in large measure due to Mr Smeall's enthusiasm for the sport. He recruited as many 'star' players as possible so as to build up the strength of the college XV. With four county players in their ranks, including Danny Harris, who gained two Welsh caps, the XV my first year there again proved superior to the arch-enemy, Loughborough College, by achieving a resounding victory in the annual match at Old Deer Park, Richmond.

Boisterous, loud-mouthed Welshmen, the majority of whom were physical education specialists, were not easily avoided. Preferring to go everywhere in a troop, I gleaned the impression they made up the vast proportion of the student body; in actual fact their numbers were not that great. This powerful minority group was most in evidence on Saturday nights. Lit up with beer inside their bellies, singing lustily and not always tunefully as they careered along the Exeter streets, these uncouth chaps were best avoided. Individually some of the Welsh students surprised me with their quiet modesty and artistic sensibilities; when in a gang they changed character and adopted the brash attitudes of foreigners abroad.

Inwardly critical of many of my fellow students, I thought they lacked polish and spoke ungrammatically or with regional accents. Educated in schools at which teachers spoke the Queen's English, I found it hard to come to terms with the fact that people from humble, working-class backgrounds could be intelligent and professionally capable, an appallingly arrogant and fallacious concept on my part. I soon learnt the important lesson that my privileged public school background had made me no better equipped to teach than anyone else. I began to judge others by their qualities rather than to mark them down because of superficial failings that had in any event been inherited.

I discovered I was to share a room in the main college building with another first-year student, a parson's son from Oxfordshire. The Freudian slip of forgetting my room-mate's name must reveal something of my negative feelings towards him. The two of us had nothing in common. I was an early riser, whereas he burnt the midnight oil. The ritual of my wet shave at what must have seemed an unearthly hour would wake him up. He retaliated by stomping about when I was attempting to get some rest. Having been inactive for most of the day, he tackled his work assignments with noise and bustle at a time when civilised folk were presumably asleep. Thankfully we never came to blows, although our lifestyles and habits were sufficiently different for us to prefer not to mix in the same circles.

It was only when I began to settle down to student life in Exeter that I realised how imprisoned I had been hitherto. The metaphorical straitjacket having been removed, I quickly discovered how socially inept I was, which galvanised me into the kind of infantile conduct that most young men would have abandoned while still in their teens. At home my mother had expected me to be the perfect boy and the perfect young man. I had been liberated at last from the guilt complexes, the duty constraints, that had plagued and restricted me up until then. The pure heaven of being able, unscrutinised, to kick over the traces led me to a number of harmless stupidities and antics that are best forgotten.

Exeter was a pleasant city in which to be based. Though not exactly throbbing with vitality, it offered after my sheltered past more excitements than I dreamed existed. The coffee bars, the Swiss Buttery, the countless pubs, of which the Dickens Bar and the Locomotive Inn were my favourites, ensured that evenings and weekends were actively employed. Dartmoor's rugged, uncanny remoteness was half an hour away, with the seaside distractions of Torquay and Exmouth no less easily accessible. On the hottest days of summer some of us were bold enough to risk the displeasure of tired lecturers as we absented ourselves from college obligations in favour of a few splendid, lazy, sunny hours in the sand dunes at Dawlish Warren.

The pent up feelings and emotions of many years needed to be discharged in order to allow me to develop a personal identity. Like a bull in a china shop, I behaved showily and with idiotic puerility in off-duty moments, drawing to everyone's attention the joyous news that a brief taste of irresponsibility was the tonic I had long awaited. I would greet other students with the Liverpudlian term of 'wacker', which led to my being branded a weirdo early on. Developing a liking for scrumpy and vintage cider, I was a pestilential nuisance after pub closing time, an opinion that was subscribed to by the owner of the Swiss Buttery, whose benign expression changed to an angry scowl whenever I entered his premises late at night.

Glad though I was to be free of the fetters of the family school that I both loved and hated, I missed certain aspects of the prep school world that were ingrained in my very being. I walked past and eyed with distant longing the three preparatory schools that were situated in and around the city. I wondered whether they were caring, cheerful places, whether they, too, struggled to pay their way and to attract and retain a capable staff. Within the walls of these establishments lived personalities of every kind, all with their joys, agonies, attributes, blemishes, secrets and desires. I felt the urge to be involved once more in the life of a school community.

The opportunity for me to work part-time at Exeter Cathedral School came unexpectedly. Through a college contact I was introduced one morning to the headmaster, Mr Reginald Pitkin. He asked whether I would be interested in teaching some history at the school to help him out whilst he was short of a member of staff.

'There is a class unattended at the moment. Would you like to sit in for the lesson and see how you get on?'

I cannot recall what I attempted to teach the boys for whom I was suddenly responsible. I know that I was excited to be back at work in the classroom.

The lesson over, Mr Pitkin summoned me to his study. 'I took the liberty of listening in on your lesson,' he told me. 'You have a good command of your subject and the boys responded well and seemed interested. I am happy for you to teach five history lessons each week, to fit in with your college programme. If you are prepared to take this on, I shall pay you at the rate of five pounds per week.'

His offer was gratefully accepted. After having been issued with a gown, timetable and syllabus, I commenced the temporary job almost at once. The extra pocket money was going to be a useful addition to my scant resources.

Mr Pitkin used to invite the teaching staff into his sitting room for a sherry before lunch, a custom we all considered very civilised. Being only an occasional visitor to the school, my knowledge of its workings and personalities was limited. The masters were of the elderly and tired or younger and idiosyncratic variety; none of them stood out as pillars of great strength. The boys were happy enough, despite the limitations of cramped facilities and lack of playing space. The musically inclined among them benefited from excellent tuition in singing as well as a wide range of instruments. The cathedral choristers, whose fees were reduced on account of their onerous duties, were, I discovered, with very few exceptions, 'as bright as buttons'.

A year later, by which time I was no longer working at the school, I was shocked to learn of Mr Pitkin's death. He had committed suicide, his body having been discovered in a warehouse near the River Exe. The circumstances of this tragedy, if correctly recounted, would match those of any of the *Tales of the Unexpected* I had heard or read.

It was said that Mr Pitkin, who had been a director of a group of hotels before becoming involved with school management, had previously been sent to prison for manslaughter, following a drink-driving incident. Whilst in Exeter jail his wife had sued him for divorce. The marriage dissolved, and there being little or no prospect of a job on his release, Mr Pitkin was desperate.

The dean of Exeter, the Very Reverend A R Wallace, a regular prison visitor, took pity on him. He was impressed with Mr Pitkin's background of an Oundle education and Bachelor of Commerce degree. As chairman of governors of the Cathedral School, the dean was convinced Mr Pitkin's financial knowledge and experience would prove valuable to the school that was in the doldrums at the time. So he took the brave step of appointing Mr Pitkin as the school's Bursar.

The elderly gentleman who had held without distinction the office of headmaster of the school for many years had not before time been persuaded to retire. So successful was Mr Pitkin in performing the duties of bursar that the dean, with even greater rash optimism, offered the vacant post to him. It can only be assumed that staff and parents were unaware of the skeletons in Mr Pitkin' s cupboard.

Mr Pitkin's drive and energy quickly enabled the school to expand and flourish; all sang his praises. What had evidently begun as a too good to be true situation came to an abrupt halt when Mr Pitkin was found to have stolen from school funds and to have interfered sexually with some of his pupils. It was no surprise when after his death it was uncovered that his Oundle background and degree qualifications were fictitious.

Sadly the well-intentioned dean was left with egg on his face in sufficient quantity for him to have learnt to be less trusting in future of his brother human beings.

It was not long before I began to investigate the local jazz scene. Live Dixieland and mainstream jazz music was to be found in a number of clubs, dance halls and pubs, in whose smoke-filled rooms the passion for syncopation gripped young and old alike. The many jivers possessed an energy that would have outdone highly tuned athletes; avid listeners, signifying approval by rocking their heads in time to the music, used the jazz experience as an innocent drug.

I first met Max, a professional photographer, in one of the most sleazy of the Exeter jazz venues. In a broad northern accent above the noisy din he shouted, 'I haven't seen you here before!'

'That's because I'm new to Exeter. I'm a student at St Luke's.'

'Does that mean that you are a rugby player?'

'I'm afraid not, but I love jazz, all kinds of jazz.'

'I play the banjo,' volunteered Max. 'I'm forming a trad band and still looking for musicians. Do you know of anyone at Luke's who plays?'

'I haven't sussed out the talent yet,' I admitted. 'But I'm a drummer and I play the clarinet a bit.'

'The clarinet!' exclaimed Max.

His animated face registered excitement at meeting another jazz fan who actually played the clarinet. In no time he was telling me with delight of his plans. It was as much as I could do not to ask to join his group there and then. We agreed to meet early the following evening in one of the college lecture rooms for him to hear me play.

Little did I know that Max was to arrange for other musicians to assemble for the audition. My experience as a traditional jazz clarinettist up until then had been so limited that I had taken the precaution of practising earlier that day.

'This is Jon,' announced Max, pointing in my direction. 'Do you know John Tidy, our drummer?' he asked. 'He's another Luke's student.'

I nodded with a glimmer of recognition.

'Larry on trumpet, Geoff on trombone and Jock on piano,' he added. 'We are without a bass player today.'

Exchanging pleasantries we began by attempting one of the old jazz faithfuls. The first chorus was ragged, but as we got into our stride we were beginning to sound more like a professional outfit. Larry blasted out the familiar tunes on his trumpet with a rustic aggression that permitted him to bemoan life's injustices in brutal musical language. Trombone player Geoff Cole, a master of his instrument, was streets better than the rest. His talent was later to be discovered by Ken Colyer, whose band he was to join in London.

After inviting me to become a member of his band, Max summed up the session with confident promises.

'We have the makings of a good trad sound. We need to brush up on intros and endings. After three or four more rehearsals, we'll be ready for our first gig. I've lots of contacts, so, providing the music is up to scratch, I can guarantee paid work.'

Max was true to his word. There were plenty of gigs to be had. With the band's repertoire and skills increasing, bookings came flooding in. The extra cash earnings made the world of difference to me. As a student with no grant and a minimal weekly allowance from my father, I was, all of a sudden, much better off than expected.

Of the band's personnel, it was Larry, an endearing rogue, who intrigued me most. He and I could not have come from more widely differing backgrounds. There developed between us an uncanny empathy that the other band members could not comprehend; he became a friend for whom I would do anything within my power. A labourer on the railways by day, Larry was known by us to be a house thief by night. Women all adored him. They were fascinated by his reckless nonchalance; his dusky Latin looks turned them on.

One day Geoff Cole's girlfriend made a pass at him. A married man much in love with his wife, Larry was not averse to having a bit on the side, especially when invitations came from females whose erotic charms appealed to him. One night in a drunken state he broke into the flat belonging to Geoff Cole's lady friend. Expecting at least a kiss to welcome him, Larry was devastated when she telephoned the police in a fit of self-righteous fury. Poor Larry was arrested and later sentenced to two years' imprisonment, previous misdemeanours having been taken into account. The night before he was to go inside, his little baby girl suffocated as she lay in bed between him and his wife. It is little wonder that this hapless and deprived guy, for whom nothing ever went right, blew his trumpet with such belligerent fierceness. He had good reason to feel angry inside.

Because of my band and illicit teaching earnings, I had more money to spend than most of the other students. The time had come for me to use this income in attempts to seek out what I had denied myself in the past.

I was not slow to spot attractive girls, whose presence distracted me from my studies. They were of all shapes and sizes: students, shop assistants, bank clerks, waitresses, well-made moorland farm lasses visiting the city from the sticks. They all appealed. A significant boon was that many of them were hooked on the jazz cult. Even a second rate clarinettist, I discovered, had female followers. Exeter was a male's paradise. I was able to forget the disappointment of the Gill rejection; there were better fish to fry.

Tom, a retired RAF Wing Commander, a mature student also training to be a teacher, attached himself to me. Scarred from a collapsed marriage, he wanted feminine company. Our researches came up with the heartening intelligence that interesting young and older ladies hung out at the Royal Clarence Hotel on Saturday mornings.

Dressed in our smartest casual gear, we entered the hotel bar the following Saturday at noon to view the talent. The room was packed to capacity with, we were delighted to see, a preponderance of ladies of the type described by our informants. Masquerading as men of style we each ordered a Pimm's. I could see Tom already had an admirer. A fetching middle-aged lady with sleek auburn hair was edging in our direction. Her eyes fixed on Tom, who was fumbling for a cigarette, she began speaking to me. She introduced herself as Joy, after which I willingly fell into the trap of doing what she so obviously was contriving to happen.

'Tom,' I said, 'Joy here is dying to meet you!'

She blushed. Gathering herself together with a self-assured directness that took the wind out of Tom's sails, she treated him to a detailed monologue that described her entire life story. She explained how she was a dentist's widow with two teenage daughters and that she had lived in Exeter for some years. Tom, captivated by Joy's engaging personality, reciprocated by recounting a shortened version of his RAF career and matrimonial disaster.

From that day on Tom and Joy were inseparable. Tom removed himself from his digs and the two of them lived together. I was welcomed always in their home as a valued friend: after all, I was the person who had been partly instrumental in bringing about the impulsive union. Tom's emotional needs well satisfied for the present, my own search for a girlfriend intensified.

Attendance at two single-sex boarding schools, as well as the lack of a sister, had caused me to view the female of the species as I would a dangerous zoological creature. Deeply conscious that my inexperience was as transparent as my trepidation, I developed an outward brashness. This deceptive tactic worked in the initial stages; as soon as my defences were uncovered, I was done for.

I experimented by taking out dozens of girls. Not one of the relationships was sustained beyond a couple or so meetings. On Saturday evenings, providing I was not committed to a band gig, I often trudged the two miles with some of my friends to the Exeter University Student Union building, where the most awful dances were held.

A lousy band jangled and banged away; excessive lighting exaggerated everyone's self-consciousness in a glare that emphasised red cheeks and facial blemishes. The absence of a bar did not help, either. Mostly plain girls sat together in grim unity, waiting to be invited to smooch under the searchlight beams on the institutional floor with dull young men like me. Why we returned to the dismal scene to be tortured further I knew not, except there was no harm in hoping it might one day lead to our meeting someone special.

My last ever visit to a 'uni hop', as we called them, proved more fruitful. To provide us with the courage we needed, we stopped off on the way at the Locomotive Inn for some vintage cider. We were in relaxed mood by the time we arrived at the makeshift dance area. An alcoholic haze dulled our senses, making the expectant girl students look strangely comical as they sat in neat rows along the room's perimeter. We swaggered insolently past the many faces, scrutinising with critical eye each one in turn, in our quest for a mate.

All of a sudden I saw a pretty redhead with blue eyes that sparkled. Any boldness deserted me that instant. Not daring to ask her to dance, I was content from a distance to study her lovely features. After long moments of indecision, I went over to speak with her. The worst she could do was to send me packing. Expecting an instant rebuff, I was happy to find that my interruption had relieved the redhead's boredom.

'I hate these dances,' she confided. 'I can't think why I ever bother to come. The men are such crashing bores.'

'Does that include me?'

'I don't know yet.'

Introductions quickly dispensed with, we began chatting away unselfconsciously as if we had been long-standing friends.

'Are you a first-year student?' she inquired.

'Yes, but not at the university. I'm training to be a teacher.'

'It gets better and better,' she exclaimed. 'The university male students are such drips!'

An endearing dimple appeared on her chin when she smiled. She was vivacious and eye-catching. To be in her company was already making me feel ten feet tall.

We strolled hand in hand to her hall of residence in time to meet the Saturday night deadline when the front door would be locked. It was not until I was about to set off on the long walk back to the other side of the city that my attention was drawn to my companion's firm, trim body, the ample breasts, the shapely legs. With sudden awareness of a glowing elation that was consuming me, I clutched the crumpled piece of paper on which the word Anne and her telephone number had been hurriedly scribbled.

'It *is* getting better and better,' I mused, remembering Anne's own words.

In two weeks' time the Christmas vacation was to begin. Anne and I saw as much of each other as possible during what was left of the term. I was sure I was falling in love with her. She responded to my displays of affection with equal eagerness. The friendship blossomed.

As Anne's home was in Jersey I knew it was unlikely she would be able to attend my belated twenty-first birthday party that was to be held in Leamington a few days before Christmas. I told her how much it would mean to me to have her there. She had already been considering the possibility.

'Of course I shall come,' she said. 'Can you arrange to meet me at Birmingham Airport?'

'I can't believe it!' I cried out, bubbling over with excitement.

Anne's three-day visit was not the lively, happy social fling that it should have been. What went wrong was mainly my fault. No woman is at ease in the company of an immature, lovesick man, whose bashfulness robs him of all fun and spontaneity. My carefree Exeter mantle having been cast aside in deference to the inhibiting influences of home, Anne was grieved to find out that the person she thought I was existed only in her imagination.

Within hours of her arrival, I could see that she wished she had never made the journey to Leamington. So intense was I that Anne's expression of boredom, disbelief and later disenchantment was deciphered by every onlooker. I introduced her to some friends at a dance the night before my party; senseless possessiveness on my part stifled her enjoyment and mine so much that we secretly dreaded the coming of age event that was to follow. The milestone that should have signalled the attainment of a manhood highlighted my shy stand-offishness that was worsened by Anne's misjudgement of me.

It was one of my mother's delights to organise domestic matters; the more intricate they were, the happier she was. Having been a headmaster's wife for over twenty years, she was prepared for all contingencies. Party guests were arriving throughout the afternoon by which time dormitory beds had been made up and a buffet tea was available in the school dining hall. Relatives as well as many of my Repton and college friends had travelled long distances. Last to show up were the musicians booked for the evening, the Cambridge University Modern Jazz Quartet. My parents doubted the wisdom of choosing a jazz band, knowing that some of the older guests would find the music far too loud.

Visitors had been allotted a dormitory in which to spend the night; the more elderly among them occupied single rooms. Chaos reigned as activity began in earnest.

'Where's a bathroom? Where can I get a point for my electric razor? Where can I? Where can I?' And so on, until water taps were running and electric razors buzzing all over the building. Raised voices of two men arguing could be heard on the upstairs landing near to our guests' dormitories. David Hardy, my father's former partner, who was to propose my toast, was remonstrating angrily.

'There was no mention of dinner jackets on the invitation,' he protested. 'What on earth am I going to wear?'

'Come in your bathing trunks if you like,' joked my father, irritating David still further. In a more serious vein he added: 'You can try on my tails. I think I have a white bow tie.'

'I'll look like some daft waiter,' complained David.

'Oh no you won't! You'll steal the show!'

David retired into his room with my father's tailcoat and matching trousers. He later reappeared, his rosy face beaming the biggest of smiles. By now seeing the funny side of the mistake, he wore the ill-fitting clothes with an aplomb that reminded us of the games of charades we had played together in past years.

With Anne's sullen help, I had opened most of my presents earlier that day. The remainder I hurriedly unwrapped before we departed for the Masonic Rooms, where the function was to be held. In all there were twelve pairs of cuff links, seven gramophone records, four wallets, some lurid ties, aftershave lotions with tantalising scents, umpteen collar studs and much more besides.

'Don't forget to write to thank all these very generous people, will you, dear?' nagged my mother with a condescension that made my blood boil.

'Will she never let me think for myself?' I mouthed in silent agony as I dashed to fetch the car.

With my parents and Anne at my side, we greeted the guests, who formed a queue on entering the Masonic Rooms, in order for them to offer their polite good wishes before gathering at the bar. To add a touch of class, my father and mother had invited some of their favourite Arnold Lodge connections to join in the celebration.

A young male guest addressed the harassed barman with the arrogant instruction: 'One double whisky, please!'

Overhearing this near blasphemy, my father rushed to the scene and with a brusqueness for which he was well noted snapped, 'If you want to drink spirits you will have to pay for them. Beer and soft drinks is all I'm providing for the young people here!'

At that point the band struck up with such deafening malice that even my more 'with-it' contemporaries covered their ears to block out the harsh trumpet blares. My aged grandmother, appalled at the din, sought refuge in an adjoining room. Anne, thankful she could no longer hear my plaintive expressions of devotion, was busy counting the minutes until 'Auld Lang Syne' was to signal her release.

The supper interval provided a pause that forced the spirited musicians to abandon their instruments. With animated chatter at last audible, the assembled crowd advanced on tables that were laden with food. Tucking ravenously into vol-au-vents, sausages on sticks, an assortment of meats, and finally devouring jellies, trifles and blancmanges, goodwill abounded. Compliments were flung at my mother who, well practised in organising children's party teas, had herself selected the menu. Grandma Bradford, now back in circulation, commented scathingly to the leader of the jazz band, 'It's really rather nice now that the frightful music has stopped!'

To attract everyone's attention, my father banged his glass with a spoon, which was the method he used for curbing immoderate hubbubs in the school dining hall. David sprang forward, notes at the ready, the borrowed clothes making him look more incongruous now that all eyes were upon him. His short speech described me in such fulsome terms that I could not believe I was the object of the eulogy. Carefully omitting any reference to my indifferent school career, he ended with stirring words.

'Jonathan has always been a trier; maybe he is conscientious to a fault. Because he works so hard, I know that he will succeed in achieving much of what he sets out to do. The best of luck to him. But it is his kindness, family commitment and concern for others that we value in particular and these qualities we shall remember most of all. Let us join together in drinking to Jonathan's continued good health, whilst at the same time we wish him happiness, good fortune and success in the future.'

I responded to David's remarks and thanked my parents for laying on the party so generously in my honour.

Had I understood women, on seeing her indifferent attitude towards me, I should have let Anne sulk on her own for the remainder of the party. With this approach, all might not have been lost. Instead of circulating as a good host should, attempting to be friendly and charming to all the other guests, some of whom I had not seen for ages, I glued myself to Anne like some wretched leech, an unwanted shadow. She found my obsessional idolising of her irritating and embarrassing. Trapped in a prison of my own creation, I was powerless to rid myself of the manacles of this first young love.

Friends and relatives, one and all, sympathise as they did with my painful dilemma, were incapable of freeing me of the miserable tensions, the stirred emotions, on what should have been the gladdest of days. Only Anne could have done that.

Anne returned to Jersey in morose mood, thankful to get away from me. So much had she come to despise me that she was unwilling even to offer a curt greeting when we later came face to face. I wondered what love was. Was it an indelible dream that transfixes every sense with an irreversibility that stings and suffocates? The great philosophers can neither describe nor define with convincing certainty the subtleties of love. All I knew was that I was overpowered by a hurt of untold depth that only time would remedy.

More of Exeter

My Exeter days were among the happiest I can remember. I was involved in numerous frivolous escapades. So plentiful were the congenial experiences that much has had to be omitted from these jottings.

The main object of attending St Luke's was for me to improve my teaching skills. Each student was expected to pursue two subjects in depth. I had chosen to specialise in French and history; it was assumed, though, that we would all be capable of teaching English, mathematics and PE at an elementary level.

Teachers the world over have complained that little useful practical guidance was given during the period of training. Most of us have had to learn the hard way, generally in the first teaching post, by a process of trial and a great deal of error. A few have fallen by the wayside at the end of a taxing probationary year and sometimes sooner; the majority have battled on to achieve competence in the end, each using an individually devised formula to cope with and stimulate a bunch of children.

Good teachers are born and rarely made. The ability to be able to mesmerise a class of children, that special electric quality, has little to do with the knowledge we acquire from books on child psychology. I have found that the mumbo-jumbo of educational theories merely confuses when I have been confronted with a specific child problem that requires an immediate common-sense solution.

The question of pupil management has confounded even the experts who cannot explain why some teachers have the ability to motivate and control a class, whereas others are hopelessly inept. This incalculable but necessary knack is impossible to define. I believe eye contact has something to do with it. The expression in the eyes signifies whether or not those in authority expect an accommodating response. A child's intuitive knowledge that the teacher is bluffing or is not confident enough to give strong leadership is all that is needed for disorder to disrupt the class-room atmosphere.

I accept that standards and attitudes have altered radically over the years. It is my firm belief still that teachers unable to manage their pupils might as well lay down their chalk and leave the profession altogether.

Children are uncannily shrewd. They will put up with any amount of chivvying from their teachers, providing such treatment is seen to be dispensed consistently, calmly and without malice. Children expect fair play and it is essential for them to get it. The well-behaved child is capable of being a rebellious pest when justice becomes the issue. The prerequisite for a teacher's success is a genuine liking for young people; without this basic concern, an essential link in the chain is missing.

A group of us visited an Exeter primary school each week. This was our first opportunity during the course to have direct contact with a class of children. Our initiation as teachers was observed by a crowd of critical students, who afterwards made disparaging noises with the dogmatism of experts. We had been warned that by the end of our training we would never again fear the presence of outsiders within the hallowed walls of classrooms where we would teach.

Each of us had to tell a story which would grip a class of eight year olds. Some students skilfully held the pupil audience with adventure tales, stories of detectives, pirates, ghosts and fiends. The very rare outstanding student separated himself from the rest with an unexplained magnetism that engrossed the boys and girls to whom he spoke. The pedestrian beginner stumbled over his words or simply lost his way in shy confusion.

The oldest of the mature students was a retired brigadier. He looked old enough to have achieved senior citizen status already. I was surprised that he was embarking upon a new career so late in life. It may have been that his wife had persuaded him to take up teaching to prevent him from getting under her feet at home. A man of obvious distinction, the brigadier must have had more than a few thrilling tales up his sleeve, based on wartime reminiscences. When it was his turn to enchant the children present, we expected a rousing performance.

'I was in command of the regiment. Our tanks were advancing towards the enemy position across the sun-drenched desert,' he began. 'German planes were pulverising us with their lethal bombs. Two tanks exploded simultaneously in a daytime firework display whose deafening crashes reverberated with tedious regularity,' the brigadier continued with the clipped decisiveness one associates with men used to controlling others.

I watched the children's faces. In the first few moments he had lost their attention completely. Speaking to them with words more suitable for an adult novel, he had failed to amend the vocabulary, add light and shade to the delivery or encourage the listeners to identify with his story. How would he cope with a class of fifty bored, unruly children, we wondered. Not very well, was the conclusion. There would be no hiding behind rank for him in the heartless classroom jungle.

Few of the lecturers at St Luke's influenced me to any great extent. My academic work was competent rather than inspired. It was seldom for there to be evidence of esoteric perception or originality of thought in the generally mechanical essays I produced. The pursuit of knowledge, the sheer joy of learning for the sake of it, were pleasures that seemed again to have eluded me. I did enough to get by but not a lot more. My potential strength lay, I thought, in an ability to communicate with the young, an objective I strove to achieve with unremitting energy.

The head of the history department, Mr J C Revill, intimidated us into buying a gigantic book entitled *World History* of which he was the author. 'If you read this work,' he promised, 'it will be invaluable to you with your course.' The inference was that we could not possibly qualify without buying a copy. So buy one we did, though it was of little relevance or help when we came to study for our finals.

A colourful history tutor was Michael Curtis, whose talent for dramatisation overlapped into the lecture room. He began one of his lectures by uttering an almighty 'Baa!' that emulated the bleating of a lamb so startlingly that we were shaken from our lethargy. 'Baa, baa!' he repeated. Our attention having been captured he continued: 'The key to the Middle Ages is sheep and the woollen industry. Baa, baa, baa!' Good teachers know that regular shock treatment is a vital tool in the process of indoctrination.

Little old Mr Jenne was a lovable tutor. Out of doors he wore a comic trilby hat to protect his shiny bald head from the elements. Minute in stature and with a distinguished white moustache, he resembled an elderly version of Charlie Chaplin.

Mr Jenne was the only member of the college French department. Though not a native of France, he spoke the language perfectly with a Parisian accent. His knowledge of French literature was so extensive that he became enveloped in a world of his own as he steered us through the great works that meant so much to him. Secondary modern and primary schools of the 1950s neglected the teaching of foreign languages. Mr Jenne regretted this. The legacy he bequeathed to us was an enthusiasm that he hoped we would in turn transmit to the children of future generations. This would be his monument.

Rag week enabled us to indulge in normally frowned-upon activities with the pretext that money raised would go to deserving causes. St Luke's and the university joined forces in the exercise.

An excited Max came up with a brainwave. 'Why don't some of us busk in the streets to raise money for the Rag?'

'A good idea,' I answered, 'but what about your photography business?'

'I can lock the doors for a week. Things are quiet this time of year. I'd much rather play jazz.'

Max, John Tidy and I set ourselves up as a jazz trio, using busy pavements and the city arcade for our performances. Joined by other musicians from time to time, we became a popular attraction. Copper and silver coins clonked into our collecting tins, as eager shoppers helped to swell rag funds.

All went well until Max decided it was time to be more daring. He marched us into Barclays Bank. We began playing. The echo in the high-ceilinged lobby was like a turned-up microphone, effectively swelling the mellow tones of my clarinet. The staff looked uncomfortable, the customers amused.

A dark-suited manager appeared from his office. Glowering in our direction with a self-important air he shouted: 'You have no business to be in this bank. I want you out of here at once!'

The curt request seemed reasonable enough to me; after all, we had not asked permission to impose our music on the manager or his customers. Max resented the interception. With a look of violent hatred in his eyes, he shouted back with such venom that we were utterly astounded. There was something about Max that was beginning to bother me.

Some of the rag stunts that were pulled off were cheeky and inventive. Four hundred students entered Boots the Chemists in the high street with alarm clocks synchronised to ring out on the dot of 4 p.m. Surprised shoppers again dug hands deep into their pockets to support the cause.

An amazing feat was when a group of mainly Welsh PE students stole trophies from the officers' mess at a local barracks, following a commando-type raid. The trophies were returned only after a payment had been made to rag funds. The subdued guardsmen were given fourteen days' jankers apiece to reward them for their slackness.

In the past, St Luke's students had traditionally sabotaged the rag efforts of their university neighbours. Rivalry had led to a number of violent incidents, in which the tough Luke's PE contingent invariably came out best.

Rag week had been a good excuse for our students to invade university women's halls of residence in the middle of the night. Armed with hockey sticks and a variety of implements, buxom Amazons fought us off to protect their honour and that of their less powerful companions. The girls enjoyed the capers as much as we did. Now that St Luke's was participating actively in rag events on equal terms with the university, harmless pranks like this would have to be curbed, if not abandoned altogether.

It was wishful thinking to assume that by dating other girls I would forget Anne. The hurt continued to nag with a power that was crippling; there was to be no substitute for Anne, no matter how hard I tried to remove her from my thoughts.

In a moment of madness, I volunteered to take part in a university drama production that was being staged as a peripheral rag event. The truth was that I had no desire to act at all. I had never before performed on stage. The sole object was to increase my prospects of seeing Anne again.

I was to play the part of a drunken nightclub owner. To add a sense of reality to my performance, I stopped off each night at the Locomotive Inn to gulp down some vintage cider before proceeding to the university theatre. Failed nerves suitably restored, I was ready to give my all. On one of the nights Anne was bound to be there. I wanted to impress her with a sparkling performance in an attempt to reawaken her interest in me.

There was to be a party for the cast after the final performance. John Stripe, our resident warden, gave me permission to return late to college as a special favour. I lingered at the Locomotive Inn longer than was good for me. My tardy arrival at the theatre needled members of the cast, who had noticed my flushed face that required no make-up titivation. I walked unsteadily to the green room.

A voice on the Tannoy system gave the warning signal: 'Five more minutes!'

'Anne's in the audience,' a St Luke's ally whispered in my ear. 'Woo her from the boards. Good luck, you romantic bugger!'

Oh God, I thought. It's more than luck I'll need. I'll want a bloody miracle.

The unexpected news of Anne's presence had thrown me completely. It was permissible for a drunken nightclub owner to stagger about on stage and slur his words. To have allowed my discomposure to ruin the first act was quite another matter. Forgetting huge chunks of the script, I brought the play to a standstill in silences that seemed unending. Only the presence of mind of fellow actors saved the day as they cleverly extricated themselves and me from a number of disasters.

I tried not to imagine the language Anne would use to describe my on-stage buffoonery. Justified in being openly derisive of me, I knew she would have written me off with a scorn that had shattered any prospect of a reconciliation.

In no humour for party merriment, I left the backstage gathering early and unnoticed. With downcast heart, I lumbered along the empty streets in the direction of the college. It was pouring with rain. The chilling wind sobered me up; unrelenting drops stung at my eyes and cheeks. The dampness irritated me. I picked up a stone and aimed it at a dustbin. The stone struck home. The noise alarmed a nearby cat, which scurried away into the darkness. A light appeared in an upstairs window. Awakened residents could hear my stamping feet. I was glad to have roused them.

By the time I entered the college it was past midnight. It made a change to disturb my room-mate, who had woken me up often enough in the past. Switching on the light, I slammed the door shut. Randomly scattering my clothes about the room, I undressed with noise and flurry. Vigorous tooth-brushing caused muffled profanities to invade the room from my now wide-awake companion. Just as I was thinking it served him right, there was a loud knock on the door. In came the warden, Mr Stripe, whose quarters adjoined our room. A blue silk dressing gown hid from view all but the maroon collar of the pyjamas he was wearing. His greasy grey hair was dishevelled; he was very angry.

'What do you mean by coming in at this hour?'

'You gave me special permission to return late after the rag play party.'

'I would have expected you to have the common sense to come in quietly rather than thunder about making noises that would waken the dead. You are gated as from tomorrow. Report to my rooms at eight every evening until further notice.'

'This is worse than boarding school,' I protested. 'I am twenty-one, you know. You're treating me like a child!'

'Might I suggest then that you learn to behave like an adult.'

My room-mate, pleased at the outcome, chortled after Mr Stripe had made his exit. Anne would no doubt have chortled, too.

Back home for Easter I met Prue, a medical secretary. She was well made, though not plump, with curves and bulges in the right regions. Healthy pink cheeks adorned a wholesome face, at the centre of which glowed teasing brown eyes. Prue was an extrovert. She was amused by my earnest manner. To help break down the barriers of stiff formality, she pulled my leg with roguish good humour.

'You take yourself too seriously,' she would say. 'You may be heir to a prep school. That makes you king of a muck heap. And a small muck heap at that!'

She made me laugh. I found myself opening up in her company. She was fun to be with. It was a dubious advantage that Prue's mother took to me instantly. When describing her mother Prue could be scathing. There appeared to be no love lost between the two of them, or so I was led to think.

'My mother's one hell of a snob,' said Prue. 'That's why she likes you. She thinks you come from the right stable. She disapproved of David because he didn't go to public school. She's glad I've finished with him.'

I was unsure whether or not I was about to take David's place. I hoped that I would. Perhaps this time luck would be on my side.

There were light-hearted evenings when Prue and I got to know each other better. We held hands, kissed and cuddled. On the horizon were the permissive sixties that heralded the removal of many of the taboos of lovemaking and sex; there was no question of our testing more basic needs as yet.

On the last night of my vacation, Prue showed me a letter she had received from David. With obvious sincerity he had expressed his distress at the break-up of their relationship. There were no recriminations; blame was cast aside. The letter combined affection and diplomacy. What shone through above all was David's mature selflessness that gave him a dignity that had to be respected. Prue was noticeably upset.

I had not met David. All I knew about him was that he had attended the local grammar school and was now an architectural student. When I returned to Exeter he would still be on the scene and available, whereas I would not.

'What are your feelings about David now?' I asked.

'It's over between us, but I can't help feeling sorry for him.'

'How does that leave us?'

'Why do you think I'm here with you?' she asked. 'It's because I want to be.'

'What are you going to do with yourself when I'm away in Devon?'

'Keep myself busy and write to you every day. I'll not change. That's a promise.'

The flame that had linked her to David in the recent past glimmered only through compassion for his sentiments. She was committed to me. I trusted her completely.

I was going to miss Prue greatly. Providing I kept myself well occupied throughout the term, I knew the time would pass more quickly. Much energy was to be devoted to the playing of jazz and a little to my work. It excited me each morning to search through the mail for Prue's warm-hearted letters that were to make more bearable the long summer weeks.

My first teaching practice of a month's duration in June was within Dartmoor's national park at Okehampton Primary School. The teaching staff consisted mainly of old biddies. None of the women had any time for Ed Watson, a male colleague, who used unorthodox teaching methods. Scornful of his qualities, they ostracised him completely. I could not understand what it was about him that they disliked so much, apart from the fact he was of masculine gender.

I took to Ed from the start and thus began a long-standing friendship. By spending time in his company, I made myself unpopular with his female critics. This did not bother me unduly. Ed and I would steal away for our lunchtime breaks to the seclusion of a moorland peak. Here we put the world to rights, discussing every topic imaginable, far away from the unfriendly staffroom.

Ed was ahead of his time. Understanding the needs of the slow learner, the emotionally disturbed, the individualist, he invented his own methods for conquering some of the childhood barriers that hindered success and about which so little then was known. As a self-taught remedial expert he had no equal. I was happy to be one of his disciples.

I was plunged in the deep end from the start. To be expected to control and capture the interest of fifty-two ten year olds may sound a tall order. My task was relatively simple because Mrs Jones, the permanent class teacher to whom I was responsible, had trained her pupils to respect authority and to strive only for the highest standards. All I had to do was follow the principles she had laid down so carefully.

Two years' experience prior to college in the private sector had given me a head start. The prescription for coping with classes a quarter of the size was little different. Careful preparation of lessons; prompt, painstaking marking of work; plans to cover the unexpected, with nothing left to chance; an abundance of praise; endless enthusiasm; the elimination of boredom. Practising the same basic philosophies that I had acquired in Leamington, I adapted easily to my new duties.

Mrs Jones was at first anxious lest my intrusion on her patch would hamper her pupils' progress. Slowly she came to trust my good intentions.

It was the children's idea to produce a class newspaper. After the appointment of an editor-in-chief, budding story writers, poets, historians, weather forecasters, artists, sports reporters and puzzle makers set to work to meet the publication deadline. An example of every child's work was included in the finished product. Mrs Jones congratulated us on our achievements. The considerable pleasure I gained from teaching at Okehampton impressed upon me that I was probably more at home in a classroom than anywhere else.

Except for morning assemblies, when he was honour bound to make appearances, the school's head, Mr Laws, spent most of the time cloistered in his office. The entire staff condemned his laziness. To relieve his lassitude and to confuse the other teachers, Mr Laws chose to arrange regular fire practices at the most inopportune moments. It was only then that like a dusty jack-in-the-box he sprang into action. He would march up and down the corridors blowing a whistle continuously. This was the signal for all to retreat to the safety of the playing field. Wearing special fire-resistant wellingtons, he carried out a roll-call to assure himself that nobody had perished in the imaginary flames before he allowed lessons to resume. Apart from the energy Mr Laws expended on these curious occasions, his contribution to the life of the school merited no compliment.

Despite staff disunity and the weakness of the head, Okehampton Primary was a fine school. It was truly comprehensive, catering for happy, relaxed children of all intellects and backgrounds; the dedication and competence of the teachers never in doubt. But for the plans mapped out for my future, I would have been content to become immersed in the life of an enchanting community such as this for the rest of my days.

The summer term ended traditionally with the college ball. It had been arranged for some weeks that Prue would attend as my partner. I managed to book a room for her at a guest house within easy reach of the college.

Prue's arrival in Exeter brought to the fore the feelings of hopeful expectation I had been forced to contain during the preceding weeks. I wanted her to be the first to know that college tutors had awarded me an A grade for my teaching. I wanted to share with her my hopes and yearnings, as well as the plans I had to improve and expand the family school. I wanted to hear more about her life in Leamington and for her to say out loud some of the sentences that had been so beautifully expressed in letters to me. In Prue I had at last a friend who really cared. The loneliness that had haunted me in the past was now a memory.

Prue's visit to Exeter was all that might reasonably have been expected, but the magic that had developed in the imagination of both of us was somehow missing. I was not unduly worried. Doubtless it would take a while for us to re-establish the friendship back to how it was in April. The intervening weeks had made us act like strangers, a temporary setback only. In spite of nagging doubts, I returned home a few days later, full of ideas as to how to make the most of the summer vacation, ideas that featured Prue most prominently.

As soon as Prue was home from work, I went to see her. Feelings of exhilaration multiplied as I thought of the pleasure-packed weeks that lay ahead.

'What do you want us to do this evening?' I asked enthusiastically.

'You're not going to like this,' she said, 'but I have to tell you that I'm back with David.'

I was paralysed with shock. Barely comprehending the meaning of her words, it was not until the implications began to register that I was able to react. I could feel I was losing control, with violent, bitter thoughts beginning to impair my judgement.

'You bitch! You bloody bitch! Why didn't you tell me this when you came to Exeter last Friday? I suppose you've been carrying on with him all the weeks I've been away.'

'It's not like that at all,' she said. 'It was only when I was with you at the ball that I realised how much I'd been missing David.'

A blush of fury suffused cheeks that would soon be wet with tears. I had to get away. Trying to be dignified but failing miserably, I made off in the direction of home. Crossing a busy street, I willed approaching vehicles to mow me down. My life was in tatters; there was nothing left.

Fate had other plans for me, however, and I avoided a traffic accident. Back home I drew the curtains tightly shut and collapsed on my bed. With unwanted sympathisers out of reach, I convulsed with sobs of childlike misery, tormented by the loss.

Battered plants find nature's timeless remedies. Battered hearts, no less resilient, are cured by optimism, the resolve of immortality. I awoke next morning to brilliant sunshine, fresh hopes, another day. When tears have dissipated and the grief begins to lift, we strive to endure, to seek beyond.

Vacation plans well and truly wrecked, I was in no humour for taking social initiatives. The distant ringing of the telephone cut short my listlessness. 'There's a bottle party in Long Itchington on Saturday,' a friendly voice was saying. 'Would you like to come along?'

'Why not! Give me the details and I'll be there.'

Why not indeed? I had a premonition that something weird and wonderful was going to happen. The suspense was quite compelling.

My friends and I, with a bottle each, drove to Long Itchington. We parked next to the outbuildings of a large country house a mile from the village centre. Our hostess, Deborah, a tall, lanky eighteen year old, bubbled with excitement as she greeted us. She was making hay while the sun shone; her parents were on holiday.

I recognised the regular party buffs, the Warwickshire set. Rich young men with flashy cars, their boastful airs and superficialities; pretty girls of gullible innocence, impressed by fast-lane opulence.

So ill at ease was I in the company of these smart but shallow people that I chose the route to drunkenness. The more I drank, the more assured I felt. It promised to be a good party.

Then Prue arrived. At her side was a tall, well-built young man, who supposedly was David. They were fondling each other. Something snapped inside me at that moment. Jealousy and lack of judgement took control. I struck out at Prue's escort, knocking him off guard. He fell to the floor with a heavy thud. Back up like greased lightning he hurtled towards me, fists clenched, expression merciless. He looked more powerful now. He would, I think, have slaughtered me had stunned spectators not rushed headlong at us both. They restrained us in the nick of time to avoid a gory massacre.

Critical eyes and scathing tongues brought me to my senses. I slunk away from the sorry scene, ashamed, depressed, humiliated. The following morning I went over to Long Itchington to apologise to Deborah for behaving so badly at her party. Her expression brightened when she saw me on the doorstep.

'Come on in,' she said. 'I'm glad you're here. You don't need to apologise. I thought you were wonderful. I only wish there was a man in my life who would fight for me in the way you fought for Prue.'

If I were not mistaken, Deborah was trying to flirt with me. By taking up wrestling, prizefighting or one of the martial arts, I would have all the girls queueing at my door.

It's an ill wind, I concluded.

A Taste of Happiness

Exeter had become like a home to me. I was in no hurry to uproot myself from the comfortable existence student life provided. The sterner duties waiting to be undertaken in Leamington were a fact of life that was bound up irrevocably as my destiny, like it or not. In a modest way, these commitments were not far different from those inherited by people of rank, whose entire upbringing assumed the burden of future responsibilities. It never occurred to me that an alternative path might have been chosen in my case. I would have preferred to have spent some years gaining experience and learning about life away from the tensions and pressures of the family school. In view of my father's age and questionable health, my conscience left me in little doubt as to what was expected of me.

I had embarked upon my final year at Exeter with the knowledge that life after I qualified would never again be as carefree or relaxed. Now was the time to let my hair down and enjoy myself.

An article in one of the national newspaper society columns announced that the Hon. Gwilym Rees-Williams was to commence teacher training at St Luke's that autumn. There was much speculation concerning his arrival at the college. His father, Lord Ogmore, a former Labour government minister, was chairman of the Liberal Party. Some of us had seen press pictures of his glamorous sister, Elizabeth, who was married to Richard Harris, the film actor. It was worth our while to engineer an introduction to the Honourable Gwilym.

A friend pointed Gwilym out to me. We reckoned he must have been in his late twenties. Wearing a dark blue blazer and striped shirt, with a tie that matched, he took on the appearance of a prosperous stockbroker. Tiny eyes imprisoned behind horn-rimmed spectacles stared out at us beseechingly. Jet-black hair exaggerated the pallor of his chinless face. With a diffident and apologetic manner, he was not at all the snooty gent we had expected.

On a Sunday morning a few days later I saw Gwilym accompanied by his fiancée, the Hon. Juno Wynn, the daughter of Lord Newborough. As they examined the notices in the college cloisters, he was being attacked with a barrage of questions by his well-to-do companion. So henpecked did he appear to be that he was utterly defenceless.

My first meeting with Gwilym told me even more about his character. I wanted to know what it was that had made him take up teaching. The chance arose for me to put this very question to him.

'Well, you know, I was sort of a banker in sort of Thailand for some years.'

'Yes, but what made you decide to give up banking in favour of teaching?' I asked.

'Well, I sort of, er, I sort of, er, I really don't sort of know at all,' was his jumbled answer.

I was amazed at the incoherence of his speech. Children would soon be making mincemeat of poor Gwilym. He was bound to be a target of their fun.

Ill at ease always in the company of conceited, pompous people, I had wrongly assumed that Gwilym would be too grand to want to mix with the likes of me. Far from being a threat to any of us, he needed our friendship. Childhood years spent in an austere, exacting Welsh household had left him reserved and vulnerable. By being led astray in a series of adventures at last he was going to have some fun.

As the College social secretary I received complimentary tickets to many of the local beanfeasts. Neglecting my obligations to the other students to further selfish ends I reserved the promising invitations for my special cronies, of whom Gwilym now was one. To enjoy free access to nurses' dances and students' get-togethers was a privilege we exploited to the full.

On Saturday nights I organised occasional dances in the college coffee bar. The college authorities were unaware that the musicians and I were pocketing the takings.

This planted the seed for a more dicey entrepreneurial idea that fortunately paid off. Most of the students had to rely on public transport to get to and from Exmouth on Saturday evenings. I discovered that by undercutting the rail fare slightly I was able to offer a door-to-door coach service to the women's teacher training college that resulted in a profit.

The combined earnings of band gigs and business enterprises enabled me to spend large sums of money on unnecessary luxuries just for kicks. Gwilym and I thought nothing of hiring expensive cars and wining and dining in the best restaurants; in fact, it was not unusual sometimes for us to have two evening meals. Having eaten a more than adequate college supper, we often went out for a lavish dinner afterwards. With hangers-on as our partners in crime, we led the life of Riley.

Conscious of my lean physique, I tried to put on weight. Exeter's culinary delights aided attempts to bulge my waistline and inflate the cheeks. My appetite had become so voracious that the skinny weakling was fast turning into a flabby monster.

A group of us one evening repaired to the Locomotive Inn with Gwilym in tow. The time had come for us to introduce Gwilym to vintage cider.

'Have you ever tasted vintage cider?' one of us asked.

'No, I haven't,' said Gwilym.

'Well, I suggest you give it a try. It's unlike anything you've ever drunk before. It's sweeter than scrumpy and less intoxicating.'

'I'll have a pint,' said Gwilym.

'You'll not regret it,' we said, egging him on.

Little did Gwilym know that it was normal for vintage cider to be served in a small wineglass. It was far too potent to drink by the pint.

'Yes, it does sort of taste rather good,' ventured Gwilym.

'Have another pint,' we urged.

'I sort of think that perhaps I sort of will,' agreed the trusting Gwilym.

We were intrigued to see the effect our knavish trickery was to have on him. Gwilym's white complexion transformed to a pinkish glow; he radiated good cheer and friendliness.

His mood changed suddenly. Pushing us aside with a pugnaciousness not before exhibited, he staggered out of the pub into the narrow street.

'The college isn't up there,' we shouted after him. 'It's down the hill, remember?'

'Piss off,' retorted Gwilym. 'I'm off to find a woman.'

Swaying precariously as he sauntered away in the wrong direction, Gwilym arrived, still in one piece, at the entrance to one of the university women's halls of residence. He forced his way in. Ribald singing drew attention to his unwelcome presence as he lurched and cavorted along the corridors, not knowing where he was. The police were sent for and, after they had taken Gwilym's details, he was hastily driven back to his College lodgings, where he awoke late next morning subdued and with a splitting headache.

Police charges were dropped. We never discovered what action, if any, was taken by the principal. Gwilym's college records doubtless bore testimony of the transgression. The irresponsible influence some of us exerted over this unsuspecting but nice guy did nothing to enhance his prospects.

A law student from the university named Alan, who was a talented modern jazz pianist, invited me to be the drummer in a group he was forming. The problem was that my drums were in Leamington. I knew that the college music department possessed a respectable kit of drums, although the poor-quality cymbals were fit only for the scrap heap. I managed to persuade the college bursar to sanction the purchase of some good cymbal replacements. He gave me the agreeable task of selecting the cymbals myself. Little did the bursar know I intended to use the drums and the newly acquired cymbals for band gigs outside the confines of the college.

Another obstacle to be overcome was when the band secured regular weekly bookings at a country club off the beaten track, some eight miles from Exeter. Like most students, I had no vehicle of my own. How was I going to get myself and the drums to the back of beyond?

The Exmouth Saturday night travel scheme was suitably adapted to meet our needs. On Wednesday evenings after college supper had been served and eaten, a coach parked outside the entrance to St Luke's. Students, members of the public and the musicians, laden with our instruments, including the appropriated drum kit, were transported in style to our new jazz haunt. The owner of the club was happy to meet the coach costs, knowing that capacity crowds would substantially increase his bar takings.

My final teaching practice was at Ladysmith, a boys-only secondary modern school in the heart of Exeter, within walking distance of the college. In marked contrast to the happy and relaxed Okehampton Primary School, this establishment was repressive in the extreme. Mr Shaw, the head, a brash Northerner, ruled his school quite literally with the rod. He would beat boys indiscriminately for a variety of offences, his theory being that good discipline was most effectively maintained through coercion rather than a combination of example and common sense.

I attended a meeting with the Ladysmith head before my month's sojourn as a member of staff was due to commence. Mr Shaw did not allow me to express opinions or ask questions during the brief interview. He blasted me with sarcasm as soon as he learnt that French was one of my specialist subjects.

'I suppose this means you can't keep order. I have yet to meet a French teacher who can. And students who teach French are the worst disciplinarians of the lot.'

I sat before him, silenced by the extravagance of his condemnation. If this was Mr Shaw's way of welcoming me to his school, I did not dare to think what he would be like when he lost his temper, which apparently he frequently did.

Mr Shaw then prepared a rough timetable of the lessons I would be taking. He handed it to me. 'The subject teachers will give you all the information you need,' he said, brushing me aside as if my presence needled him. Before I retreated to the passage that led to the school's main entrance, he fired a parting shot: 'Make sure you send any boys who misbehave to my office without delay. I guarantee that once they've paid me a visit, they'll not play up again!'

'Thank you, sir, I'll remember that,' I answered, pretending to take heed of the advice I had been offered.

Of one thing I was certain. Under no circumstances would I send miscreants to Mr Shaw for punishment.

Because Mr Shaw regarded French as a Cinderella subject, he begrudged spending money on resources for the teaching of the language. This state of affairs was the despair of the school's sole French specialist, who received no support from any quarter, not even his colleagues. My heart sank when it came to light that there were only seven French textbooks to be shared between a class of fifty restless fourteen year olds. As I planned my schemes of work, I did not need to be an Einstein to see why unruly behaviour in French lessons at Ladysmith had become so prevalent.

The boys' initial hostility, an expression of their hatred of French, came as no surprise to me. I wanted them to appreciate that French was a living language and that to learn it could be fun. Discarding the textbooks, I concentrated on the oral approach, which was as yet unknown to them. By the end of the first two lessons many of the boys were able to ask and answer in French simple questions concerning their names, ages and the weather. Minor errors were disregarded. To encourage effort and participation, bonus points were given to those with promising accents. With the aid of chalk and talk and vocabulary notebooks, we jotted down a number of the commonest French words. A shop was set up and the boys were taught how to buy and sell items of food and stationery, using the make-believe francs they had designed and cut out in art lessons.

Apathy gradually receded. To my surprise and relief, occasional cries of satisfaction and approval were audible. A tousle-haired boy with a strong Devonian dialect commented with a triumphant look on his face, 'And now I can see why we learn French!'

Four of the boys had actually visited France the previous summer. They were encouraged to note down their experiences, whilst their classmates prepared suitable questions about the

French way of life. As a supplementary member of the panel, I volunteered answers whenever there were embarrassing silences.

This led on to a map of France being displayed. The pupils plotted the major cities, ports, airports, rivers, mountains and seas on maps they sketched with the care of draughtsmen. We discussed the country's industrial products, its wines, its dependence upon agriculture and some of the events and characters that had highlighted a fascinating past.

I recognised it was necessary for me to be more of an entertainer than a teacher in order to keep the pupils' interest alive. This was sustainable during a four-week teaching practice. To maintain the strenuous acting role as a permanent teacher at Ladysmith, with negligible resources and an antagonistic head, would, I think, have proved impossible.

My college French tutor, Mr Jenne, was a welcome visitor at one of the earlier lessons. He toddled absent-mindedly into the classroom. He gave me a friendly nod as he sat quietly at the back to observe me in action.

The lesson over, he took me to one side. 'You seem to be coping remarkably well. Ladysmith is known to be a tough school. I wouldn't last a week here myself and that's the truth. If you can make a go of it, you'll survive anywhere,' he said, revealing the familiar toothy grin that so endeared him to us.

Mr Pyatt, whose class I understudied throughout the practice, was a man of military precision. He had arranged the class into six separate groups for mathematics.

'You will need to divide your time equally between the groups in each of the forty-minute lessons.'

'What do I do about the boys who don't understand the work covered or who run out of things to do?' I inquired.

'It's simple. They carry on working through the textbook questions until it's time for them to be taught the next topic. The strugglers can always transfer to another group.'

I did not bother to ask what was to happen to the boys who were already in the lowest group. No useful purpose would have been served by my questioning the obvious defects in the system. Pupils requiring special attention were left wanting. It was contrary to school policy for these ill-fated individuals to be singled out for extra help during breaks or lunch hours. On the one occasion that I broke this rule, Mr Pyatt was so enraged that he threatened to inform my tutors.

It irritated me beyond measure that the exclusive aim of the Ladysmith teachers was to subdue the pupils into silent submission. Fear was the overriding feature. Mr Shaw would lurk outside my classroom door in the hope that he would have a pretext to haul out troublemakers for a caning. It became a matter of honour for me to maintain good order, so as to avoid the need for his savage intervention. Weaker members of staff, of whom the permanent French teacher was a prime example, relied on Mr Shaw to discipline the malefactors. An endless stream of ashen-faced youths stood awaiting their fate in the dingy corridor. Passers-by listened in horror to the agonised shrieks that emerged in response to the debasing thwacks of the perverse correction.

Two days before the teaching practice was due to end, I witnessed a barbaric act of sadism.

I was enjoying a chat over a cup of coffee with some colleagues in the staffroom at morning break when the door burst open. With one hand clutching the throat of a smallish youth, in came Mr Shaw. His other hand wielded a cane that he was applying with frenzied force to various parts of the boy's anatomy. Buttocks, legs, arms, chest and shoulders, all were brutally and sundry times assaulted.

'Take this, and that,' yelled the hysterical head, still striking at the victim. 'This will teach you a lesson you'll *not* forget.'

Twenty years later Mr Shaw would have been locked up for his actions. The mesmerised staff, who had seen it all before, looked on helplessly, restraining fruitless anger.

There were no regrets when I bade farewell to Ladysmith, an episode of my life not easily forgotten.

I could not help but notice a lovely brunette, who was window-shopping outside one of Exeter's largest stores. Outshining all the other females in the street, she carried herself with the proud bearing that derives from a stylish background. Bowled over by the impact of her comeliness, I stopped to have a gawk.

Aware of the interest I was taking in her, she turned to face me. Judging me, I supposed, to be a man of innocuous innocence, her lips loosened to a smile; limpid brown eyes scanned me quizzically.

Not wanting to waste a one-off opportunity, I plunged in there and then with the corniest of openings: 'Where have you sprung from on this sunny day?'

Instead of stalking off haughtily, which was what I had expected, she did not budge.

'I only arrived in England yesterday. I am a stranger here,' she answered, betraying traces of a sexy foreign accent.

'This calls for a celebration,' I urged, with masterful decision. 'I'll give you a guided tour of Exeter. But first, how about a cup of tea?'

'I know that you English like your tea. I shall be pleased to take tea with you,' she said with impeccable politeness. 'As for the guided tour, we had better wait and see.'

Looking like a cat that had stumbled upon the cream, I escorted my companion to an intimate café in Cathedral Close. We seated ourselves at a corner table, self-possession fast deserting me. I knew that only with the greatest difficulty would I persuade my gorgeous captive to prolong our tête-à-tête.

'Where did you get that wonderful tan?' I asked.

'I have just returned from skiing in Zermatt. I go there every Easter. Do you ski?'

'I've never had the chance, but I'd like to try it one of these days.'

'You really must. You would find it most invigorating and it is so good for your health.'

'What is a beautiful girl like you doing in drab old Exeter?' I continued awkwardly.

'I am here at the university just for a term to improve my English. I am training to be an interpreter at Geneva University and my visit to England is essential to my course.'

There was no doubting that her spoken English was astonishingly fluent. When she told me that to qualify as an interpreter meant speaking perfectly at least three languages after a gruelling five-year course, I could not help but marvel at her mental stamina.

After the initial shyness had evaporated, a rapport was developing between the two of us. She informed me her name was Odette and that her father, a Hungarian count, practised as a dentist in Geneva. I gave Odette a potted version of the tedious life I had led before coming to Exeter. Being an only child herself, she understood the burden of parental expectations, a problem she had not yet solved herself. Romantic urges stirred within us that same evening when we walked beneath a darkening moonlit sky.

The relationship prospered. We became close friends, occasioning for me and Odette untold happiness. We talked, laughed, caressed, argued, mollified. The route was perilous as we probed the secrets locked inside our tender souls. Odette was loving, lively, jealous, mischievous. Her vacillating moods excited, tantalised.

I was again playing clarinet in a small jazz outfit led by Max. The fresh sound we attempted to give to well known evergreen melodies was praised by Acker Bilk, who listened to some of the recordings. Our new style of playing was in constant demand within a wide radius of the city. Odette enjoyed and supported these musical interests, often accompanying me on gigs.

For the ensuing weeks, Odette and I were inseparable. The upsetting nightly partings increased the value of our meetings, without which nothing would have seemed worthwhile. Unspoilt virgins, we were too scared to perform an act of loving intimacy to consummate our precious bond. The physical veto led to ugly moments, with tensions rising high. We rowed frequently, but took pleasure from the peaceful interludes that followed. Ours was a volatile union. It was not unusual for us to be on cloud nine in the evening, having been at loggerheads throughout the day.

I had never relished the prospect of examinations. The feeling of alarm increased with finals only weeks away, knowing as I did that insufficient preparation might well cause my downfall at the last fence. Very few evenings during the period of my training had been devoted to serious study in view of unrestrained socialising and my musical engagements. Had I left it till too late? Intensive preparation was undertaken in the same manner as I had tackled past challenges. My main subjects necessitated much revision and concentrated study, without which the qualification I had set out to achieve would be forfeited.

With the help of my tape recorder, I memorised relevant historical facts. The reel-to-reel tapes repeated time and again the basic information that I needed for the likely essay topics. Coincidentally, some years later I took part in a radio discussion on the subject of hypnopaedia, or sleep learning, which reminded me of my attempts as a student to learn subliminally.

The self-disciplined approach with which Odette pursued her own studies was an inspiration. She would refuse to see me in the evenings until all work tasks had been done. Her knowledge of French literature was considerable. With patient thoroughness she taught me all she knew of the works of Racine, Molière, Victor Hugo, Flaubert, unravelling the puzzling aspects in a most bewitching way.

Odette was there with me in spirit as I waded through the examination papers that were crucial to my future. The day of judgement was at hand.

At the college ball Odette looked ravishing. She wore a black low-cut evening gown that clung seductively to her slim, well-contoured body. Judging by the lecherous male glances, she was the evening's belle. Oblivious to all but each other, we treasured the vanishing moments in a state of ecstasy.

I did not want to believe my days at Exeter were over. Examinations successfully completed, far from being uplifted, I was bitterly upset to be leaving the untroubled life to which I had become attached. The real world was unlikely to be any easier than the one I had left behind. It grieved me that the pull of duty continued to tug so hard. I was beginning to resent it.

Odette

The anticlimax of my departure from Exeter was quickly alleviated. Odette came to stay with us for three months before returning home to Switzerland.

In the familiar environment of Arnold Lodge, I quickly re-established myself as an assistant master for the remaining weeks of the summer term. Odette was intrigued to see how keenly I tackled my teaching duties. The transformation from an extrovert and outrageous student to a conventional and serious-minded schoolmaster had not been overlooked.

Odette took a great interest in all I did. She watched me coach and play cricket with the boys. The more I tried to explain the rudiments of the freakish game, the more I managed to confuse her. On several occasions she took charge of French classes at the school, assisting pupils with the speaking of the language, a necessary skill that was sadly lacking in those times. Odette's zestful personality made her an instant hit. Even the most recalcitrant of learners began to take an interest in French.

Odette and I would have liked to have gone away on holiday for a few days on our own. The idea would have appalled my strait-laced mother. I was able to imagine what her verbal reaction to the scandalous suggestion might have been. 'It simply isn't done! My parents wouldn't have dreamt of allowing your father and me to go away together before we were married.'

The obvious retort of 'The war is over, Mother dear,' would have cut no ice. It would not have been worth the hassle to have argued the toss. Despite my being twenty-two, I was still dominated by Mother's desire for me to live up to her rigid expectations. To appear to bow to her superior judgement made life a lot easier.

We were joined by Odette on our family holiday. First we stopped off for a few days as guests of one of my mother's closest friends in an enchanting Cotswold cottage. Impelled by romantic yearnings, the two of us escaped on country walks and trips to nearby towns as often as we were able. The closeness that had engulfed us in Exeter was deepening. We were in love, a simple, outmoded, hesitant love that was unquestionably genuine.

Odette's bedroom adjoined mine. Last thing at night she would tap the wall to signify that I was foremost in her thoughts before sleep finally took over. '*Bonsoir et bonne nuit, mon petit renard*' ('A good night's rest, little fox') she would chirp with high-pitched fervour. I signalled back with a knocking at the wall and my own mellifluous flirting.

Odette enjoyed pulling my leg. A favoured custom was for her to tease me with endearing messages when we were alone together. '*Je t'aime un peu, beaucoup, à la folie... pas du tout.*' ('I love you a little, a lot, madly... not at all.') Childish though these affectionate whisperings were, the way in which she fluttered her eyelids as she warbled sweet nothings in my ear made me want to gobble her up with kisses.

As invariably happened on our annual holiday, we ended up in Worthing, so as to be near to my father's sister, Marjorie. My mother protested that she would have preferred a more exciting vacation itinerary. My father's reluctance, however, to choose a more stimulating spot caused him, with predictable wilfulness, to park his car outside the same imposing Victorian hotel in which we had stayed so often in past years. It was here, in the company of mainly geriatric guests, that we were to spend the next few nights in rooms that overlooked the sea.

Most evenings Odette and I made for the gleaming lights of nearby Brighton, whose lively atmosphere appealed to our young tastes. Quite by chance we discovered a club at which modern jazz musicians of national repute were playing my kind of music. We seated ourselves near to the stage, eager to delight in the sensational sounds that the masterly line-up was producing.

Keith Christie was blowing his trombone with the effortless competence of the genius I knew him to be. The slick backing provided by the rhythm section, enhanced by piano-playing expert Dill Jones, created a jazz prescription that was truly memorable. Gasping with an emotion that would have been surpassed only by a sexual climax, I was enthralled by the sheer magic of the sound.

'I'd do anything to sit in with this group,' I murmured to Odette, with a longing that was agonising.

'As your clarinet is at home, you'll have to play drums instead, won't you?'

'You must be joking,' I said laughing. 'I'm not in their class.'

'Leave it to me. I'll tell them you are a celebrated Parisian jazz drummer and that you would like to sit in with them. But remember, you don't speak English.'

During a short interval, when the musicians were sipping beer and puffing at their cigarettes, I was mortified to see Odette get up and advance towards them.

With a charm that captivated all the band members in one fell swoop, she announced immodestly, 'My boyfriend over there is Claude Luther's drummer. I would like him to play a number with you, if you will permit it. His name is Jean Vertou. He is, as I am sure you will know, one of the best jazz drummers in the whole of France.'

After receiving a nod of approval from the drummer, who had also been completely taken in by the deceit, Keith Christie invited me to join them. I sat myself behind a dazzling array of drums and cymbals. Grabbing a pair of rhythm brushes, I responded to the warm welcome offered me with a brand of broken English that was in keeping with the part Odette had so mischievously forced upon me.

A fast-moving intro by the rhythm section, of which I was now a key member, got us off to a swinging start. I was in my element. Not for one moment did I feel out of my depth alongside these jazz stars, so intent was I upon matching their proficiencies.

Keith Christie gave the signal for each of us in turn to feature in four-bar solo spots after which, with stage lights blinding me, I unburdened pent-up feelings by bashing hell out of the percussion instruments in a frenetic and lengthy drum solo that was met with rapturous applause. This must have been one of my finest ever moments, a reckless, thrilling moment, when the world of fantasy was in control, with Odette, my loving witness, proudly savouring the uniqueness of our feat.

Odette and I returned to Leamington with the secret desire to become engaged. The marriage would have to be delayed until Odette's university course had been completed. I wanted to see an engagement ring placed firmly on her finger, to guarantee her allegiance to me during the long years when we would be apart. We made up our minds with absolute certainty that nothing was to destroy our plans, despite the resolution to hide the news from everyone until Odette had met up again with her parents in Geneva.

One morning after breakfast, as Odette was reading the paper, I noticed she was looking strained and tense. The pallor of her face shocked me.

'What ever is the matter?' I asked.

'I need to talk with you as soon as possible. I think I'm pregnant.'

We made our way to the privacy of Odette's bedroom. She sat herself awkwardly on her unmade bed, no longer able to hold back the tears that were running down her cheeks.

'What makes you think you're pregnant?'

'My period is very late and I have felt sick in the mornings for the best part of a fortnight. It is not my imagination that something strange is happening inside my tummy.'

'You can't possibly be pregnant,' I said. 'We've never made love, so how can you be?'

'But we have often kissed,' persisted Odette.

'So what?' I retorted with biting sarcasm.

'Kissing on the mouth *can* produce babies. It's a known fact,' wailed Odette, who by now was hysterical with distress.

'If you are pregnant as a result of kissing, it must be the miracle of the century.'

'Don't make fun of me. I know that my fears are justified.'

It was not until Odette received comforting reassurances from a medical expert that she was not expecting a baby, that she was prepared to dismiss her fears. The stomach pains soon disappeared and colour returned to her cheeks. I was shaken by her vulnerable naivety, as well as the depth of her sensitivity. It was obvious that Odette would have to be handled with kid gloves in future.

I cannot remember how it was that Gwilym stumbled back into my life. News reached my ears that he had failed to qualify as a teacher and that he was temporarily unemployed prior to taking up a position with the Ministry of Defence. Concerned for the safety of our homeland and for those I held most dear, I trusted that the security that previous generations had fought for so courageously would not be obstructed by Gwilym's injudicious actions.

I invited Gwilym to stay with us for a few days in Leamington. His visit coincided with a number of parties to which I managed to wheedle invitations on his behalf. There was something about Gwilym's gullible nature that made him easy prey. We all indulged in taking the piss out of poor Gwilym, despite there being no malice in our intentions.

A friend of mine, David Howell Jones, who had just come down from Cambridge, had arranged a get-together at his home to celebrate his birthday. When the party was in full swing and after much alcohol had been consumed, we concocted a plan that once again was to take advantage of Gwilym's simple-mindedness. We indoctrinated him with the mischievous idea that the occasion had been laid on entirely in his honour and that later in the evening it would be only right and proper for him to deliver a speech of thanks. Grunting incoherent sighs of both pleasure and surprise, Gwilym was taken in by the deception, hook, line and sinker.

When some of the guests were about to take their leave, I nudged Gwilym in the ribs and whispered: 'Don't forget to deliver your speech before it's too late!'

'I suppose I sort of ought,' was his mumbled reply.

It was obvious from the giggles of derision behind his back that all were itching to see and hear Gwilym make a fool of himself.

Clearing his throat with a self-conscious cough, he raised his voice to subdue the lively chatter.

'Ladies and gentlemen,' began the painful preamble. 'This is my first sort of visit to Leamington Spa, or should I say Royal Leamington Spa. I was sort of thrilled to know that David had sort of arranged this, er, event especially for me and I sort of thank him very much indeed. Hopefully I shall have the opportunity to reciprocate this, er, smashing hospitality one day when some of you sort of come up to London.'

The claps and cheers that followed signified our mocking approval of Gwilym's confused prattle, a recognition that pleased him greatly. He gurgled with delight at being the centre of attention, totally oblivious to the callous ridicule.

As elder son and heir to his father's title, it seemed incredible to us that Gwilym might one day be making speeches in the House of Lords. His maiden speech some years later, on the subject of devolution, was listened to with rapt attention by noble peers of the realm, who gave him a fairer hearing than he had ever received from his cruel mates.

Odette was disgusted by our treatment of Gwilym. She nagged and lectured me during the days that followed, determined to make her point.

'You are nothing but a bully, you and your silly friends. How can you expect me to love and respect you when you behave in that contemptible way?'

Odette's unpredictable, fiery nature caused me to be on my guard at all times in case I said or did something that might cause ructions. It was not that I was frightened to express opinions; peace and quiet I much preferred to stormy clashes, because I knew that Odette's arrogant ways always maddened me.

'Show me the respect that my social superiority deserves. Remember that I am a full-blooded aristocrat. You are a mere pleb, a social climber,' she would say.

'Full-blooded aristocrat, my foot!'

She infuriated me whenever she used this tack. The facetious quips became more frequent in response to my growing impatience.

'What makes you so important, Miss High and Mighty?' I asked.

'It is because I am La Comtesse Odette Nagy de Bergénie, and I have reason to be proud of it.'

'How come you are a countess?'

'My father is a count. All the sons and daughters of continental counts and countesses automatically assume a title.'

'That must make them ten a penny. In England titles are not doled out like confetti as appears to be the case with you lot.'

There was no doubting that Odette was a mischievous handful. Our future promised to be full of incident. Dullness was one word that had already been scrubbed from the marriage agenda. Far from our ever being bored, the tempestuous relationship brought us pleasure as well as anguish. I was proud to introduce Odette to my friends, all of whom were impressed by her vitality, quick-witted intelligence and repartee.

Odette was eager for me to meet her family in Geneva. Her parents' apprehension would have been justified had they known I was to be introduced as a prospective son-in-law, who had it in mind to whisk their only daughter away to a foreign land. News of our designs was not going to reach their ears until a few days before my intended visit.

The plan was that I was to spend three months living with Odette's family in exchange for the hospitality she had received in Leamington. My father was prepared to release me from my teaching duties for one more term, providing I undertook to pursue a course that would improve my French. Reassuring my father that she would see to it that I would be completely fluent before I returned to England, Odette also gave her personal guarantee that I would attend a number of lectures at Geneva University.

Odette seldom spoke of her family. A married half-sister living in Paris, whose mother had taken her own life, had been referred to only once. In marked contrast, however, she would constantly remind me that she was the favourite niece of Ugo and Sophie, a wealthy, childless couple, who lived in a huge house that was full of priceless antiques in a fashionable part of Geneva.

'They are millionaires, you know,' boasted Odette. 'When they die, they will be leaving everything to me.'

'Big deal,' I said, strongly disapproving of Odette's mercenary Swiss attitudes.

My interest in Aunt Sophie took a different turn from the day that Odette brandished a letter from her in which specific reference was made to me.

'Aunt Sophie was so pleased to receive your photograph,' said Odette. 'She thinks that you look *sympathique*, very *sympathique*. She wants to meet you.'

If I played my cards right, the chances were that I would have at least one influential ally when I arrived in Geneva. The thought, too, that I, an impecunious schoolmaster, would one day be marrying an heiress led me to conjure up some fanciful notions.

Preparations for Switzerland were more complicated than I had anticipated. Up until then nobody had ever suggested I dressed sloppily or that my appearance was less smart than that of the average student. Odette viewed me critically, bewailing the fact that I did not possess a dark blue suit.

'In Geneva we are likely to be invited out to dinner by friends and it is vital for you to wear a smart suit,' she urged, as if she were issuing an edict.

'I have a perfectly good dark suit, as well you know.'

'Not that scruffy, creased one, the one your mother bought for you at Burtons. That will never do!'

'Why the hell not?'

The insulting comments halted on the day I appeared wearing a new dark blue suit.

'You look fantastic,' exclaimed Odette. 'Aunt Sophie will find you even more *sympathique* in the flesh than in the photograph I sent her. But there is still one more thing you will need to do.'

'What now?'

'Remember always to place a white handkerchief in your breast pocket, with an inch only visible to complete the effect of the ensemble. That is what all chic men in Geneva do.'

Carrying out her absurd instructions to the letter, I sought her final seal of approval.

'How's that look?'

'*Sympathique*. Oh, so *sympathique*.'

'I suppose you want me to bring my dinner jacket as well,' I said, irritated by the fuss and palaver that had been created by the suit issue.

'Only the very affluent have dress suits in my country. You *must* bring it with you. Our friends will think you are from an upper-class English family. They will envy you.'

'I cannot imagine why I love you, Odette. You are nothing but a vile snob!'

For two days peace reigned, after which Odette gave me a series of lessons in basic table manners that would prepare me for the honour of eating with her sophisticated father and mother. A public school education and fastidious parents had at least ensured I knew how to hold and manoeuvre properly knife, fork and spoon. It never had been my habit to eat from a knife or to chew noisily with mouth wide open.

'I'm not some wild animal that needs training before being allowed to mix in polite company,' I thundered, greatly vexed.

I was beginning to wonder what I would be letting myself in for in Geneva. Odette's parents sounded very difficult to please. They clearly expected nothing less than the highest of standards from their guests. The thought of undue expectations was not a little daunting.

The time came for Odette to return home to Geneva. One day she was there at my side, larger than life, with every moment packed full of bustling activity; on the next she was gone. The quiet brought about by her absence made me feel woebegone and abandoned. The vibrancy of her personality had captivated my very soul in ways that had given purpose and meaning to an expressionless life.

My father was unaware that Switzerland was the most expensive country in Europe, despite the ample exchange rate of twelve Swiss francs to the pound that we took for granted at the time.

'You will have to make do with forty pounds to cover your expenses for the trip,' he declared. 'After all, as you will be staying with Mr and Mrs Nagy, your expenses will be negligible.'

On the face of it, my father's contribution was going to be more than adequate. Neither he nor I could possibly have guessed that fate had it in mind to fashion some startling happenings.

Early one evening, a few days before I was due to leave for Geneva, my mother shouted out: 'You're wanted on the phone. It's Odette.'

'Hello,' I said, 'is everything all right?'

'Of course it's all right. I have a wonderful idea. Why don't you spend two nights in Paris, instead of flying direct to Geneva? I shall meet you at the airport and will deal with the hotel booking in advance. We can see the sights together. Doesn't it sound lovely and romantic?'

I had already seen most of the noteworthy sights of Paris with my friend, Peter, but this stop-off plan promised to be a great deal more exciting.

'I'm sure I can alter the flight arrangements,' I said. 'I'll let you know what time I'm to arrive in Paris next Tuesday. I can't wait to see you. Love you!'

Continental Mishaps (1) – Paris

Airports lacked the vulgar, cattle market image we associate with them nowadays. My flight to Paris from Heathrow, the first time I had been airborne, was a civilised and comfortable adventure. Even economy passengers were provided with a service that was outstanding in quality. I was wrapped in wonderment as we were carried through sun-filled territories, way above the clouds. So entranced was I by this magical mode of travel that the journey was completed before it seemingly had begun.

Odette was as good as her word. She was waiting for me at the barrier; she bore a forlorn and troubled look that immediately aroused my curiosity. The moment she set eyes on me her face flashed a fulsome smile before a more serious expression erased the jubilant guise. The embrace that was to follow, loving though it was, lacked the untamed spontaneity I had expected from her. There was something altogether very different about Odette.

Pleasantries quickly dispensed with, and betraying an eagerness close to impatience, I asked, 'Where are we going to stay?'

'I have booked a room in a small hotel next to the Folies-Bergère. It is near to the Place d'Opéra, which is very central. It will suit our purpose.'

I knew exactly what my purpose was. Excitement mounting, I bundled my luggage into a taxi that sped us through busy streets to the Montparnasse district of Paris.

The hotel concierge handed us the key that was to unlock the door that separated the drab third floor bedroom from the dimly lit corridor. The only item of furniture in the room, other than a chair, chest of drawers and worn-out wardrobe, was a single iron bedstead covered with torn, crumpled sheets and a solitary blanket. The absence of a bedside table and telephone added to the sense of isolation, which made our illicit intentions the more appealing.

'I don't think we're going to be very comfortable in this bed,' I remarked.

'You're jumping to conclusions,' protested Odette indignantly. 'You are staying here with me, aren't you?'

'Of course I'm not.'

'Where's your room then?'

'Not here, I'm staying with friends.'

'With friends, you say. You inveigle me on this mad excursion to Paris; a lovely and romantic time we were going to have. Then you dump me in the tattiest hotel you can find, only to tell me you are staying with friends. Bloody hell, Odette, who are these friends and where do they live?'

'They are just friends. You are making an issue out of nothing at all. They have an apartment only minutes from here.'

'Why can't I stay there too?'

'Because it is a tiny apartment with not enough space for the two of us.'

Odette's explanation seemed plausible enough. Perhaps I was misreading the vibes. Instinct, however, told me something was radically wrong.

Odette left me to sort myself out. For what seemed for ever I awaited her return from the secret quarters about which she had insisted on being tight-lipped. Unable to make contact with her, I had no option but to remain in the dreary room. I bit my nails, unable to concentrate on more useful activity. When at last she reappeared, seething inside I accompanied her to a nearby restaurant, where she had decided we were to eat. I was determined to discover what had changed Odette's attitude towards me in less than a week.

Throughout the meal I remained confused and upset by Odette's detached indifference. Sombre and furtive, as if she had something to hide, she expressed none of the warmth that in England was open and unprompted. There was a restiveness in her manner that increased my feeling of unease. We drank our coffee in silence, each eyeing the other suspiciously. She had become a remote stranger, whose love for me appeared to have perished all at once. What was it that had brought about this change?

I must have been reading her thoughts. 'It's nine o'clock,' she said. 'I am tired after the journey and think we ought to have an early night.'

'The flight from Geneva would have taken less than an hour. How can you be so tired?'

'I did not fly. I came by car. Daniel drove me.'

There was a long, awkward silence. I had heard of Daniel before, described by Odette as her platonic boyfriend from Geneva. I had never regarded him as a threat. But now the warning signals were clear enough. This was the explanation I had been seeking.

To my horror, Odette strode off at a brisk pace, leaving me alone on the pavement outside the restaurant. She turned and called back casually: 'I'll telephone the hotel concierge early tomorrow morning to let you know when and where we are to meet.'

I stood open-mouthed, confounded by her callousness. Her dismissal of me was unmistakable, a heartless brush-off. It was as if the past few months had counted for nothing. With wild thoughts racing through my head, I contemplated the futility of a life without Odette. In a dumbstruck stupor I roamed the Paris streets for many hours. Physically and emotionally drained I returned at last to my grim base, to be haunted by nightmares that depicted weird, pernicious images. My energy depleted and spirits crushed, early traffic noises awakened conscious thoughts to a renewed awareness of my desolation.

Breakfast was served in a windowless room next to the hotel foyer. I stared at the hot croissants and petit pain that remained uneaten on the plate in front of me and drank my coffee with the preoccupied air of one tormented. The frustration of having to remain in the confines of a smoke-filled bar area whilst waiting to be summoned by Odette increased my sense of panic.

She had promised to be in touch early that morning. By mid-day still there had been no contact. Imagination was running riot. I conjured up extravagant forebodings as I paced up and down like a caged animal. Assuming the worst, I took it that our relationship was dead and over as far as Odette was concerned. Left to my own devices in a strange city, armed with an outgoing plane ticket for

Geneva, I assumed that it was up to me to find my own way back to England, never to set eyes on Odette again.

The poet in me wanted to write her a Churchillian note, such as the one sent by the articulate young Winston to Muriel Wilson after she had jilted him. The lack of Odette's address removed for me the possibility of an emotive letter.

And suddenly everything was changed. 'Monsieur Hall,' said the concierge, interrupting my thoughts. 'I have Mademoiselle Nagy on the telephone for you.'

Odette explained she would be waiting for me in ten minutes' time in the Place d'Opéra. Instant relief evaporated the anger that was pent up inside me. During the wretched hours of the previous night all had been despondency and gloom. In the more optimistic light of day, now that Odette had resurfaced, the clouds of despair were lifting. I was prepared to forgive her for each and any of her improvident actions.

The atmosphere at lunch was strained. I could see Odette was about to say something that would upset me further.

'Tell me what's on your mind,' I said. 'I think I can cope with anything now.'

'I do not intend to hold the truth back any longer,' she began deliberately. 'Daniel and I are leaving by car for Geneva later this afternoon. You will have to spend this evening on your own, but I shall be home in time to meet your flight tomorrow with my mother at Geneva Airport.'

'Is there any point in my coming to Geneva now?'

'I don't see why there should be any reason for a change of plan. My parents and I are still keen to repay you for your hospitality in England.'

'You know damned well that the only reason I accepted your invitation to stay was because we had decided to get married. Has all that changed?' I asked, trembling by now with emotion.

'I don't know. I really don't know. My parents are putting pressure on me to remain in Switzerland. They think Daniel would be an ideal choice of husband for me. They have nothing against you, of course, but they would never be happy for me to live in England.'

Trying to remain calm, I entreated her with one vital question, the answer to which would influence the pattern of my entire future. 'Do you love Daniel?'

'Yes, I think I do.'

Abandoning restraint, I lashed out with a torrent of abuse. 'You selfish cow! You unbelievable, calculating bitch! So much for the romantic Paris trip you were so fucking keen to engineer. Do you ever think of anyone but yourself?'

'I have heard quite enough. I am going back to the apartment,' she said, raising her eyebrows with a haughtiness that made me burn inside with fury.

'I'm coming with you to find out just what's going on in this hidden refuge of yours.'

'Please yourself. But don't behave like an idiot. It is my half-sister's apartment. Up until now she had been told you were a nice, well-mannered Englishman. I should prefer her not to be disappointed.'

Odette paid the café bill with flamboyant relish, as if to emphasise my financial dependence on her. She got up from the table and hurried out on to the busy street. It would have been easy to have lost Odette in the crowd, but I was close on her heels, determined to pursue her. I could feel myself becoming more and more agitated, with a violent anger building up inside me. I was intent upon a confrontation, indifferent to the consequences that were likely to ensue.

Odette entered the hallway of a large apartment block that was situated a few hundred yards from where we had been eating. By the time she had pressed the lift button, I was at her side. She had no means of keeping me in suspense any longer. We entered the lift together. Up we travelled to the eighth floor. Odette and I stepped out on to a landing. Turning right and walking along a wide corridor, Odette unlocked the door that led to her private hide-out.

The entrance lobby was cramped, confirming what Odette had said about the size of the apartment. A woman, whom I assumed to be Odette's half-sister, emerged from one of its rooms. I had difficulty in assessing her age, because grey hair and gaunt features masked a youngish face. She fixed me with a discerning gaze as she beckoned me into the living room.

'I am Nicole,' she said. 'You must be Jonathan. Odette has told me such a lot about you.' She too spoke perfect English, and despite my simmering wrath, I was beginning to feel more at ease as we indulged in innocent small talk.

'With the name Jonathan, I take it that you must be Jewish,' she said.

'No, I'm not. Why ever should you think that?'

'Jonathan is a popular *prénom* or first name for Jewish males in France. Did you not know that?'

Fascinating though this information was, I could not prevent my attention from being diverted when suddenly my eyes focused on a suitcase by the window. The words DANIEL GIRAUD were printed in large black letters on the canvas covering.

So it was not my imagination that I had been cheated on by Odette. The ugly facts were self-evident. Only a simpleton would allow himself to be tricked and humiliated in this manner. Suffocated by a sinister inner turbulence, I was gripped by an evil force that was taking control of my emotions. Barely conscious of the potential dangers, and with an insane impulsiveness that caused my witnesses to gasp with horror, I forced open a glass doorway and flung myself out onto the balcony. Climbing over the railings I crawled onto a narrow ledge, the perfect spot for a suicide fall.

'I am going to throw myself down. For God's sake keep away,' I yelled out threateningly.

I am unsure whether this was merely a dramatic warning or the menacing gesture of a distraught young man who had every intention of killing himself. A cousin of mine, Brian, the elder son of my father's twin brother, had not long before ended his life by throwing himself into the path of an oncoming express train. Brian's impetuous, obsessional and often volatile temperament was in many ways quite similar to my own, a fact that underlined the need for Odette and Nicole to treat with extreme urgency the matter of my rescue from the roof.

I do not know how long I remained out there suspended precariously on the ledge. A paranoia over heights added to my miserable predicament. Had I succumbed to the temptation of looking down, an attack of vertigo might well have resulted in the pavement observers being treated to a fatal consequence. Instead the animated chatter of the onlookers reached fever pitch as they hungered with deafening candour for a tragedy. I had neither the courage to jump nor the common sense to retreat indoors. Fear paralysing me, and with sweat saturating my clothes, I gripped the railings so firmly that the knuckles of my fingers tightened to a bloodless white.

Odette's initial reaction was to try to shame me into seeing reason.

'You crazy, immature fool! This is the behaviour of a child. Stop playing games and come inside at once so that we can talk sensibly.'

In no way swayed by her words, I stiffened my resolve. Nothing would induce me to yield to Odette's blandishments.

Odette halted her attempts to assault me with her tongue, while she and Nicole considered what strategy to adopt next. I almost plunged to an inadvertent end when I lost my balance, thereby causing Odette, who was by now on the balcony, to change her attitude.

'I beg you to come back inside,' she pleaded. 'I am sorry for the awful way I have behaved towards you. If only you will give me the chance, I can explain everything.'

Numbed with despair, I was barely capable of taking in the meaning of her words that smacked of trickery. Refusing to give in or feel any remorse, I would rather have died than be susceptible to Odette's wily ploys.

The trancelike state was broken when, all of a sudden, strong hands grabbed me from above. Three helmeted men in dark blue uniforms dragged me to the safety of the balcony, to which they had gained access from the apartment itself. It all happened in the twinkling of an eye before I had time to catch my breath. I had been rescued by *sapeurs-pompiers*, who, in addition to fighting fires in France, deal with masses of emergencies. The firemen escorted me to a van, whose jarring siren noises rang out with persistent clarity, a metaphoric advertising of the suicidal act that never was. Having deposited me at the nearest gendarmerie, the firemen had completed their mission. Warning sirens scattered the traffic as their vehicle hurtled away in the direction of the next calamity.

An impatient officer lectured me for wasting police time. He made it clear that Paris was no place for young Englishmen, especially those of the deranged, egocentric variety.

'Get the hell out of here and go back to England' is an approximate translation of his advice to me.

Unburdening my soul to him, I gave an account of the sorry saga that had preceded the rooftop drama. Expecting no sympathy whatsoever, I was astonished to discover that the police officer was greatly moved by my tale of woe. Uncharitable thoughts vanished the instant he realised my desperate exploits had been brought about by passions of the heart. Holding my hands tenderly, and tearful eyes disclosing a deeper sentiment than I would ever have imagined possible, he offered me words of solace.

'You poor young man. The best thing you can do is to leave France at once and try to forget your sweetheart. Catch the next plane to London. Life is too precious to allow it to be endangered by a girl who does not deserve your love.'

Inspired by his support and honest wisdom, I decided to return to England without delay.

As I was leaving the gendarmerie, Odette sprang out from behind one of the entrance pillars. Fatigued and on edge, she approached me with extreme caution, unsure whether I intended to ignore her or attack her with my fists. Putting her arms round me and looking into my eyes with a grave intensity, she was at last able to tell me how she really felt.

'Without you I am empty inside. I have and feel nothing. I know that now,' she said simply. 'I do not love Daniel and never have. I was trying to make you jealous. You have no idea how my world began to fall apart the moment I knew there was a possibility of losing you. I cannot alter the last twenty-four hours, but I promise to make it up to you in the future. Please, please come to Geneva. My parents so much want to meet you.'

After all that had happened, I found it hard to believe the sincerity of Odette's words. The sensible course was for me to follow the policeman's advice to cut and run. In matters of the heart, common sense rarely rules our actions; my only wish was for Odette to reciprocate my loving feelings totally.

I was putty in her hands. Optimistic hopes were already erasing the gruesome memories of the recent past. In a fit of impulse and against my better judgement, I reversed my plans and opted for Geneva.

Odette was elated.

'There's one bad piece of news,' she said.

'What's that?'

'The *sapeurs-pompiers* are going to send you a call-out charge for four hundred francs.'

'Good God,' I exclaimed. 'The balance left from my father's allowance won't even buy us fish and chips.'

Her eyes twinkled impishly as she teased: 'There are no fish and chip shops in Geneva. We'll be eating caviar instead!'

Continental Mishaps (2) – Geneva

My shameful and reckless behaviour at Nicole's apartment had frightened me more than I dared admit. The novelty of being on course for Geneva again was fast diminishing, especially as deep down I sensed Odette had been manipulating me for her own selfish reasons. No matter how great these misgivings were, I was encouraged by a faith that everything would pan out happily, culminating in a fairy tale ending.

I was met by Mrs Nagy and Odette at Geneva Airport. If daughters really do turn out to look like their mothers, I had cause for concern. Mrs Nagy was no oil painting. An overweight woman in her early fifties, she was of dowdy appearance. For the most part her lips remained closed with a defiant tightness; on the rare occasions she ventured a smile, she displayed an array of discoloured, tombstone teeth that looked intimidating. Camouflaging her apprehension, she gave me a cordial rather than an effusive welcome. We shook hands formally and made for the car.

The short drive highlighted the austere, clinical buildings, whose impersonal drabness reflected Calvin's sixteenth-century influence that still dominates Geneva. The lake glistened invitingly, forming as it did a theatrical foreground, draped in the distance by thick clouds that concealed Mont Blanc from our view. We drove along the quayside, Odette pointing out the Richemond and the Beau Rivage, two lovely hotels that overlook the Brunswick Gardens, hotels noted for sophisticated luxury and the excellence of their cuisine.

'That's Château Banquet over there,' exclaimed Odette, as we approached an imposing block of flats close to the lake. The car was deposited in the underground car park from which a lift took us up to the Nagys' spacious second floor apartment. In view of the fact there were only two bedrooms, Odette had generously given up her room to me and was to sleep in the living room.

Odette was impatient for me to unpack so that she could give me a whistle-stop tour of her precious Geneva and the surrounding district. In the process of showing me some of the local landmarks, she proved herself to be a reckless driver, with a propensity for emergency stops and near misses that scared me to pieces.

'For Christ's sake slow down,' I shouted at her, 'or we'll both be corpses before the day's over.'

'You were the one with the death wish, remember,' she snapped.

'That's as may be,' I said, 'but with you at the wheel I've no choice in the matter and it'll be murder this time.'

Mr Nagy looked tired when he arrived home later that evening from his surgery. A plump and not very tall man of at least sixty, he offered me a terse welcome, taking little trouble to disguise the concern he must have felt at having to provide lodging for an excitable young Englishman who had designs on his daughter. His eyes darted about suspiciously, manifesting an impatient irritability which suggested that, like his daughter, he would not suffer fools gladly. Were he ever to be crossed, I judged that he would be a merciless and uncompromising adversary. I was wary of Odette's father from the outset.

I dreaded my first meal in the Nagy household, when Odette's lesson in table manners would be put to the test. At dinner that evening I sat upright like a ramrod, exhibiting the impeccable deportment I had been told was expected of me. In marked contrast, Mr Nagy slouched at the table with an oafishness that was barely imaginable; he guzzled the food in front of him in a way that likened him to a chimpanzee. Using hands or whichever feeding implement best suited, he shovelled the contents from his plate into an oversized mouth, spluttering indecipherable French words with such speed that most of what he said was lost on me. Whether Odette had been naive or rascally when preparing me for this charade, I never did discover. Hungarian count or not, Mr Nagy's behaviour was not in keeping with the twentieth-century aristocrat he professed to be.

Towards the end of the meal Mr Nagy held forth with such rapidity that again I could not comprehend what he was saying. His gesticulations implied that Odette was to interpret a message intended for me.

'My father says,' she began uneasily, 'that he will pay the four hundred franc bill the fire brigade will be sending to Nicole. He also says that he will allow you to stay here for three months, as agreed, providing you conduct yourself sensibly and promise never again to attempt to do yourself an injury.'

I mumbled incoherent words of gratitude that were met with scornful snorts from my surly host.

'He's got me over a barrel,' I thought. To have begun my relationship with Mr Nagy by being in financial debt to him had placed me in an insufferable position. My initial impression that he was a man to be reckoned with had indeed been correct, but he was cunning as well. I was going to need to be on my guard at all times lest he attempted to banish me from his daughter's life altogether.

Mrs Nagy was deferential towards her husband, never seeming to be completely at ease in his company. It was as if at any moment she expected his simmering temper to erupt and for a cruel tongue to shower her with oral abuse. My presence may have added to Mrs Nagy's discomfort, although her manner suggested she was used to being the target of bullying tactics.

The atmosphere in the Nagy household was stiff. The ritual of shaking hands several times a day was the accustomed acknowledgement of the various comings and goings. Ready for bed, in faltering French I thanked Mr Nagy for his tolerant welcome. After being shaken by the hand in the same manner as had been the tradition each evening after prayers at my prep school, I retired for the night.

'It's time to get up,' Odette whispered sweetly in my ear early next morning. 'We shall need to leave for the university as soon as you are ready. Do you want me to get you coffee or tea?'

After shaving hurriedly, I slipped into casual trousers and a sweater. Viewing me with a critical eye Odette remarked cuttingly: 'You can't go to the university dressed like that. Why aren't you wearing your dark blue suit?'

'Don't be ridiculous. I'm a student, not a male model.'

'Please yourself,' said Odette, 'but don't say I didn't warn you when you discover that Geneva is different from other universities.'

Odette was dressed up to the nines. She could not have been smarter had she been attending a fashionable wedding. Puzzlement dominated my thinking as we travelled first by bus and later by tram beyond the Old Town to the university campus at the opposite end of the city.

The spectacle I perceived as we approached the steps that led up to the university's entrance baffled me further. Out of jazzy sports cars and chauffeured limousines stepped stylishly attired young men and women. Like clones, the men wore dark blue suits. The female students, all in high heels, and extravagantly coiffured, displayed tailored suits and pretty dresses. It was a veritable mannequin parade. So incongruous was the presence of these elegant undergraduates that my attention was diverted from the vast majority, who, turned out in the informal gear one expects of students, were making their way to the various lecture rooms.

'Now perhaps you can see why I wanted you to wear a suit,' said Odette pointedly.

'Not everyone takes themselves as seriously as you do. It's obvious there are two categories of student here, those who dress to kill and the ones who are down to earth and sane.'

'I am glad you have noticed that we Genevese pride ourselves on our appearance,' declared Odette, 'and that it is the foreign students that are slovenly and scruffy.'

'It seems that I am one of those scruffy foreigners and I much prefer it that way.'

Odette had told me it was not necessary to enrol in order to attend lectures at the university. The system was sufficiently informal for me to be able to follow whatever course I desired without being challenged. She had it in mind for me to sit beside her at some of the interpreter's school sessions, which is why she wanted me in my Sunday best.

Odette was studying in-depth English, German and Spanish. 'Only eight per cent of us will qualify as interpreters,' she explained. 'Most will become translators or will give up before the end of the five years. We need to be much more than fluent in these languages. We have to be familiar also with the technical terms in a great variety of specialist subjects.'

Three days at her side increased my respect for Odette's intellect and determination. Her linguistic skills highlighted my own inadequacies, so common to most Englishmen. So advanced and unremitting were Odette's university commitments that the lectures I attended confused rather than helped me. I felt like an instrumentalist in a symphony orchestra who had yet to learn how to read music. My standard of French at college had been tolerable; any confidence, however, that I had possessed in my ability to speak and understand the language was fast diminishing.

'My so-called studies at the university are doing me no good whatsoever,' I grumbled to Odette one evening. 'I honestly think that my French is a great deal worse than when I left England.'

'I have noticed an improvement already,' encouraged Odette. 'It is because you are surrounded by spoken French all day that you feel inadequate and out of your depth. In next to no time you will have been immersed in the language to such an extent that it will become second nature to you. Trust me!'

Not sharing such optimism, I insisted it was pointless for me to continue to follow the same studies as Odette. My aim had been to achieve no more than reasonable fluency in French. Odette discovered a course at the university, designed specifically for foreign students, that satisfied my needs admirably. Thanks to the demands made by an exacting lady tutor, my fellow students and I quickly began to master some of the more subtle features of the French language.

My first meeting with Daniel was when he joined the Nagys one Sunday. After picnicking in the autumn sunshine at a favourite local beauty spot, we inhaled the intoxicating air as we clambered along hillside paths that commanded spectacular views.

In his mid-twenties, of medium height and slimly built, Daniel was of nondescript appearance. The short-cut hair highlighted a sallow face that bore signs of a fading suntan. Prim, humourless and lacking imagination, he came dressed for the weekend jaunt in a dark blue suit. The statutory white pocket handkerchief was displayed in the desired manner.

Daniel ignored my presence, whilst devoting attention to flattering Odette as well as ingratiating himself with her parents. Far from being impressed by the man, I likened him to other Swiss clones, whose bearing and behaviour symbolised a self-righteousness I was beginning to despise.

'Daniel is such a nice young man,' enthused Mrs Nagy, focusing a toothy smile in my direction. 'He's a qualified engineer, you know, and his career prospects are excellent.'

'The big-headed bastard's also a natty dresser, especially on Sunday afternoon rambles,' was my private quip.

'Oh yes, Mrs Nagy, he has any number of talents. Odette thinks he's the cat's whiskers.'

My literal translation into French of cat's whiskers removed Mrs Nagy's wide grin in an instant. I had flummoxed her completely.

Odette was a complicated young woman, unable to decide what it was she really wanted. The rigid home upbringing caused her to crave to be freed from the tyrannies of parental domination. It was her inbuilt need to part from the life neatly mapped out for her that had drawn her closer to me during her stay in England. The strain of trying to please her parents, as well as giving vent to her true feelings, was the cause of her developing ambivalence.

Had I possessed a more mature worldliness and the courage of my own convictions, I might have succeeded in luring Odette away from her Swiss roots. Intent upon shattering a future that had promised so well, Mr and Mrs Nagy littered our path with obstacles, using base intrigues to achieve their purpose. With united opposition mounting, it became clear I was to play the part of the sacrificial lamb in this human tragedy and that Daniel would very likely end up with the heroine.

Odette, busy with her studies, kept me at arm's length. She regarded me as a playmate, there to be picked up or cast aside, according to her mood. The two of us were drifting apart, a fact that caused a deepening sadness to destroy what little confidence I had. I was troubled by Odette's changing attitudes. Whenever I attempted to assert my independence, she needed to be convinced of the permanence of my love. Had my responses been less predictable, I am certain it would have been possible to have unmasked her vulnerability to my advantage.

I felt very isolated in Geneva. Apart from when I was at the university, I spent long hours in solitude, lacking the will to channel usefully my frustrated energies. I read a lot and wrote countless letters, some of which were sent to people with whom I could claim only tenuous connections.

One such letter was to a buxom nineteen year old from Birmingham named Pat, whom I had met some months previously. We had twice indulged in a marathon of sensual gropes which gave me cause to hope that more and better was to follow. Her muscular frame, broad shoulders, massive tits, slim waist and sturdy legs had endowed her with the body of a superb athlete. She was a magnificent specimen of womanhood that encapsulated all that was desired for my initiation as a lover. I had hoped my letter to Pat was not too late to relight a delicate flame that had all but been blotted out.

> I did not know how much I was going to miss you. When I return to England, can we arrange to meet? Do please write soon.
>
> Love
>
> Jonathan
>
> PS. Does the invitation to stay the night when your parents are away one weekend still stand?

Instinct had already taught me it was wise to keep options open. I impatiently awaited Pat's reply. Meanwhile, in view of Odette's growing disenchantment, I wanted to find out what consolation there was to be had in Geneva.

Living under the Nagy roof hampered my ability to socialise as a free agent. It would have been out of the question for me to have brought a lady friend back to the apartment. Odette still wanted to possess me. Unwilling to give anything of herself, she was unscrupulous enough to use every dirty trick imaginable to prevent me from finding the comfort of an alternative friendship.

I was greatly at odds with myself. The emotional love I had committed to Odette was being superseded by a need for sheer physical lust, a need that was unlikely now to be fulfilled by her. The arousal pains in my groin were so urgent that I was beginning to understand what it is that causes frantic men to assault or even rape in return for lewd moments of sexual gratification.

Daily visits to the university made me more aware than ever of my need for an Odette substitute. One that would titillate my more sensitive regions was what I had in mind. This was easier said than done. The continental glamour girls with whom I was rubbing shoulders all appeared untouchable somehow. What time would any of them have for a wet-behind-the-ears Englishman with scarcely enough Swiss francs for the most basic evening out?

A Swedish blonde with long, curvaceous legs attracted my attention with disturbing regularity. Her shapely beauty was admired by all the male students on the campus. Lacking the confidence to make a pass or even speak with her, in silent fascination I watched the firm thighs tighten and the calves bulge with perfect symmetry as she glided up the stairs inside the university.

In the past, in answer to the question: 'Are you a tit or leg man?' I had been unsure of my preference. From that time onwards I knew for certain that my predilection was for legs.

Rather than have my every movement scrutinised by Mrs Nagy, I preferred to spend most daytime leisure moments away from the apartment. An avid walker, I discovered the Old Town antique shops, restaurants emitting fondue odours, chintzy backstreet souvenir stalls, banks and finance houses, innumerable bridges, the lakeside paths. A chill of abandonment passed over me as I trudged along ill-disposed streets in the soulless city. The strange thing is I was able to identify with the dirty old men, those pitiful figures in long, shabby raincoats. Intense loneliness was the common thread that linked me to them. We all hungered for the unattainable, the forbidden fruits. The old men were alive with just their memories; for me erotism was a song as yet unsung.

I first saw Eva inside a bookshop near the city centre. A wholesome-looking teenager with an attractive, high cheekboned face, she had inherited a voluptuous build, huge breasts and legs that could crush a watermelon. She was the physical duplicate of Pat from Birmingham, the girl who had not so far responded to my letter. Memories of naughty frolics with Pat led me to wonder what it would be like to indulge in a programme of energetic exercises with the well-made creature who was standing right beside me.

Unable to bring myself to make an innocent advance, I kept my distance, endeavouring to observe her discreetly. Detecting my interest and with brazen forwardness the seductive stranger began walking towards me, smiling radiantly.

'Haven't I seen you at the university?' she began.

'I was sure I recognised you, too,' I replied. 'That's why I was staring at you so rudely. I do apologise.'

'There's no need. I have only been in Geneva for a few days. I know virtually nobody as yet and am eager to make some friends. My name is Eva and I come from Holland.'

I could not have hoped for a more promising opening. Determined not to waste this rare opportunity, I arranged to meet Eva for a drink the following evening. So stunningly eye-catching was she that I was elated at the prospect of what might come next. To achieve the success I had long hankered after, the meek approach I generally adopted would need to be replaced by more forceful insistence. I had twenty-four hours in which to plan my strategy.

With great glee I told Odette of my date with Eva.

'You'll have to cancel it. My parents have arranged to take us out to dinner tomorrow evening,' she snapped resentfully.

'This is news to me. Even if you're not making it up, I refuse to let Eva down. It will be a much cosier party without me in any case, especially if Daniel is there.'

'I can see what my parents mean when they say that you are rude and ignorant, as well as being a suicidal maniac. No one can blame them for telling me to end our relationship.'

In spite of Odette's snide lecturing, I met Eva as planned. Our chosen rendezvous near to the university was a bar frequented by young people at which live music was being played.

Brainwashed into thinking that a dark blue suit was the only dress acceptable for me at a social occasion in Geneva, I made my appearance in the mode of a tailor's dummy, hoping to impress my new Dutch friend. The other men were all wearing casual clothes; suits and ties were definitely out. Having again misjudged the situation, I felt a prize idiot, so much so that my intended boldness was erased in an instant.

Conversation was stilted, indicating that the two of us had little in common. After a couple of drinks, I could see Eva was bored in my company. That she was eager to get away was patently obvious when she said: 'As I live on the other side of the lake, I really must be going now. It's a very long walk. Thank you for a lovely evening.'

All was not lost. The gentlemanly thing to do was to offer to walk her home. Perhaps in the privacy of her apartment she would reward me with a coffee and a cuddle. It was certainly worth a try.

'You can't go back all that way on your own. It's not safe. I'll walk with you,' I said gallantly.

'I'm quite capable of looking after myself, but if you insist, we shall at least be able to hear each other speak away from that noisy bar.'

Encouraged by her words, thinking it may have been the venue rather than my company that she had objected to, it seemed I was still in with a chance.

It had turned cold that evening and I regretted I was without my overcoat. We walked briskly along empty streets that next day would buzz once more with feverish activity. Faint lights twinkled and beckoned us as we crossed the bridge to the other side of the lake, where the city's perimeter separated Switzerland from France.

Arriving at the house in which Eva was renting an apartment, we had reached the end of our march. With no offer of a drink to revitalise me for the return journey, Eva delivered a cursory 'goodnight'. She slammed the front door shut, leaving me alone in the driveway. Cold, angry and frustrated, I began the long traipse back to Château Banquet.

It maddened me beyond measure that my bashful performance had wiped out Eva's interest in me. At that moment the loss of a limb would have been preferable to tongue-tied inexperience. No matter how hard I tried, I was still unable to be the confident man about town that females drooled over.

There was a distinct chill in the air. I quickened my pace, aware that it was starting to rain. Gently at first, the spots dusted my face, then all of a sudden the heavens opened. In true Swiss fashion, the cloudburst caused gushing water to transform the roadside gutters into a murky stream. So mesmerised was I by the force of the deluge that I was unaware until the storm subsided that my suit had been ruined.

Back in the Nagys' apartment, I must have looked like a drowned rat. Odette was amused, if not euphoric.

'Serves you right,' she mocked. 'It has proved a very costly evening for you. Your one and only suit's a write-off. I hope Eva made it worth your while!'

My relationship with Odette had soured to such an extent that we seldom communicated. Her parents became increasingly antagonistic; begrudging my very existence, they succeeded in making me feel that I was an intruder.

My only way of dealing with what had become an untenable situation was to attempt to mix in a social circle that had no connections with Odette's family. The fact I was reserved and did not make friends easily worsened my plight. I came into contact with a number of English students at the university, all of whom had so much money that I felt ill at ease in their company. I defended my failure to get along with them by carping at their arrogance. What in reality held me back was my sense of worthlessness. Lacking the aid of a friend or confidant, I brooded incessantly on the unhappy circumstances. In spite of my yearning to be accepted, intense reticence had created unassailable defences that were impossible to infiltrate.

A German girl, Heidi, who had attended Exeter University, was now studying in Geneva. It was a relief that she and Odette had been no more than acquaintances. I had only ever spoken to her briefly, but the thought appealed of getting to know her better. Exeter had been so agreeable for me that to be able to reminisce with a personable young lady might help to lift my spirits.

Heidi accepted my invitation to paint the town red. This time I planned that nothing should go wrong. After careful scrutiny, the bedraggled suit was pressed and brushed. Misshapen and no longer the elegant garment it once had been, in view of my plan to treat Heidi to a special evening out, the only option was for me to wear it.

I was in lively mood when we met at a bar in the Old Town. Two brandies later I was friskier than ever, behaving in the manner of a seasoned toff. Heidi played safe and stuck to tonic water.

Next we headed along cobbled streets in the direction of La Tour, a well known nightspot. Emanating from the club's interior came modern jazz sounds that were enticing. Impatiently I ushered Heidi in. The vestibule led into a plush lounge bar; the jazz quintet switched to playing music of a soulful mood. Knit together, inseparable as twins, two listless dancers shuffled their way around the tiny pear-shaped floor.

Nostalgic thoughts of jazz exploits in Brighton two months previously came flooding back. Drumming was the one skill that I could demonstrate with confidence. If I were to succeed in impressing Heidi, it would help to draw her to me.

With a glass in my hand, I sauntered over to the tenor saxophone player, the leader of the group. Using the best French I could muster, I told him I was a jazz musician and that I had missed the opportunity of playing so much I was experiencing withdrawal symptoms. Betraying visible impatience, he viewed me glumly. Remembering how I used to hate it when would-be drummers wanted to have a go on my percussion instruments, I could understand the reason for his frostiness.

'You must think it an awful cheek,' I said, 'but I should be very grateful if you would let me sit in on drums for just one number. I know what I'm doing and promise not to drown the other instruments.'

'If you want to play the drums, you will first have to buy me a large whisky,' was his response.

Bribery and corruption, I thought, but it appeared that he had agreed to my request, albeit grudgingly.

In next to no time I was back from the bar with a double whisky in my hand. The idea of playing jazz once more was a blissful prospect. Heidi was on edge, wondering whether I really was a bona fide drummer. Never doubting that I would give a masterly performance, I was amused at her mistrust of me. Far from being the cause of embarrassment, I was hoping to delight her. Not imagining for one moment that the bandleader would renege on his promise, I waited to be summoned for my turn behind the drums.

The band played three more numbers; not once did the leader's eyes meet mine. After a short interval, the music continued.

'It is obvious you are not going to be asked to join in,' volunteered Heidi. 'It is best to forget it.'

'I'm damned if I will.'

Perturbed by Heidi's cynical presumption, I finally cottoned on to the fact that the musicians had been ridiculing me. Had I been on my own it would have been bad enough, but I was maddened that my companion should be witness to such discourtesy. Patience having expired, I rose, this time determinedly, to restate my desire to play the drums.

'You said I could join you on drums if I bought you a large whisky. I honoured my part of the bargain, so what about your promise?'

'This is my band and my nightclub. I decide what happens here. I will not allow you to play the drums until you buy me one more whisky.'

'This could go on all night,' I retorted angrily.

'Take it or leave it. It's up to you.'

Common sense should have led me to take Heidi's advice and drop the whole idea, but pig-headedly I would not let the matter rest. When I came back with another whisky, the bandleader finally gave in.

'Okay,' he said, 'you come and sit in now!'

Shrugging his shoulders mockingly, the drummer stepped down from the rostrum. I seated myself on the drum stool. I checked that the bass drum and high hat pedals were easily accessible and that the snare drum and cymbals were of suitable angle and height. Discreetly I then tapped the various drums and cymbals to get the feel of them, as is normal when a drummer uses someone else's kit.

I signalled to the leader that I was ready. He responded scathingly, 'The party's over. You have played the drums, young man. Go back to your lady friend.'

The injustice and boorishness of the snub was incomprehensible. I had been deceived by a confidence trickster into buying drinks at exorbitant prices, way beyond the scope of my budget. The fact that Heidi had observed the humiliating spectacle made matters ten times worse.

Too shamefaced to rejoin Heidi, I made straight for the bar. I thumped my glass on the counter with such force that it cracked and broke. When I tugged at a wire that was suspended from the ceiling, a sin of monumental proportions had been perpetrated. The head barman was the first to intervene. 'You have unplugged Radio Télévision Suisse. It was set up for tonight's broadcast.'

What followed was more like a comedy film than a real-life drama. An army of Italian waiters rushed forward. Grabbing hold of me, they began to push and drag me in the direction of the exit. Meanwhile the owner, who by now had laid down his saxophone, had joined in the scuffle. He was prodding me in the ribs and seemed to be enjoying the diversion. Freeing one arm, I planted a punch that connected with his belly. When I came to, I was sprawled out on the pavement.

The absurdness of the situation caused an exhilaration that had temporarily quelled my anger. Before taking leave of the club's exterior, I had to retrieve my overcoat that was hanging in the foyer; negotiations for its return were likely to prove tricky. In the doorway was a glass partition that was secured by a metal grille. Spying out on me from behind the slats was one of the waiters.

Banging the door to attract his attention, I called out, 'Will you please give me back my overcoat?'

The door opened. Out stepped the waiter without the overcoat but armed with a soda siphon that he proceeded to squirt liberally over my ill-fated suit. He chided me with 'Bloody fucking English!' before seeking safety back inside.

In an uncontrollable rage I smashed a plate glass window, causing my right hand to bleed profusely. Realising I had gone too far this time, I raced towards a taxi that was parked a few yards up the road. Hot in pursuit, carrying menacing-looking implements, was a line of waiters, intent on revenge. After I was captured by my assailants, the taxi driver amended his route and dropped us off instead at a nearby police station.

I had been unaware that Switzerland was a fascist state and that law and order was a national preoccupation. Having enjoyed neutrality during two world wars, the Swiss were past masters at protecting their own interests.

The waiters gave two burly police officers an overblown version of the nightclub incident. When they went on to say I had carried out a vicious attack on the club's owner and had caused him severe injuries, I made vehement protestations.

'That is nowhere near the truth. I may have behaved stupidly, but there was extreme provocation and I think you ought at least to hear my account of what happened.'

'We are not going to believe anything we hear from a drunken Englishman,' snarled one of the officers.

'All I want is fair play. Don't you believe in justice in this country?'

Without more ado, one of the officers clutched at my neck; his colleague gripped my arms. I was frogmarched along a passage to a police cell and was propelled roughly inside. I had assumed I was going to be left in peace to simmer down, but such optimism was ill-conceived. Taking care not to inflict damage on my head and face, using fists and boots in a well-practised manner, the bully boys punched, butted, kicked and shoved. My body was treated like an expendable football; battered and shaken, I collapsed in a state of shock.

'You know what Swiss justice to expect next time,' said one of the officers scornfully as he locked me in the cell.

When I awoke, stiff, aching and shaking with fear, I mused on the extraordinary events that had taken place since I had left England. Were I to have given a detailed account of the happenings to a friendly listener, I would have been dubbed a liar. I compared the rough treatment meted out by the Genevese police with the sympathetic reception I had been given by their Parisian counterparts. With the exception of Odette's Aunt Sophie, who had gone out of her way to be friendly, I had discovered nothing to commend the Swiss people.

Before early morning sounds were audible, my captors returned to the cell. My contact address having been noted, I was released with a blunt warning ringing in my ears: 'You are going to be charged and it is likely you will be sent to prison.'

Crestfallen and hung-over, I limped my way back to the Nagy apartment, knowing full well that I was in for a remorseless telling-off.

Odette was the first to confront me. She looked strangely triumphant, as if my disordered appearance and state of inebriation proved I no longer deserved to be a recipient of her family's benevolence.

'Heidi has already told us of your escapades at the nightclub and of your arrest. My father is sick with anger. He asked me to let him know the moment you were back.'

I was horrified to learn that Odette and Heidi had been in cahoots all along. If Heidi's account of what had happened was as highly coloured as was the waiters' rendering to the police, I had cause to be very fearful of the outcome.

Mr Nagy manifested himself, his ill-tempered, glowering expression making it plain I was in for a rough ride.

'From the first I did not like you,' he began, 'but I put up with you for the sake of Odette. To be woken up twice in one night, all because of your senseless, violent behaviour, is the final straw. You have abused my hospitality so outrageously that I am not prepared to harbour you under my roof any longer. I want you out of the apartment at once. I forbid you ever again to have any contact with my daughter.'

Later that morning I visited the British consulate. I managed to see the deputy consul, who sat po-faced and non-committal as he listened to my extraordinary tale. Without finding a solution to my troubles, he helped me to obtain a small bed-sitting room near the university, though I had no idea how I would be able to afford to pay the rent. He warned me, however, that at the very least my disorderly conduct would result in my having to pay a fine.

I returned to Château Banquet to collect my things. Odette was there with her mother. After I had finished packing and was in the process of departing, Odette accompanied me to the apartment building entrance. Turning towards her, with anger welling up inside me, I called out, 'You got me to Geneva under false pretences, you bitch. I came with love in my heart; we had a future together and you know it. You have allowed your parents to rule your life and the reason they favour Daniel is that they're too selfish to part with you. Your father doesn't have a clue what really happened last night. To throw me out into the street like this without knowing the facts is utterly unfair. I feel like killing the bastard.'

From the time of my birth I had been institutionalised. Despite the disadvantages of living within a community, there had always been someone with whom I could speak and someone to provide for my physical needs. People noises, too, I had taken for granted. Once I was installed in the comfortless bedsit, I realised for the first time in my life how it felt to be entirely alone. The ability to cope domestically and to be independent in the adult sense were skills I had yet to acquire. I was scared rigid.

Thoughts then turned to the matter of my finances. Checking pockets and wallet, I discovered I had fifty Swiss francs and a ten pound sterling traveller's cheque. That was all. Rent to be paid up front would gobble up most of my resources, with nothing left for food. How I was going to subsist on what amounted to peanuts I did not know.

I investigated the possibility of a work permit. In the same way that it is complicated for foreigners to purchase properties in Switzerland, the Swiss mania for officialdom and paperwork prevented me from applying for a job without stirring up a hornets' nest. When aged eighteen, Aristotle Onassis, having escaped massacre at the hands of the Turks, made his first million in Buenos Aires, where he was unable to speak the language. He would not have been daunted by constraints of bureaucracy and would have found an effective means of evading the rules and regulations that were hampering me. The zip had been knocked out of me to such an extent that I had no desire to attempt to deceive the authorities.

A few days later, by which time I was living on little more than bread and water, I was walking disconsolately along the street in the direction of the university. A police car drew up alongside me. Out stepped two officers. Grabbing hold of me, they bundled me into the back seat. 'You are under arrest,' said one.

I was taken to an interview room in what must have been Geneva's main police station. An undersized man in plain clothes sat behind a desk, with official-looking papers in front of him. A uniformed policeman guarded the doorway. It was not until my interrogator spoke that I began to realise the gravity of the situation.

'You are charged,' the little man said, 'with threatening to murder Monsieur László Nagy of 8 Château Banquet and for causing a breach of the peace four nights ago in the Old Town. You will be kept in custody pending a court hearing. I must also inform you that Monsieur Claude Baronetti, owner of La Tour nightclub, is bringing a private action against you for damage caused to his premises and he is claiming compensation for the physical injuries he sustained in the affray. After your fingerprints have been taken, you will be removed to the cells.'

Odette must have repeated my words to her father out of context. She knew perfectly well that my threat to kill him was an idle one and had been said flippantly. In view of the menacing nature of the remark, and the fact the police were now involved, only a miracle was going to save me from imprisonment. As for Mr Baronetti's claim for compensation, I was outraged at the thought of the deception. Built like a prizefighter and as tall as a giant, he was in no danger of being beaten up by me, although I knew that any courtroom would be full to overflowing with witnesses eager to testify in his favour.

The ill-fated events had come about so rapidly that I was unable to digest the fact I was on centre stage, depicted as the villain of the piece. So dejected was I by this time that I had abandoned any hope of receiving equitable treatment. My family and England seemed a world away; there was no one to whom I could turn.

After my fingerprints had been taken, much to my surprise I was led back to the interview room. Sitting in the same seat that I had occupied was Odette. She was wringing her hands and contorting her face, in a state of extreme agitation. Swollen, tormented eyes accentuated dried-up tears that had smudged her make-up. Did I detect a beseeching look? What was the purpose of her visit? Forgiveness perhaps. Like it or not, Odette was my only hope.

'I shall leave the two of you together,' said one of the officers in a conspiratorial tone.

Wondering what was going to happen next, I waited for Odette to enlighten me.

'My father was taken ill after I told him of your threat to murder him,' she began. 'I merely repeated to him your words and he took them literally. I found myself in an impossible position. To save your skin I have told him and the police that I was lying. I never meant to harm you, even though I was angered by the things you said. My parents are furious with me. The police are considering taking action against me now. By the way, you look awful. You're as white as a sheet.'

'You don't look too good yourself. It must have taken a lot of courage to lie on my behalf. I can't tell you how much I appreciate what you've done.'

Before withdrawing, she handed me an envelope. 'I gather you are about to be released. I'll no doubt see you at the university.'

Bemused by Odette's selfless act of loyalty, an act that must have caused her personal anguish, I realised I had never stopped loving her. To have jeopardised the relationship with her parents in this way was the proof I needed that she too still cared.

Overjoyed to be free, I regarded the dingy bedsit as my sanctuary, a much more commodious place than a prison cell. In a few days' time my funds would be exhausted. Mr Baronetti's specious claims would, I knew, be pursued with vigour, resulting in a judgement made against me. The police, too, would go ahead with the breach of the peace indictment. The common-sense solution was for me to return to England as soon as possible.

I telephoned my parents from a call box across the street.

'Hello, this is Jonathan,' I said.

'It's good to hear from you,' answered my father. 'Are you enjoying Geneva?'

'Very much. I've had a whale of a time and my French is greatly improved.'

'How's Odette?'

'She's fine and she sends her love. I'll have to be brief because I am running out of coins. I plan to come home within the next couple of days as I am itching to get back to work.'

'That is good news. We can do with you here.'

'Must go now. Love to Mum. See you tomorrow or the day after.'

Remembering the envelope that Odette had handed to me at the police station, I retrieved it from my pocket. Inside was the long-awaited letter from Pat, the erotic idol of my fantasies. Scanning the missive for the salient features, I discovered our liaison was not over and done with as far as she was concerned.

> I had given up hope that you would contact me. I am longing for you to return to England, so that we can continue where we left off. My parents will be away for a fortnight just after Christmas. Does that sound promising? I can't wait.
> With much love
> Pat

A few days earlier I would have been delighted with Pat's answer. Now I was not so sure. Still deeply committed to Odette, I was not ready to plunge headlong into another relationship. Only when the hurt had lessened, with the healing process under way, would my thoughts return to Pat.

By surreptitious means I managed to get word to Odette that I would be leaving for England the following day. Her reply was delivered to my lodgings.

> Aunt Sophie will be collecting you tomorrow at 11.30 hrs and will be giving you lunch. Afterwards she will take you to the airport.
> Your loving
> Odette

Aunt Sophie's big-hearted gesture was typical of her. She was not going to allow me to sneak away from Geneva like a fugitive.

Arriving next morning in a roomy estate car, complete with two Great Danes, she drove me to her imposing residence.

The dining room table was laid for two. My delight was immense when Odette suddenly appeared. Dear, sweet, wily Aunt Sophie had contrived for us to spend a final hour together. In a clandestine atmosphere highly charged with a mixture of lamentation and romance, Odette and I ate little of the food that was placed before us. Robbed of what could have been a loving marriage, we shed tears for one another in the saddest of farewells.

Having completed the ten-minute drive to the airport, Aunt Sophie parked the car. She was unable to disguise how much the recent developments had upset her.

'Odette has always been our favourite niece,' she confided. 'She may be volatile and highly-strung, but you know as well as I do that underneath the veneer is a heart of gold. László Nagy has a lot to answer for; I detest his autocratic ways. I know that Odette is in love with you. It's a tragedy because I can see you love her, too. Memories of Odette will linger and the wounds are bound to ache for quite some while.'

'I shall never forget your kindness to me, Aunt Sophie. I know you'll keep an eye on Odette. Thank you and goodbye.'

'*Sympathique* was the word I first used to describe you,' she reminded me. 'My opinion has not changed. Never surrender your sensitivity; it's the greatest quality a man can have. Good luck.'

Free as a Bird

Cocooned in the safety of home and England, I tried to erase the hapless memories of Geneva from my mind. That was until Odette's letter arrived.

Resting on the hall table was a solitary envelope, which bore Odette's easily discernible handwriting. I was alarmed the letter was addressed to my parents and not to me. My father and mother knew nothing of my Paris or Swiss exploits; it was better left that way. Seizing the envelope, I whisked it away to the privacy of a loo. Perusal of the contents made me thankful my presence of mind had spared my parents the humiliation of having to share in my anguish.

Odette had not minced her words. Exonerating her father's actions, she made me out to be an utter scoundrel. So plausibly expressed were the contents of her letter that my parents would be compelled to take her side. The epistle concluded defensively:

> My parents were hospitable and generous to Jonathan at all times, so much so that he was more than repaid for the hospitality I received from you in England. Even the fire brigade levy was paid for by my father, so please don't judge us harshly. Jonathan will doubtless offer his own interpretation of what happened, but I give you my word that I have summarised the facts precisely.

I cannot imagine what, other than a guilty conscience, had induced Odette to write that letter. Less than a week ago we had parted on amorous terms. Calculated to distress my parents, her bitter onslaught was like an arrow in my side. No useful purpose would have been served by my handing the letter over. Burning the grisly evidence, I buried the charred remains well out of sight.

I joined forces with two endearing mischief-makers. David, whose birthday party I had attended with Odette and Gwilym in the summer, was the ringleader. He was aided and abetted by

John, an engineering graduate. The three of us had one thing in common; we were seeking female company.

Sophisticated David brandished all the characteristics of a city gent. His overt displays of male chauvinism raised a few eyebrows. Girls were only ever popsies, tarts, floozies or totty, as far as he was concerned. He informed us that the plural of the word totty had no 's' on the end.

We met in the café at Bobbies department store on Saturday mornings. It was David's suggestion that John and I should each prepare our own totty list, which noted in order of preference the names and telephone numbers of the females we wanted to take out.

'Who is your first choice?' asked David.

'Pat Donovan. She gave me the go-ahead signal in a recent letter. What about you?'

'Lucy is my number one, with Mary at the bottom as number seven.'

'You're scraping the barrel with Mary,' broke in John. 'She's got droopy tits and a bitch of a mother who won't allow you in after 9 p.m.'

I went home to dial Pat's number. She must have been lying in wait by the telephone, so immediate was the response.

'Is that you, Bob?' she asked cheerfully.

'No, it's Jonathan. I'm just back from Geneva and thought it was time I rang. I was glad to get your letter. I wondered whether you would like to join me for a drink this evening.'

'I'm afraid I can't. You're seven days too late. Last Saturday night I met a smashing guy and now we're going steady.'

Pipped at the post by a hair's breadth, I referred again to my totty list. There were seven names to go. Two were away for the weekend; three had already been dated; the remaining two gave an outright no. Downcast though not defeated I conferred with David, who had by this time taken it upon himself to be my mentor. He had succeeded in talking Anne, his number four, into joining him for the evening.

'Why don't you call that au pair girl, the one who's staying with the Wrights in Milverton Hill? I think her name is Barbara,' he suggested.

'Do you mean the ugly German girl with the biceps? She's over six feet tall and as wide as a door. Isn't she supposed to be a shot-put champion? I'll have to protect myself with armour plating if I'm to take her out.'

'She's not that bad,' urged David. 'You never know your luck. She might be so grateful that you'll be hugged to death before she's through with you!'

David's playful enthusiasm led me to strike while the iron was hot.

After a grilling from Mrs Wright, who went to great pains to point out that she took the duty of watching over her au pair girls very seriously, I was at last put through to Barbara.

'Do I know you?' inquired a gravelly voice.

'Not exactly,' I said, 'but I'm a friend of David Howell Jones and John Gater.'

'That no good,' she said, stumbling for her words. 'Please to tell me what you want.'

'The three of us are meeting for a drink tonight. Do you want to come along with us as my guest?'

'David I know and I no like. John I know and I no like. You I no like even if I no meet. Please not to telephone again. Bye-bye.'

The affront of having been turned down by the least prepossessing girl in town was eased only by the relief of not having to suffer the embarrassment of being seen with her in public. When I told them of the rebuff, David and John laughed uproariously.

'Your reputation must be in a sorry state,' teased David. 'Better luck next time!'

John came up with a bright idea. 'Bottle parties are definitely in,' he said, 'so why don't we arrange one? There's virtually no preparation involved. Just think of the crumpet we can invite!'

'Three cheers for all the totty,' interjected David.

'And where do you propose we hold this thrilling event?' I asked, knowing full well what the answer was going to be.

'In your father's school, of course. The gym is ideally suited,' enthused David, with a waggish grin.

Before giving David and John the green light, I broached the matter with my father.

'David, John and I want to invite a handful of people for drinks next Friday evening. Do you mind if we hold the party in the gym? It is likely to be a very quiet affair.'

My father's reply was to the point. 'I have had bad reports of what party-goers of your age group get up to these days. Also I never have liked the idea of the school premises being opened up to a bunch of strangers. You may use the gym only on condition that you do not disturb us or the neighbours. If there's any damage or mess, I'll make you responsible.'

The bush telegraph effectively spread the news. Not discriminating between the disreputable, the eligible, the rabble-rouser and the prude, word-of-mouth invitations reached the ears of young people in their hordes. It was no skin off David's nose or John's for that matter if the whole of Leamington attended. A barrel of beer was purchased; crimson crêpe paper was draped round the strip lights to dampen the gaudy brightness. My mother was sure that our guests would appreciate being served with ham sandwiches. Despite my contrary view, she produced a tray load of the kind of institutional doorsteps one associates with the worst of school match teas; these we placed out of harm's way on the piano.

'Why don't we convert the loft above the gym into a rest room?' suggested John.

'Whatever for?' I asked.

'Couples must have somewhere to go when passions are aroused,' exhorted David.

Tables and chairs in the loft classroom were stacked in neat rows along the walls. Mattresses from dormitories and all the gym mats we could lay our hands on were transported up the rickety stairs, in readiness for what seemed was going to be an orgy.

After pub closing time on the allotted day, young men and women turned up at the school's rear entrance in an endless stream; gatecrashers outnumbered the legitimate guests. All were intent upon exploiting the grounds and shabby school buildings in pursuit of their own merriment.

Within minutes the party was in full swing. Instead of entering into the spirit of the occasion, as self-appointed custodian I found myself trying to quell the mindless antics of a drunken mob. My father's reservations had been more than justified. It was fortuitous that my parents' bedroom was at the front of the building. Had my father decided to join us for a nightcap, he would have blown a gasket and me with it.

The gymnasium and surrounding area resembled a battlefield when all had departed in the early hours. Vomit, urine, broken bottles and countless cigarette ends fouled nearby paths and garden areas. A whiff of sex, rubber sheaths and Durex packets were the lingering signs of debauchery in the squalid loft. The barrel of beer had spilt over the floor of the gymnasium, the crêpe paper having fallen into the puddle. My mother's carefully prepared sandwiches had been trampled by dancing feet into the slimy mess.

The fact that the school had broken up for the Christmas holidays was the one redeeming feature. With the absence of Saturday school I was able, with relative peace of mind, to sleep in late before applying my mind to the mopping up.

I was awoken by a thunderous knock on my bedroom door. In stormed my father.

'Get up this instant!' he roared. 'I cannot imagine why I ever entertained the idea of handing the school over to you. You are doing your best to destroy it.'

'Whatever do you mean?'

'I'll tell you what I mean,' persisted my father, who by now was shaking with fury. 'I had an appointment with prospective parents at ten this morning. Nice people with three sons. They seemed impressed until I took them across the playground to the carpentry shop and gymnasium. Their opinion changed the moment they saw the disgusting state of everything. If word gets out of what happened here last night, it could close the place. You spend weeks gallivanting about the continent at our expense. Now that you're back, instead of pulling your weight and earning your keep, all you think about is parties and your own enjoyment. Your mother thinks we've been too lenient with you over the years, and I agree with her. We've a mind to sell up and leave you to paddle your own canoe.'

My father's castigation caused me to feel the misery of guilt, as well as the need for repentance. Knowing as well as anyone that the school was in dire straits, I was deeply ashamed that my actions had given rise to scandalous consequences. I vowed never again to err in this way; the lesson had gone home to roost.

There was enough cleaning up to occupy an army. Single-handed I removed the glass, erased the telltale evidence, washed floors, swept paths, restored to their rightful places the tables, chairs, mats and mattresses. Apart from the stubborn red stain on the gymnasium floor that no amount of vim and vigour would shift, the reinstatement process was complete.

The veil of evening darkness had descended. It was with a languid pride that I was viewing my handiwork when David appeared.

'John's been in bed all day with a thick head,' he said glibly. 'He was so smitten with one of last night's totty that he's meeting her tonight.'

'I'm glad someone enjoyed himself,' I retorted sharply.

'I came to help you tidy up,' continued David unabashed, 'but can see there's nothing to be done. They were a cleaner lot than I imagined. A pity about the floor, though. Will you ask your father if we can book the gym again at Easter?'

The Christmas mail brought with it the usual cards. In addition, I received two ominous-looking envelopes with a Geneva postmark. In the first letter I was informed that the Genevese police had decided not to pursue the breach of the peace charge, but that it was incumbent upon me to meet in full within fourteen days the cost of the replacement of the nightclub's plate glass window.

The other letter was from Mr Baronetti's solicitor. It stated in threatening terms that Mr Baronetti was claiming five thousand Swiss francs to compensate him for his physical injuries; failing my willingness to comply with the demand, I would be issued with a court summons, in which event the amount of the claim, to include all costs, would be substantially higher. Thinking that, no matter what, luck was never on my side, a windfall came my way. A second cousin had left me five hundred pounds in her will. The arrival of the cheque was as unforeseen as it was propitious.

Since reading law at Cambridge, David had been doing his articles with a firm of solicitors in Warwick. Not wishing to forfeit the entire legacy to Geneva without a murmur, I asked David what action he thought I should take.

'Strictly speaking, you should settle the bill for the window repair,' he said, 'but whilst you are in England, there is nothing they can do to enforce payment. Mr Baronetti's claim is obviously a try-on, although if the matter went to court one cannot tell what the outcome would be. If I were you I would throw away the correspondence and spend the legacy as you wish. Take a genial totty out to celebrate and why not buy a jalopy? But don't ever go back to Switzerland. If the police are sharp enough, you'll be arrested and it could get very nasty.'

And so it was that I came to purchase my first car, a pea-green Morris 1000. 'Green's unlucky,' exclaimed my mother, with undue pessimism. My father, on the other hand, relieved I would no longer have cause to use his vehicle, was far less circumspect.

Drinking and driving in those days was generally accepted. People who practised a strict moral code in other aspects of their lives were seen to do it flagrantly; we followed their example. Thinking nothing of consuming several pints and driving when quite sozzled, we sped home in separate cars from our regular haunt, the Dirty Duck in Stratford.

Before the three of us set off in a state of bleariness, David would say, 'I'll race you. The last to touch base will buy first round tomorrow!' It is a miracle that our destiny was shaped in such a way as to circumvent a tragedy.

Familiar faces appeared with humdrum regularity at all the social gatherings, no matter where we went. Nevertheless, things were looking up. Whenever it was in his power, David would engineer a ruse with the intention of surprising us. He arrived at one of the cocktail parties wearing a genteel suit that concealed his fleshy build. Cheeks flushed, he beamed a sportive smile that laid bare his patent animation. Accompanying him there was a winsome stranger.

'Who's the totty with David?' I asked John.

'Search me. Never seen her before. She can't be a local.'

I could see that David was wending his way in my direction. My inquisitive look revealed the interest I was taking in his up-market companion.

'I don't think you've met Elizabeth Innes,' said David breezily. 'Jonathan's the brave bugger who laid on the bottle party I was telling you about.'

'It can hardly be said the party was my idea. David was the instigator and I'll have you know it got me into a lot of trouble.'

'What sort of trouble?' asked Elizabeth.

I began to explain what had happened on the fateful Friday night before Christmas.

Huffing and puffing with indignation, David exclaimed contemptuously: 'We ought to provide Jonathan with a soap box at Speakers' Corner. I've heard this story so many times that it gets more tiresome each time he repeats it. Rather than suffer the inflated details yet again, I think I'll see which of the genial totty have turned up this evening. Give me a shout, Elizabeth, when you want me to rescue you.'

Suitably fortified after emptying another glass of sherry, David made a beeline for the group of people responsible for making the loudest clamour.

'You don't really want to hear about that awful party, do you?' I asked Elizabeth.

'No, of course I don't, but it would make a change from legal talk. I seem to meet nothing but lawyers these days. What do you do for a living?'

'I'll give you three guesses.'

'I would say you're either an accountant, a doctor or a banker.'

'Nothing as high-flying as that, I'm afraid. I'm a dreary schoolmaster. Are you disappointed?'

'You don't seem at all dreary to me. Do please tell me more.'

'There's not a great deal to tell, except that I teach in a prep school, coach games and help with a number of extra-curricular activities. A very mundane existence, I'm afraid, but I do find the work very satisfying.'

'There's no need to belittle yourself. I promise that I'm not being patronising when I say I've always wanted to meet a schoolmaster.'

'Let's change the subject and talk about you instead. Do you have a job or are you still a student?'

'I had set my heart on being a ballerina. For years I slogged away for hours each day at ballet school, but was forced to give up because I have weak ankles. In those days I was super fit and everyone used to call me Skinny Liz. Now that I'm having to work as a secretary in London, I miss the dancing more than ever.'

'It's sad that a quirk of nature has prevented you from fulfilling your ambition. How long have you known David?'

'I met him only last week at some professional men's club in Warwick. My stepfather is a member, so is David's boss. I'm sure David only joined in order to meet the right people.'

Elizabeth and I were spontaneously attracted to each other. The appeal was not just physical; there was a spiritual affinity as well. She possessed that rare beauty often to be found in those of Latin origin. The wistful smile, the sad countenance, indicative of deep suffering, made me want to protect her from life's buffeting. I somehow knew we would meet again.

During the two years when I taught as an unqualified teacher, my pupils had been guinea pigs and I had regarded myself as a charlatan. Providing school owners with cheap labour, gentleman amateurs and unpractised school leavers had always been employed in private schools; retired officers from the services were among those most highly favoured. A plum-in-the-mouth accent, sporting proficiency, an acceptable school academic record, together with the ability to provide controlled leadership to a group of boys, were the foremost qualities required of such men. Evelyn Waugh's comic depictions in *Decline and Fall* of a preparatory school in the mid-1920s were not all bogus exaggerations. Thirty-five years on from Waugh's short-lived experience as a prep school master, the worst private schools were still employing individuals whose references obscured a disreputable antecedence.

Had there been a nought-to-ten scale that graded Britain's preparatory schools for their attributes in 1961, Arnold Lodge would, at best, have gained no more than two points. A local rival establishment blessed with spacious grounds would have earned a much higher rating, if its popularity with Warwickshire's middle-class parents was anything to go by. Our survival prospects were so precarious that it was going to take an abundance of ingenuity, hard work, determination and wishful thinking to prevent us from going under.

The first priority was to improve the calibre of the teaching staff. This was not going to be easily achieved because the grim residential accommodation that was supposed to be a perk caused all the superior job applicants to look elsewhere. My father paid his permanent teachers, other than his most senior assistant, a hundred pounds per term, irrespective of their age and experience.

To ease the school's cash flow problems, no salary payments were made until the last week of term. A mature teacher in his fifties once asked my father for a fifty pound advance at half-term. With ill grace he handed over a cheque to the embarrassed teacher, admonishing him with the words 'That leaves a balance of fifty pounds at the end of term. What you've received now you can't have again. I hope you'll manage your finances better in the future!'

A much bigger income was needed for it to be possible to remunerate a quality team of teachers that would help raise the school's academic standards, described by Her Majesty's inspectors as 'modest at best', from the bottom league. It was a chicken and egg situation. Apart from basic decorations and repairs, no structural improvements had taken place at the school since my parents had arrived in Leamington. I was convinced it was essential for us to express our faith in the future by embarking on a building programme.

'When viewing the school, parents expect to see a tangible indication that more and better facilities are being provided,' I urged my father.

The thought of having to spend money always caused my father to become restive and ill-tempered. 'Your mother and I have coped for twenty-seven years without getting into debt. I don't intend to change my policy now, not for you, not for anybody.'

'Surely it's better to invest in the future than to sink without trace?'

'We have survived all this time without going broke and there is no reason why we shouldn't continue in the same vein. What parents want is a sound education for their sons, not gimmicky new buildings, all chrome and plate glass, like the secondary modern up the road.'

'A sound education requires investment as well. Fee-paying parents have a right to expect more than tatty desks and an outmoded syllabus. Unless we are seen to provide something better than our competitors, we're unlikely to remain in business for long.'

Much to my surprise, now that I was qualified, my father was beginning to trust my professional judgement. He gave me my head in ways that must have seemed incautious. It was only over matters of finance that we clashed. After weeks of argument, my father took the unprecedented step of committing the school to a fifteen hundred pound loan from the bank. Plans were drawn up for the building of a modest single-storey block and the provision of some showers. The decision to go ahead with the project helped to raise morale. Imperceptibly at first, the school's standards and reputation began to improve; numbers gradually increased. Word was getting about that Arnold Lodge was at last changing its image.

Up until then drama as an activity had featured very little at the school. The senior master, Tom Southam, had been busily directing rehearsals throughout the Lent term for a play that was to be staged by the boys at Lillington Community Centre. Two days before the first performance, the centre was badly damaged in a fire. To add authenticity to the set, Mr Southam, who was known for his impulsive strokes of failing genius, had borrowed from a local store a suite of furniture, which was gutted by the flames.

Unaware of the significance of Mr Southam's furtive negotiations, my father asked him, 'Am I to assume that all the borrowed items were insured?'

'I'm afraid not. I was planning to deal with the matter but was so busy with rehearsals that I never got round to it. The problem is that the store's managing director expects the school to pay in full for the furniture that was lent.'

The absence of an apology for this folly maddened my father beyond measure. 'If I deduct from your salary the amount owed, you won't be earning anything for at least eighteen months,' he said bitingly.

The production's venue was finally switched to the town hall. My father noticed that the newly devised set contained some familiar pieces of furniture. There were pictures, photographs, a pipe-rack and other ornaments, too, that were easily identifiable.

So incensed was he that these items, some of which had a high sentimental value, had been surreptitiously removed from his study that words failed him when an unrepentant Mr Southam stated with dogmatic obstinacy, 'The stage looked so bare without any props that I assumed you would not mind my using one or two of your own oddments to brighten things up.'

When the irrepressible producer was no longer within striking distance, my father let rip with: 'Will no one rid me of this turbulent beast?'

It would have served no useful purpose to have sent Tom Southam packing. No schoolmaster worth his salt would have taken on his onerous duties under the employment conditions that existed at that time.

Still harbouring vivid memories of Repton days, I could not imagine that self-assured men with good Oxbridge degrees would ever wish to teach in a run-down enterprise such as ours. I knew it was essential for the ablest pupils in their final two years at prep school to be nurtured and inspired by teachers who had achieved academic excellence themselves.

A different expertise is required in dealing with younger pupils. No matter what a child's individual needs are, however, the value of the well-organised, dedicated teacher can never be overestimated.

Fee-paying parents were soon going to expect better value for money from the schools they supported. Their most pressing demand would be for ineffectual dilettantes to be replaced by professionals. Products of lesser-known universities and the training colleges were beginning to infiltrate the portals of the more prestigious private schools, where hitherto Oxford and Cambridge credentials were vital. This new source of teacher talent, untapped by many of the private schools, was beginning to revolutionise the atmosphere and scope within the independent sector. If we were to avoid the collapse of our family school, it was going to be necessary to recruit men and women with vision and enterprise. Much had to be accomplished, with little in the way of financial resources available, a mission that would have daunted all but the indefatigable.

The insouciant experiences of Exeter had given me a new-found confidence. Despite the obstacles that glared threateningly from every quarter, I managed to quell past melancholia in favour of more assured attitudes. Leaving no stone unturned in attempts to improve the existing state of affairs, I began to analyse every facet of school life with a compulsive doggedness.

The pupils I had taught before my Exeter training would have been intimidated by my restless obsessiveness. In addition to throwing myself wholeheartedly into my work, I now found time also to play hard. Evenings out with pretty young ladies, among whom was the intriguing Elizabeth, provided light relief. The better use of leisure moments improved my effectiveness as a schoolmaster and I quickly discovered that children responded more positively to a cheerful approach. Free of emotional encumbrances and not yet burdened with a headmaster's cares, this brief period can undoubtedly be looked back upon as the most agreeable of my entire career. Worthy of being preserved was the strong family atmosphere that existed at the school in those times. Expansion in later years brought with it the outward signs of success, a success that sadly emphasised the gradual diminution of the personal touches that matter so much.

I was responsible for coaching the school's 1st XI cricket team. Even if the players lacked batting or bowling skills, I knew that slick, alert fielding could win matches. Challenging practice sessions to improve the boys' catching and throwing techniques began to pay dividends. I would not allow my protégés to use their feet for stopping the ball. 'Get down and use your hands, you lazy chump. You can kick the ball as much as you like when the soccer season starts next term!' Another bee in my bonnet was the state of the players' kit and their appearance. I believed that the smartest team began with a psychological advantage. 'Shame the opponents by being much better turned out than they are. It'll be worth at least two wickets!'

A long summer afternoon spent at the cricket field with the sun beating down was to my mind, the perfect setting in which to earn a living. Trips to matches against other schools, especially the more rural ones, are remembered with a nostalgic joyfulness. Umpiring in unspoilt surroundings, with the regular knock of leather on willow; eating cream cakes and cucumber sandwiches on well-mown lawns; doting parents of players indulging themselves peacefully, with the aid of comfortable deckchairs, binoculars at the ready; returning to Leamington triumphant because of victory and dejected after defeat. These are some of the precious moments that require recapturing and savouring for fear of being lost for ever.

Speech day and prize-giving always took place on the last day of the summer term. Several times my father had concluded his address by quoting a famous soldier, who at some public school jamboree had commended the qualities of integrity, courage and enthusiasm.

'By integrity', my father elucidated, 'he meant speaking the truth. By courage he meant moral courage, which is standing up for what you believe to be right, even in the face of great temptation. By enthusiasm he meant being determined to put something into life and not just taking something out of it.'

Commendable though this message was, I was embarrassed when I overheard parents say it was a pity that the headmaster made the same remarks year after year.

'Isn't it time you changed the theme of your speech? We're all tired of hearing about integrity, moral courage and enthusiasm,' I said unkindly.

'As you're such an expert, I'll leave you to prepare my report and speech this time. It's not easy to be original every year when you've been at it for as long as I have!'

Making straight for my typewriter, with frenzied inspiration I bashed out a draft speech for my father's approval. Despite my delight at the result, what I had in fact produced was a naive, unpolished discourse that was inappropriate from every point of view. So preoccupied was my father with other burdensome duties that he accepted the draft without a murmur.

Addressing the assembled speech day gathering, my father declared, 'The time has come to move away from complacent, old-school-tie speeches about leadership that can bore us so much on occasions such as these. There is the danger that advice of this nature, no matter how well intentioned, may no longer have any relevance to the world in which we now live.'

The guest speaker, Air Marshal Sir Lawrence Pendred, who was grandfather of two of the boarders at the school, was greatly bewildered by my father's utterances. Having planned to talk on the very subject that my father was censuring, Sir Lawrence changed his theme completely and instead stressed the need for volunteers in various fields of public service. Relieved that his ordeal of having to ad lib was at last over, he sat down, unable to conceal his displeasure. It was appalling bad manners not to have sent Sir Lawrence a copy of the text of my father's speech in advance, a public relations error never to be repeated.

As he left the hall, my father was accosted by one of his most nit-picking parents, a tall, distinguished-looking man with a glossy black beard that was shaped like a spade.

'Headmaster,' he exclaimed pompously, 'today's speech was undoubtedly the best I've ever heard you give. I really must congratulate you.'

Soho

Working men and women with ungenerous holidays point the finger of envy at teachers, who are blessed with greater access to extensive leisure periods than the majority. During long summer vacations we can write, travel or indulge in our hobbies, knowing that for at least six weeks the doing of our own thing will not be interrupted by work.

The last I had heard of Max, the banjo player, was that he had joined the well known Nat Gonella Band and was based in London. An unsolicited letter from Max tempted me with an offer I could hardly refuse.

> Why don't you spend part of your holiday with me here in London? I promise that you will take part in the most fabulous jazz sessions with some of Britain's top musicians. For the sake of convenience, bring your clarinet rather than the drums. I am counting on you not to let me down!
> Yours,
> Max

A telephone call settled the arrangements. Two days later I was on my way to Earls Court. Parking near to the dilapidated Victorian dwelling that Max had given as his address, I made for the main entrance. Unable to identify Flat A, I randomly pressed one of the doorbells. The front door was opened by a young man with long, greasy hair and an unkempt beard.

'Does Max live here?' I asked.

'He may do, but what business is it of yours?'

'Max is expecting me. We're old friends.'

'Well, that's different. I thought you were one of those prying officials. You can come in if you like, but you might have a long wait. We don't see much of Max when he's busy screwing some bird, but when he's browned off it's not unknown for him to doss down here.'

Hoping Max would soon appear, I stepped inside and was shown into a large ground floor room, whose windows looked out on to the street. Most of the floor was taken up with blankets and sleeping bags. My guess was that at least eight people slept in that one room. Clothes and miscellaneous objects were strewn about in untidy heaps; a smell of stale tobacco permeated the atmosphere. Perching myself on a ragged sofa, I was able to observe the comings and goings of a number of hippie-like males, none of whom gave the impression of belonging there.

It was not long before Max showed up. Neatly dressed and with his usual short back and sides army-style haircut, his appearance had little changed, though his facial expression was greatly altered. Barely acknowledging me, his eyes betrayed a wildness that was intimidating. A belligerent attitude highlighted his apparent contempt of the world and the people in it.

'So you made it,' he said, with cold disinterest.

Allowing no time to catch up with each other's news, Max led me out of the building and began striding off in the direction of Kensington High Street. I remembered Max as lively, enthusiastic and above all friendly. Now he was quite the reverse. In response to my questions he gave inapposite, terse answers. He showed not the slightest pleasure in my having made the effort to visit him. Then suddenly, as if any obstacles had been swept aside by the turning of a switch, he began chattering away with his accustomed zest.

'I used to spend a lot of time busking in this street. The police moved me on because I hadn't got a licence. I almost had a punch-up with one of the bastards.'

'I thought you were playing with the Nat Gonella Band.'

'I was, but I decided to leave. As a busker I can please myself.'

His old spirit seemingly restored, Max talked nineteen to the dozen, giving me no opportunity to get a word in edgeways. I was bothered by his sudden swing of mood, which reminded me of the occasion when he had berated an Exeter bank manager, behaviour that had been totally out of character.

Max dismissed my question of 'Where am I going to stay to-night?' with vague indifference.

'I don't much feel like kipping in your flat, with all those strangers,' I remarked.

'It's not my flat and I hardly ever stay there. I merely use it as a contact address; mostly I sleep rough in and around Soho.'

The crowded room or even my car was a preferable sleeping place to a Soho street. I was beginning to wonder whether I would have cause to regret having come to London.

'I thought I was going to have the chance to play some jazz,' I said, indicating my disappointment.

'Play jazz you will. You remember Geoff Cole, don't you? He's still with Ken Colyer. They're playing tonight at the 100 Club in Oxford Street. With Geoff on trombone, you on clarinet and me on banjo, it will be just like old times.'

Clasping our instruments, we arrived later that evening at the celebrated jazz venue, ready for action. When asked for our admission money, Max protested rudely.

'Musicians don't have to pay; in any case we're guests of Ken.'

Sensing Max was not the bosom pal of Ken Colyer that he pretended, it was with diffidence that I followed him. He pushed his way into the club's darkened interior that was crammed to overflowing with gyrating jazz enthusiasts. Assuming that Max would be content to listen to the music for a while, I was alarmed when he swaggered up to the maestro and demanded, as if it were his right, for the two of us to join in with the band. Having sworn I would never again inflict my unwanted musical offerings on others, I found Ken Colyer's withering look enough for me to want to abandon Max and return to Leamington.

We mounted the dais. The audience, who had not paid good money to be entertained by a makeshift group, looked on disapprovingly. I could tell from Geoff Cole's offhand manner that this was not the first time he had been vexed by his former friend's pushy antics.

I had not picked up, let alone played, my clarinet for nearly a year. To be expected to take my place alongside some of the finest jazz players in the land, before a crowd of well-informed spectators, was a daunting prospect. The first number, 'Pennies from Heaven,' went well enough, but whether my tiring lips were going to stand the strain of playing for long, after a lapse of several months, was quite another matter. Worst of all was the discomfiture of being bullied by Max to perform when our fellow musicians offered an ungracious welcome. What had promised to be an electrifying jazz experience was a sorry let-down from my point of view. It mystified me that Max was so changeable and aggressive; something was undoubtedly wrong with him.

Back at Earls Court, I assumed Max was going to inform the flat occupants I needed somewhere to stay for the night. Before leaving me stranded on the doorstep, he called out, 'They may be squatters but they're my mates. All you have to do is mention my name and they'll let you in; if there are any problems, ask for Pete. Two of the blokes are light-fingered, so hang on to your cash. Another most definitely is *not* heterosexual. Watch out for him, especially in the middle of the night. Must go, Jon, I'm off to see my bird.'

I awoke early, relieved to find my money had not gone missing. There had mercifully been no homosexual skylarking in the squatters' 'dormitory', as far as I was aware. In his present mood, Max was capable of such sick humour that his malicious warnings were best taken with a pinch of salt.

Surprised that Max had returned from his nocturnal wanderings, I stumbled across his sleeping form whilst making for the loo. The foul state of the toilet and washing facilities showed that the inmates ignored all rules of domestic decency. A group of drop-outs they undoubtedly were, for whom a scrub and purge to remove the sweaty body odours was long overdue.

Max was in an ugly frame of mind when he ultimately surfaced.

'Shitty women. They're all the bloody same,' he expostulated, seething with anger. 'Claire and I have had a final bust-up. She says I'm a no-good loser.'

'There's nothing to stop you going back to being a photographer, if it's security she's after,' I said, doing my best to humour him.

'Don't patronise me, Jon. We all know you were born with a silver spoon in your mouth. You haven't got a clue how hard it is for me to struggle, just to keep body and soul together. My illness makes it doubly hard.'

'What illness? You've never spoken to me about an illness.'

'Forget it! You'd never understand. Nobody does. It's something I'm having to learn to live with.'

I lowered my voice, so as to prevent our exchanges from being overheard by the others.

'If only I knew what your problem was, I might be able to help. In view of what we've been through together in the past, surely you feel able to confide in me.'

'You always were one for putting your flaming oar in and coming to the wrong conclusions. Either stop meddling in my business or bugger off home.'

His harsh remarks wounded me to such an extent that I was inclined to leave Max to wallow in his bitterness. A sixth sense told me he was at his wits' end. To have turned my back on him when clearly he was in a desperate state would have been no less than a betrayal. I tried hard to puzzle out the nature of his illness. A hardy physical specimen, Max looked well enough; it was his mental state that worried me.

Brushing aside his dolefulness, he sprang into action, positivity restored.

'We're going busking, Jon. You'll be surprised how profitable it can be!'

My heart sank, not because I was averse to the idea of sampling the life of a street musician, but my companion's boorish irascibility was a serious feature I could hardly ignore. It was plain that, as long as I remained in his company, I would continue to be drawn into compromising situations.

'You say you don't have a licence. What happens if the police turn up?' I asked.

'We'll just have to keep out of their way. Don't forget that Soho is the playground of the criminal fraternity; the police aren't going to be interested in two harmless buskers.'

'I hope you're right, but if they do make a nuisance of themselves, for God's sake don't lose your temper.'

'What's happened to the daredevil playboy I knew in Exeter? I've been busking in Soho for weeks now and I've had no problems. You may not have the chance to busk again, so why not cheer up and be grateful for the opportunity.'

Max chose as our first port of call a street on the edge of Soho, no more than a stone's throw from Piccadilly Circus. We were in the middle of playing one of Acker Bilk's current hit numbers, in the presence of some inquisitive passers-by, when a police officer appeared. He advanced towards us, his face exuding distaste. After cautioning Max, the officer reminded him of past offences, including one of violence that had led to his conviction for causing grievous bodily harm.

'If you continue to flout the law with your troublesome antics,' advised the officer, 'I shall again be forced to apprehend you. I hope your Pied Piper friend will have the good sense to keep away from you.'

Overcome by frenzied anger, Max raised his fists threateningly, a defiant gesture that symbolised his hatred of authority and his exasperation at being chided in front of me. No useful purpose would have been served by my attempting to intervene or to reason with him. During the tense moments that followed, I was fearful that he was going to strike the officer. Slowly, Max backed off, fists no longer clenched, his eyes still menacing yet terror-stricken, a hideous, choleric red.

'Unless you are able to control that vile temper of yours,' said the officer, 'my guess is it won't be long before you are shut away for a very long time.'

It was foolish of me not to have recognised how dangerous was my proclivity for befriending erratic, out-of-the-ordinary people. Max had lied to me so blatantly that I was no longer able to believe a word he said, even though I knew he was not culpable for his actions. To avoid disaster from striking, it was obvious he needed urgent help. The unwelcome truth began to dawn on me. I was the one person Max had chosen to deliver him from the demons threatening his sanity; he was abandoned, unprotected, distraught, spiritless. It would be for ever on my conscience had I left him in a fit of pique.

I tried to steer Max away from his reckless busking plan. With cavalier bluntness, he refused stubbornly to heed the police officer's warning.

One of the world's centres of corruption and depravity, Soho has an identity of its own that makes it in a way autonomous. A small proportion of the men and women who live and work there are engaged in the marketing of porn or in catering for deviant sexual appetites, through girlie shows and prostitution. The vast majority of Soho's workforce goes about its daily business in law-abiding ways. This is how it has always been; little in essence has changed since the days when Max and I took to serenading bystanders in the litter-filled streets.

With flagrant boldness, Max led the way, choosing as locations for our forbidden renderings the least sequestered spots. Business could in no way be described as brisk. A few miserable pennies was all there was to show for our hard day's efforts.

'Just you wait until tonight,' said Max. 'At pub closing time you'll see where all the jazz fans have been hiding. They can be very generous when they've a mind.' Not believing a word of it, I braced myself, heart in mouth, ready for yet more bother.

We positioned ourselves near to the entrance of a crowded pub. As if in answer to our dulcet calls, two other musicians appeared from out of the shadows. One removed a tenor saxophone from a well-worn case; the other held a trumpet. The power and depth of the session men's instruments helped to neutralise the plaintive effects of my lone clarinet; despite the lack of a rhythm section, we were swinging away breezily when the pub patrons began to spill out onto the street. So pleasingly temperate was the climate that August evening that the jovial drinkers, in no hurry to make their homeward journeys, delighted in the musical fun. The feelings of elation that our playing aroused in the well-disposed listeners caused me to banish from my mind any thought of the perils of our unlicensed trade.

Jubilant and exhilarated, Max was in buoyant mood. The least thing, a chance remark or misinterpreted glance, would, I knew, have shifted him from his cheery state to one of melancholia. Not once during the noisy display of impromptu jazz was a policeman to be seen, which was just as well.

We were amazed to discover the collection tin was filled with coins; there was a pound note as well. Counting the takings with scrupulous care, Max donated an equal share to the session men, a magnanimous gesture which I could never have predicted.

'That leaves us with eight pounds, eleven shillings and threepence,' said Max. 'Not bad for twenty minutes' blowing. I told you that busking was profitable. Do you not believe me now?'

For two more days I shadowed Max along a labyrinth of streets, in and out of alleys, courtyards and on to Soho Square. No matter where we went or what we did, the climactic success of our first night's busking was never reproduced. Angry and disillusioned, Max blamed the whole world, never himself, for the sorry situation; his depression was unshakable. There was nothing I could do to harness in him the faintest optimism or to get him to reveal his innermost thoughts. My patience having eroded, I made a final attempt to reason with Max.

'I've nothing against busking, but what's to stop you applying for a licence and doing it legitimately? It's only a matter of time before you're involved in another fight and where will that get you? You can't expect people to show you any sympathy until you make an effort to help yourself.'

'I've already told you that I'm ill, sick as hell, in fact, and all you can do is preach.'

'We're back to where we started, Max. You won't explain about your illness, so how can you expect me to understand?'

'Seeing as how you know all the bloody answers, you tell me what to do.'

'I'm not going to *tell* you anything. What I do feel is that you need to get away from London for a while.'

'I've nowhere to go.'

'You're not using your brain, Max. You know that your parents would love to have you home. Your mother's one of the sweetest ladies I know; she'd like nothing better than to be able to look after you.'

I had seen enough of his home set-up to know that Max's parents were a caring couple. His father, though confined to a wheelchair, never complained; his mother, a North Country lass with a heart of gold, was homely and down-to-earth.

I was convinced she was more capable than anyone else of helping Max to regain his mental equilibrium. Slowly he began to realise there was no alternative but to accept my advice.

Had I left Max to travel home under his own steam, I am certain he would not have budged from London. I saw it as my responsibility to drive him to Exeter; only when he was safely under his parents' roof would my conscience be clear.

Before the installation of a motorway network, car journeys from London to the south-west were long and wearisome. Try as I did to engage Max in conversation, my sullen passenger refused to speak throughout the drive. By the time we arrived at his parents' small terraced house, I was convinced that his hatred of me was giant-sized.

Max was sent out to purchase some food items from a nearby shop. As soon as he was out of earshot, his mother helped me to piece together some of the mysteries of his jumbled life.

'Thank God you've brought Max home,' she said. 'We've been trying for weeks to contact him. We've had no address, no telephone number, no means of getting in touch. We thought he was dead. Max has been undergoing treatment for depression for years; we've told no one until now. In his manic state he is often violent. The depression is even worse. Twice he has tried to take his own life; we've been living on a razor's edge. Max often talks about you. He always says you are his only true friend, the one person he knows he can trust. Thank you for sticking by him, for not leaving him alone in London.'

Humbled by the praise that had been dispensed in my favour, I was abashed to think how close I had been to deserting my jazz buddy. I dread to think what might have happened had I let him down.

Nice

My visit to the south of France three years previously had left a profound impression on me. The Côte d'Azur allured me with a magnetism that compelled me to journey there again. Two of my friends were so impressed by eulogistic descriptions of Nice that the three of us were soon making plans to take a holiday there.

I was to fly direct with Jeremy, whose cynical outspokenness steered people's attention away from his withered left arm, of which he was deeply conscious. Tony, an up-and-coming business executive, with aspirations to be a successful playwright, decided for reasons of economy to travel by train.

We all met on the evening before our departure to discuss last-minute details.

'We'll expect compensation if Nice turns out not to be the paradise you've painted it to be,' Jeremy said to me.

'You'll not regret coming for one moment. Just you wait and see!'

The Nice-bound evening flight departed three hours later than scheduled. In consequence, it was nearly midnight when Jeremy and I began searching for a room in the old part of the city. Frequented by layabouts, fearsome-looking bruisers and limbless beggars, the seedy backstreets bore ominous signs of danger. Weighed down by our heavy cases, we hunted high and low without success for a place to stay.

At long last our prayers were answered. We were led up to the one vacant room by the manager of a small hotel we discovered opposite the Lycée. The need for a roof over our heads exceeded the disappointment we felt when we discovered one of us would have to sleep on the floor. To my mind this was a preferable alternative to sharing a bed with Jeremy, had the bed been large enough, which it was not.

'Let's toss for it,' I suggested.

Jeremy won the doubtful privilege of sleeping in the lumpy bed. Resting my head on a pillow, I settled myself as comfortably as I was able on the hard floor. All was well until Jeremy got up in the small hours to search for a lavatory.

Back in the room he began shrieking out with such horror-struck frenzy that I feared for his life.

'Christ Almighty! I've stepped on a scorpion. The bloody thing's stung me. Send for a doctor! Quick!'

Switching on the light, I could see that the insect's squashed remains were fastened to the spot where one of Jeremy's bare feet had trodden. Edging their way in the direction of my pillow, inches from where my head had been, were several hideous-looking brown insects. They were cockroaches.

Jeremy's recovery from near death was instantaneous. There was nothing for it but for me to abandon dignity and share the tiny bed with him for what was left of the night. Avoiding the cockroaches, for which I had ever since army days developed a deep-seated aversion, I opened the shutters to let some air into the stifling hot room. Shortly after 3 a.m. the market began to set up on the adjacent square with bumping, banging, crashing and shouting sounds through which only the deaf could have slept.

'You told us Nice was a paradise. There's nothing I've seen so far to commend it in any way,' said Jeremy.

'I admit we've got off to a bad start. By the time we meet Tony this afternoon our luck will have changed. I know it will.'

The manager, who attempted to be all things to all people, was the hotel's waiter, receptionist and handyman. Providing us with an above average quality continental breakfast, he laid bare his soul by recounting his entire life story, warts and all, from which we gleaned that, although of Danish descent, most of his misspent years had been confined to Nice and its environs.

In answer to the question, 'Can you provide us with an extra room for the next few days, preferably a twin-bedded one?' he responded with fulsome civility, 'Of course I can. There's nothing I will not do for my English friends. From now on I want you to call me Pierre.'

Not wishing to be in bad odour before the holiday had scarcely begun, we thought it wiser not to complain about the cockroaches. A plain-spoken female American guest gave us the low-down.

'If you stay long enough to be able to ignore the primitive conditions, including the cockroaches from next door's bakery, you'll find the food here is excellent value for money. The owner, Madame Ducroix, does all the cooking herself.'

A prodigious worker, Madame Ducroix bustled about with unrelenting energy, her preoccupied air giving the impression that the worries of the world rested heavily on her shoulders. The two men in her life were as languid as she was assiduous. Her husband, a wizened old man, who wore the same dirty vest throughout our stay, spent most of the day staring vacantly into space. Endowed with the energy of a pudding and the build of a sumo wrestler, the son and heir, Jules, slumbered most of the daylight hours away in the lobby's most capacious chair, until he condescended to take the Alsatian guard dog for its daily saunter.

Tony stepped down from the Paris train, bubbling over with unbridled excitement. His arrival in Nice signalled the start of an action-packed fortnight, throughout which his chirpy good humour was unquenchable. He and I were so determined to enjoy ourselves that not even Jeremy's grouchy moods were going to dampen our spirits.

The humid August heat was like a furnace. Fanned by a gentle breeze, we spent many hours lazing on the pebbled beach, the beautiful and the ugly flaunting their ill-assorted, near-naked forms for all to see. We took in the parks, the squares, the churches, the museums; we visited exquisite villages in the hills behind the coast; we scrambled down the hillside track from Eze Village to the tranquil beach below.

In Monte Carlo we listened to a cockney tourist's painful attempts to obtain a cup of tea at a quayside bistro. 'A cup of tie,' he requested.

'Tie?' queried the waiter. *'Je ne comprends pas.'* After several abortive attempts, perspiration dripping from his puzzled brow, the frustrated cockney spluttered unrepeatable profanities before leaving in disgust.

Overwhelmed by Tony's wicked sense of fun, I empathised with his crass partiality for the absurd, whether it was the cockney's unfulfilled longing for tea or the knowledge that Jeremy's hotel bedroom continued to be infested with cock-roaches, whilst ours was clean as a whistle. We cracked our faces with indecent laughter whenever we caught sight of the man in the dirty vest and the sumo wrestler. Jeremy, who despised our callous frivolousness, was not so easily amused.

Each evening Pierre served up succulent meals with Provençal recipes, after which, in mellow mood, we made for the more glamorous regions of the city, where pleasure-seekers gathered in their thousands. There is nowhere in the world to equal the nocturnal ambience of the Mediterranean. For the cost of a drink, disturbed only by persistent hawkers laden with their tawdry wares, we would sit and watch the ambling passers-by; some in colourful evening finery, others with their scant clothing soiled and creased from a day in the sun.

Searching for a suitable spot from which to watch the nightly spectacle, we strolled along the Promenade des Anglais, the less salubrious Rue Massenet, as well as streets close to the seafront that to this day bear the names of distinguished French ancestors. Avoiding the gaudy cafés, we seated ourselves at a pavement table outside a backstreet bar whose modest charges invited our custom.

Opposite the bar in a cobbled alley stood a dozen or so young women with faces caked with make-up, brazenly flaunting their erotic charms. One was as black as the ace of spades; another possessed the slanting eyes of the inscrutable Oriental; a third was probably Arab. Of every size and shape, the streetwalkers provided a choice that suited a plethora of partialities: tall, diminutive, busty and lean bodies on sale to the highest bidder. A middle-aged woman strutted back and forth in front of us, her eyes flashing a defiant stare each time she passed. Short in stature and of sturdy build, she was more hardbitten than the rest.

'I think I'd choose the tart who's old enough to be my mother,' said Tony. 'I've always fancied a bit of rough. Which is the one you'd pick, Jonathan?'

'The tall one with the black stockings, stilettos and the shapely legs. I could do with an hour under the sheets with her.'

'You're mad to think of going with any of those hussies unless you want to end up with the clap,' warned Jeremy.

'Stop being so bloody sanctimonious! You don't honestly think we're being serious, do you?' snapped Tony, unaware I had not been joking.

A Repton contemporary once told me that when he was sixteen his enlightened father had employed a high-class hooker, whose job it was to give his son lessons in the art of lovemaking. My Victorian upbringing offered me no such benefits. On the one occasion my father took it upon himself to reveal to me the facts of life, a well-timed telephone call stopped him in his tracks, so that he never progressed beyond a stumbled sentence.

To keep up with my vaunting friends, a sense of pride had led me to brag about my female conquests. In reality, far from having been sexually liberated, I was still a virgin. Approaching the ripe old age of twenty-four, starved of what a man needs most, with natural urges near to bursting, I came to a decision that was coldly calculating, lustful and compelling.

My temptress was young and beautiful. Assuring myself it was now or never and that it was foolish to let a golden opportunity pass me by, I stood up and advanced towards the leggy hustler, my heart thumping loudly like a deep-toned drum. Disbelief remodelling their faces, Tony and Jeremy looked on in a state of utter shock.

I was gladdened by the sweetness of the street girl's manner. She gestured me to come closer.

'Hello, *chéri*,' she said. 'You want a nice time? I make it good for you.'

She gave the appearance of being the most obliging of the prostitutes, one who would be patient, encouraging, mindful of my greenness, the ideal teacher.

'How much?' I asked, attempting to pass myself off as a well-versed client.

'For you, *chéri*, forty francs for my services and ten for the room.'

Fifty francs was equivalent to half my weekly earnings; it was cheap at the price if it was going to lead to the long-awaited breakthrough.

No more words were spoken. From a discreet distance I followed her to the brothel's entrance. Up three flights of steps we went, the echoing clatter of the sharpened heels demolishing the silence. On the landing, installed in a curious boxlike hideout, was a wrinkled old woman. Her toothless gums grinned at me mockingly. Half a century ago she could well have been a call girl. Long since pensioned off, she was now a concierge and cleaner.

'Ten francs for the room and five for a *préservatif*,' she squawked.

Making off with the contraceptive packet, safely away from the spooky hag, I entered the tall girl's bedroom. In contrast with the stark exterior, the room itself was generously appointed. At the far end stood a massive bed. Devoid of harsh vulgarity, the thick carpet, cushioned chairs, matching brocade curtains and softened lighting combined to create an effect of warmth and luxury.

Discarding my clothes, I was taken by the girl to the en suite bathroom. Stepping out of her skirt and knickers, she sat astride the bidet in stockings and suspenders and washed between her legs. I looked on, entranced by her magnificently contoured figure, impatient to achieve my crucial ends. She massaged my penis gently, before unrolling the sheath down its extended length. She drew my naked body to her. Deft fingers eased me deep inside. I needed to prolong those special moments; the tactile probing; the rhapsody of kisses, the tantalising foreplay. For admission to the fellowship of manhood, I was entitled to be taught the proper way.

'Take off your top and let me hold you, feel you, love you,' I whispered longingly.

'Get on with the fucking, never mind the loving. I've given you more than enough time!'

Heedless of the fact she might have wrecked my chances of a healthy sex life, her crude words dealt the bitterest of blows. She got up and left me on the bed panting, pleading, cursing. Before I was conscious of her movements, the door had banged and she was gone.

I became aware someone was standing over me. The scrawny crone cackled with delight as she appraised my state of nudity. Appalled to think that she was about to take over where her cruel accomplice had left off, I charged into the bathroom cubicle, dressed, was down the stairs and back onto the street in record time.

I was hailed by Tony, who looked decidedly uncomfortable.

'How did you get on?' he asked.

'It was the best screw I've ever had.'

'It will serve you right if you catch gonorrhoea *and* syphilis from the filthy whore,' teased the sadistic Jeremy. 'The umbrella treatment will have you screaming with pain.'

'Just like when you were stung by the deadly cockroach. With your imagination, it'll be a venomous snake next time!'

At breakfast next morning Pierre was even more affable than usual; we could tell he was leading up to something.

'I've always had a liking for sea food and escargots,' he declared. 'Do you eat escargots in England?'

Jeremy remembered once having tasted the delicacy, whereas Tony and I had to admit we were disgusted at the thought of snail-eating.

'I'll tell you what,' said Pierre. 'After dinner tonight, I'll treat the three of you to escargots at a sea food restaurant I patronise. You can't leave France without being a little daring. Oysters when they are in season, langouste, bouillabaisse, fish soup, moules, escargots, crab, frogs' legs: they're all worth a try.'

'Jonathan's tried most things already,' goaded Jeremy.

'It's food he's referring to,' I asserted angrily, blushing more than slightly.

After Pierre had disappeared into the kitchen, Jeremy's hectoring continued.

'The clap has an incubation period of up to ten days, so if you experience a burning sensation when peeing or have a discharge, go straight to the nearest quack. He'll push a tube up your pipe with opened ribs, like the ribs of an umbrella. It's then drawn out backwards to remove the infection. I'm told it's worse than torture.'

'That's quite enough,' complained Tony, wincing unmistakably, 'or you'll convince us that you've had the clap yourself. Don't worry, Jonathan, the umbrella treatment hasn't been used for ages; all that's needed for a cure these days is a hefty dose of penicillin.'

'Seeing that I wore a sheath, I'm not in the least bit worried.'

Jeremy pointed out with glee that sheaths often split and that I would, like it or not, have to suffer the uncertainty of not knowing for the remainder of the holiday whether I was going to contract the dreaded venereal disease.

Tabooed as a subject on Tony's insistence, the badgering and baiting mercifully ended. During the days that followed, in the privacy of my own thoughts, I dwelt long and often upon the gruesome possibilities outlined by Jeremy, regretting the risks I had taken.

Pierre's evening duties completed, he was ready to escort us to La Cave Niçoise, one of the region's most popular eating places. The head waiter greeted Pierre flamboyantly, his expression lightening with an impish grin. Four bottles of red wine had been placed in readiness on our table.

Pierre began lecturing us on his best-loved subject. 'After forty years in catering, there's very little I don't know about food and wines. It isn't true that white wine brings out the flavour of fish or shelled food better than a red. I drink red with everything.'

By the time we were on the way to finishing our first glass, Pierre was at least three drinks ahead of us. The more he indulged himself, the more he waxed eloquent.

'The black market prospered in Nice during the war years,' he continued. 'When the franc no longer had a value, commodities of every kind became the currency. Food and alcohol would buy a multitude of goods and services; after all, what's the good of having a car with petrol and an engine if you're starving to death? A roof over my head and a full belly is all I've ever wanted.'

It was at this stage that a plate containing a dozen snails was deposited in front of each of us.

'These I can guarantee are the best escargots to be found in Nice,' said Pierre.

'Dip your bread into the garlic butter and mop up all the juices. It's the perfect combination. Washed down with wine, nothing could be better.'

Despite our apprehension, feeling outrageously decadent, we surprised ourselves by delighting in the culinary adventure.

When a circular dish appeared, filled to the brim with the largest bouillabaisse fish stew imaginable, we wondered whether Pierre had taken leave of his senses. Madame Ducroix had already cooked us an excellent four-course dinner. What we had expected from Pierre was a snack, not a gargantuan banquet. Rude though it is in France to use the word *plein* to express the fact one has eaten more than sufficient, it was an appropriate way to describe our bloated condition. Oblivious that we had withdrawn from the gastronomic contest, Pierre continued to tuck in gluttonously until the tureen was emptied.

Just as we were hoping Pierre would ask for the bill, thinking that his munificence had already been excessive, he made a shock announcement. 'You haven't lived until you've sampled the best cheeses. I've ordered a selection I know will tempt you. Some of the names you will recognise; the others, I suspect, are not obtainable in England. Boulette d'Avens, époisses, brie, chaource, fourme d'Ambert, gaperon, reblechon, Roquefort. Raclette from Savoie is my favourite. It delights me to see how much you enjoy French food. I have never before met young Englishmen with such good appetites. Two more bottles of the house red, waiter, if you please!'

Going through the motions of picking at the cheeses, our token gesture of good manners, we finally reached the point at which we were unable to swallow another mouthful. Pierre's voracity, however, was unstoppable. A dedicated trencherman and imbiber, he had no intention of giving in until his plate was bare and every drop of wine was gone.

The mission stout-heartedly accomplished, Pierre slumped in his chair, his eyes watery and bloodshot, the crinkled face a mass of purple veins. Inhaling deeply, he clutched at his head, as if about to have a seizure. Gurgling, gasping, spluttering, he collapsed on the floor in a crumpled heap. Greatly alarmed lest our generous host had breathed his last, we made frantic signals for the head waiter to come to help us.

The fact that one of his regular customers had been taken ill did not appear to trouble him. After talking inconsequentially to some Italian diners, he deigned to come over to our table.

With typical French arrogance he asked, 'Does there appear to be a problem?'

'Pierre needs to be admitted to a hospital,' said Tony. 'We think he may have had a stroke.'

'There's nothing wrong with Pierre that a good night's rest won't cure. One of these days booze will see the end of him, but I fancy he'll survive tonight. A slap on the cheeks will bring him round. I then suggest you take him home and get him straight to bed.'

Holding on to Pierre in the way warders guard a prisoner, we steadied, pushed and dragged him along near-empty streets. Insensible to our presence, blinded by drunkenness, he lurched and swayed about erratically. The weird cavalcade halted at the hotel entrance. Discovering he had lost his key, our fuddled friend hammered his fists on the door, demanding instant entry.

The door was opened by Madame Ducroix, who looked anxious and exhausted. What puzzled us was that, far from being outraged by Pierre's intoxicated state and tardy homecoming, she welcomed him with a protective tenderness that we would never have imagined. In the manner of a solicitous nurse, she ushered him into a bedroom.

Before turning out the light Tony asked, 'Do you think the two of them sleep together?'

'They may share the same bed, but they're not capable of *doing* anything, not at their age. They must be over sixty!'

We had not expected to see Pierre back on duty. At breakfast, displaying the unctuous smile of the true professional, he behaved as if nothing had happened. When, however, he bent over us whilst placing coffee and croissants on our table, a stench of foul breath that combined the worst features of drains, a distillery and stale garlic met us head-on. His deathly pale face made him look as ill as he must have felt.

'Pierre has obviously been on another of his benders,' observed the American female guest. 'When the hotel's busy and the responsibilities get on top of him, the only way of keeping him off the hooch is to lock him up. Madame Ducroix would never cope without him, though. Despite his drunken sprees, Pierre is infinitely more use to her than the pathetic duo sitting over there!'

In his native Stratford, Jeremy had been an agreeable enough associate. On holiday, he was a totally different character. As each day passed, he became more and more irritable. Interspersed between long periods of silent self-analysis, the fault-finding increased to such an extent that Tony decided to initiate a showdown.

'I thought we were here to enjoy ourselves. What the hell's up with you, Jeremy?'

'I'm pissed off with Nice, the hotel, the heat, everything. I can't get back to England fast enough.'

'There has to be more to it than that,' I said, exasperated by his negativity.

'If you *must* know, I'm in love,' confided Jeremy. 'I met this girl, Julie, at a party and I've been thinking about her ever since. I've decided to go back to Stratford before someone else muscles in. I know of at least two other blokes who are after her!'

On the pretext of forestalling Julie's attempts to fraternise with other men, Jeremy cut short his holiday. At the airport he made no effort to conceal his spirit of optimism that had been rapidly and miraculously restored. The sheer delight at leaving behind the two companions with whom he had been so out of tune gave him further cause to celebrate.

My encounter with romance began when Tony and I stopped off for a beer at an open-air nightspot on the Promenade des Anglais. Sitting at a nearby table were two stunningly attractive females. Dark haired, expensively dressed and oozing sophistication, they were a ravishing pair.

'They must be mother and daughter,' said Tony. 'As well as looking sexy, the mother's ripeness is a real turn-on.'

'What is it about older women that appeals to you?'

'I like the thought of all those years of experience. You can keep the novices!'

Preferring the idea of a liaison to its practical application, Tony was content to watch his female discovery from the safety of his seat. I invited the younger woman to dance. We began shuffling about the floor to the live music.

'Are you French?' I asked.

'No, I'm Greek. My stepfather is English. He's an army officer and is stationed at Catterick.'

'So that's why you speak such good English. How long have you been in the south of France?'

'My mother has been renting a villa for the month of August. Why don't you join us at our beach tomorrow? We're always there by midday. You will find us at Villeneuve-Loubet-Plage; it isn't far from here. I'm Stella. What's your name?'

The thought of a rendezvous with Stella excited me immeasurably. I was heartened that the suggestion for us to meet had been instigated by her. Convinced that the dull ache in the pit of my stomach was proof I was already falling for the delectable Greek girl, my engrossing desire was to see her again.

Leaving Tony to his own devices after an early lunch, I made a short cut through the flower market and was soon heading in a westerly direction along the esplanade. Not one of the many private beaches between Nice and the airport seven kilometres away bore a name that faintly resembled Villeneuve-Loubet-Plage. I regretted not having researched its whereabouts in advance. Some way beyond the airport I accosted a fisherman, who was mending his nets in the St Laurent-du-Var harbour.

'Can you tell me the way to Villeneuve-Loubet-Plage?'

'Make for Cannes, then ask again,' he said, beaming a smile that indicated his pleasure at being able to assist a guileless foreigner.

Knowing that Cannes was more than thirty kilometres from Nice by road, my morale plummeted to an all-time low. Unwilling to catch a bus or hitch a lift until I knew more precisely where I was heading, I legged it in the sweltering heat until I found myself in the seaside resort of Cagnes-sur-Mer. Here I asked again for directions to the elusive beach.

'Carry straight on for three kilometres, after which you must take a turning on your left. It's a two-minute walk from there.'

At once I realised that the seaman had been referring to Cagnes not Cannes; it was his local dialect that was the cause of the confusion. I continued my jog, confident I would in next to no time be lying in the sun at Stella's side.

I must have been wearing blinkers to have lost my way after the explicit directions I had been given in Cagnes. I have no idea how I ended up at the small inland town of Villeneuve-Loubet, but end up there I did. To my alarm I discovered that to get to the beach with that same name involved a four-kilometre hike across vineyards, meadows and rugged countryside. In no mood to capitulate, my heart still set upon achieving the goal that was by now an obsession, I quickened my pace.

When at last I arrived at the Villeneuve-Loubet-Plage entrance, I was horrified to discover that sunbathers were packing up for the day and already departing from the beach. There was no sign of Stella. It was obvious my long-drawn-out excursion had been nothing but a wild goose chase. Not knowing the address of the villa, there was no point in my hanging about. I decided to have one last look for my lady friend before returning to Nice by bus.

There was something familiar about two bikini-clad females lying at the water's edge, their well-rounded bodies the colour of ebony. My exhilaration was immense when I realised they were Stella and her charming chaperone.

'We thought you weren't coming,' said Stella, unable to hide her pleasure at seeing me again. 'We were about to return to the villa, so you very nearly missed us.'

'When you said the beach wasn't far away, I assumed it was in Nice. It's taken me five hours to get here on foot, including a senseless detour of my own invention. I could do with a nice cool drink.'

Suitably fortified, using my most eloquent powers of persuasion, I asked Stella to return with me to Nice for the evening.

'This is the last day of our holiday,' explained her mother. 'We *have* to stay in tonight to tidy up the villa. Our flight leaves early in the morning.'

On seeing my disappointment, Stella came up with an alternative suggestion.

'If I travel back on the bus with Jonathan, the two of us can have a talk and exchange addresses. It's the least I can do after he's walked all this way. I'll catch the next bus home, so as to help with the packing.'

Back at the hotel, Tony could see I was in exuberant mood.

'Does the Cheshire cat grin mean you've scored a bullseye?' he enquired.

'In a manner of speaking, yes.'

'Come on, spit it out!'

'Do you want the good news or the bad news?'

'Let's start with the bad news.'

'Stella and her mother are leaving for England tomorrow.'

'That's scuppered my chances with the mother! What's the good news, for heaven's sake?'

'Stella is to start a course at a secretarial college just off the Cromwell Road in London. She will be living at her parents' flat in Twickenham. She's already invited me to visit her.'

'Will her parents be there, too?'

'No, they'll be at Catterick. Stella will be on her own.'

'Not for long, I trust. At least next time you won't have to pay for it!'

Whilst Tony was travelling back to England by rail, I spent a solitary day in Nice with plenty of time to luxuriate in our never-to-be-forgotten adventures. Just as I was thinking how tame it now all seemed by comparison, I was approached in the vicinity of the bus station by a young lady whose dazzling good looks were so mind-blowing I would defy any man who passed her by not to turn his head to steal a second glance.

'How would you like to take me on the bus to Monte Carlo?' she asked.

Greatly flattered though I was by her proposal, it was as much as I could do to stammer in reply, 'I'm afraid I can't. I've a plane to catch.' Knowing that I had the remainder of the day free with nothing more interesting in mind, I surprised myself by the terseness of my response.

Seemingly unconcerned that I had turned down her offer, the golden-haired stranger, taking my expensive suntan to mean I was an expert on all matters relating to the Riviera, wanted to discover whether I was acquainted with any of the millionaires in town.

'Arthur Krantz flew in from New York yesterday. Do you happen to know where he's staying?'

'I've never even heard of him, but you can always try the Negresco.'

'You must know Pablo Picasso,' she said.

'You mean Picasso, the artist? I know of him, of course, but I've not met him. Why do you ask?'

'I've been his model for the past three months; he's an absolute sweetie. Sitting like a statue, though, day after day, gets a bit tedious. I could do with some light relief before resuming my art course in London. Arthur knows exactly how to treat a lady. Perhaps he'll find the time to take me to Monte Carlo.'

'I hope you succeed in tracking him down.'

'Please don't go yet, you look like a real nice guy,' she persisted.

She produced a card on which she wrote her name, London address and telephone number. 'I'm returning to Hampstead next week,' she continued. 'Give me a call. I'd love to meet you in England.'

Time spent with Picasso's nude English model would have seemed a harmless enough way to occupy the hours on an otherwise uneventful day. Had I given in to her hypnotic sorcery, there would have been no going back. Although my friendship with Stella had barely begun, I was convinced the relationship was going to ripen. A persuasive conscience left me with no option other than to remain faithful to the ideal of making this happen. Whether through prudishness or fear or more simply because I was already in love, I destroyed the card with the name and contact details of the enchantress, an action I was well aware I might live to regret.

So eager was I to see Stella again that my memory of our two brief meetings had attained fanciful proportions. Lost in thought as I queued to board the London flight at Nice Airport, I became aware of a fellow passenger being pushed in a wheelchair on the tarmac alongside me. It was Sir Winston Churchill.

Crisis Time

My father's physical condition had been declining for as long as I could remember. The smoking habit he acquired as a teenage soldier soothed him at times of stress, as did his evening tipple at a nearby hostelry. At breakfast in the school dining hall, with not a qualm of conscience, he would puff away at a cigarette, immersing himself in the daily newspaper. The impressionable young boarders, whose propriety he prided himself on nurturing, listened in alarm to the explosive cough that hacked away incessantly.

Worse still was his unquenchable need to smoke in the presence of his paying customers. During parental interviews or when accompanying visitors around the school, he was rarely to be seen without a cigarette in his mouth. Greatly concerned that he was flagrantly abusing his health, my mother and I remonstrated with him to cut down. Knowing him to be a stubborn man, it did not surprise us that our exhortations were of no avail.

Handicapped by a damaged lung and unfitness generally, my father became breathless after the least exertion. The family doctor, as well as recommending a reduction of the smoking, urged my father to lose some weight. These warnings, too, he disregarded.

Meanwhile, life went on. I had married and the school continued to tick over happily enough until one night soon after the start of the Summer Term. The well-ordered routine of the entire community was thrown off balance when fate struck the inevitable blow.

A telephone call after ten at night or before six in the morning generally brings bad news. My wife was quick to pick up the receiver. 'It's your mother,' she said. 'She sounds upset.'

I knew at once that something had happened to my father. What I did not realise was that home life from then on would change so drastically that our right to privacy as newly-weds had been immutably surrendered.

My mother was more self-possessed than I would have expected when she recounted the shattering news.

'Daddy's had a coronary. It's been touch and go, but he's now in a stable condition. Dr Edmondson was with him for two hours and couldn't have been more thorough. He doubts whether Daddy will ever be well enough to teach again, let alone cope with his other duties. I hoped and prayed the responsibilities of the school were not going to be forced upon you suddenly like this.'

'Are you at the hospital?'

'Daddy refused to go to hospital. He said the only way they could remove him from the school was in a box.'

I found myself reeling from the shock, unable to take in the implications of the news. It is hard to express how ill-equipped, afraid and overwhelmingly desolate I felt. In the manner of an inexperienced actor, survival depended upon the way in which I enacted my most demanding role. To cast aside the mantle of youth in favour of a maturer identity required a star quality performance. How long I would be able to deceive the staff and a discerning public into thinking I was tailor-made for the job, a born and bred headmaster, was a question I was repeatedly to ask myself.

The gossipmongers of Leamington and district were out in force, with their callous thoughts and judgemental attitudes. Their verdict was unanimous. 'Johnny Hall couldn't run a piss-up in a brewery. Now that Dougie's on his last legs, he might as well sell the place. It'll only be a matter of time before it folds.'

Surrounded by this background of cynicism and mistrust, it is little wonder I was scared beyond belief of the trials that lay ahead.

My father was determined to make a comeback. I clung on to the slender hope that he might one day recover sufficiently to be able to take over the reins once more. Aged sixty-seven and all at once a frail old man, there would have been a tragic outcome had he burdened himself again with the pressures he had endured uncomplainingly for nearly three decades. He grudgingly conceded the time had come for him to step down.

It was comforting for me to know that his guidance was close at hand. I regretted the wasted years when he and I should have made more effort to get to know each other better. He was a man of immense character, whose shrewdness and experience up until then I had taken for granted. So valuable was he as a friend and stabilising influence that the possibility of his demise haunted me with a persistent eeriness.

A prospective parent from Cheshire with three Eton-bound sons, who had visited more than a dozen educational establishments, including Oxford's Dragon School, regarded the headmaster's age as a key criterion in the selection process. A schoolmaster friend had advised him to choose a privately owned prep school with a young head. 'The headmaster', he had said, 'in these circumstances is unlikely to retire or move elsewhere. You would be secure in the knowledge that your boys are able to complete their preparatory education without disruption.'

Won over by this dubious assertion, the parent opted for Arnold Lodge because I was the youngest headmaster he could find.

My young age did not always work to my advantage. During the early stages of my apprenticeship, I remember greeting my first prospective parent with the nervousness of an incoming batsman. Mr Veale, a self-assured industrial consultant, glowered at me so disapprovingly that I was made to feel no better than a worm. I found myself apologising for having to stand in for my father and lied that it was only a temporary arrangement. The expression on Mr Veale's face said everything. He resented being interviewed by a fledgling, who was not much older than a pupil. Angry to be wasting his time, he cut short the interview with an abruptness that deeply bruised my faltering nerve.

I was twenty-five years old but looked a great deal younger. Immature, emotionally erratic and of questionable intelligence, I was unqualified in every sense to cope with the burdens of the office of headmaster. I yearned for my deficiencies to be replaced by useful attributes. Energy, however, I possessed in abundance, together with an inborn desire to pay attention to the minutest detail. Supplementing these qualities with a burning enthusiasm and a willingness to work my socks off well into the night seven days a week, success was still achievable.

I have never got over my reticence on public occasions. When confronted with large numbers of people I become tongue-tied to such an extent that it is as much as I can do to string a number of words coherently together. Small talk is a skill that to this day I have failed to master.

Lack of confidence is a shortcoming not easily concealed. At my first headmasters' conference, I was cowed by the strident voices of the suave delegates, many of whom exuded the imperious assertiveness one associates with men in command. Representing some of Britain's most celebrated schools, the lofty heads treated me to pompous descriptions of the institutions they had steered to unrivalled excellence. So out of my depth was I made to feel that my prime desire was to be suddenly older and wiser, even if it had meant eroding some of the precious early years.

To have to stand up and speak before an audience has been the cause of great discomfort. Preparing for speech days always took hours of exacting rehearsal before I was ready to deliver my orations. A parent once praised me with these words: 'You make public speaking sound so easy!' What he did not know was that I had put myself through hell to achieve the delusion.

I was no less meticulous with my preparation for routine commitments, whether it involved officiating at school assemblies, chairing meetings or giving pep talks. Not once during my thirty years as headmaster or principal did I risk leaving anything to chance.

Few people were aware of the strain incited by these self-imposed demands. Life would have been a great deal happier had I been able to loosen up and laugh at myself more freely; the austere early training had taught me to expect the task of attempting to build up the school to be a herculean one. The search for perfection was an obligation from which I could not escape, no matter how costly its relentless pursuit would later prove to be in physical and human terms.

Having suffered two nervous breakdowns by the time I was twenty, I was well aware the responsibilities with which I had been prematurely encumbered were likely to stretch me way beyond my limits. For my marriage to survive and flourish, an instant exit from the school to a more tranquil lifestyle was essential. I was deeply conscious of my inability to cope with the professional challenges, although the trauma of my father's illness had made me oblivious of my young wife's needs or of how the rapid changes were already affecting her.

It was wrong of my father and mother to have invested such high hopes in my capabilities. Their presumptions were not only unreasonable, they were also unfair. It was assumed that, as a dutiful son, I would carry on the family tradition. Had I walked away, it would have meant destroying the little kingdom my parents had cultivated. The school had for so long been an intractable obsession for all of us that my resolution to stay with it was as inevitable as was destiny itself.

Not long after my father's coronary, I made an important decision. I had concluded that it was out of the question for me to be able to manage the school on my own. The idea of taking on as a partner a prep school man with a good track record was, I thought, a sensible compromise. My father was unenthusiastic. 'Before the war your mother and I were in partnership with David Hardy, as well you know,' he said. 'When David pulled out, giving us no notice, the business only survived because we drew virtually no salary for years. Partnerships are even more dicey than a marriage, believe you me. It's far better to keep the school within the family.'

Ignoring my father's advice, I immediately arranged a consultation with the London educational agents, Gabbitas and Thring. Within a matter of days, I had received the names of a number of aspiring partners, together with their curricula vitae.

I met three of the candidates. David Prichard, who was then on the staff of Monkton Combe Junior School near Bath, was the most impressive. A graduate of Pembroke College, Oxford, he possessed flawless credentials. Presenting himself as a model of probity, he made me wonder what part, if any, I would be allowed to play were he to join us. He was sophisticated, streetwise and frighteningly ambitious. Although chronologically he cannot have been much more than three years my senior, his superior manner caused me to suppose I would not be capable of matching any of his talents.

A man acquainted only with the highest standards, Mr Prichard had no reason to approve of what he saw when he cast his eyes around our strained community. He was nevertheless astute enough to recognise the potential that existed. With irritating superciliousness, he argued that his management skills would swiftly bring about a transformation. He was prepared to consider a partnership, with the condition that he owned a fifty per cent stake in all developments and acquisitions that took place subsequent to his appointment. He was neither looking to invest any capital himself, nor had he given thought to the goodwill element, which was by no means worthless. So heavily was the suggested deal weighted in Mr Prichard's favour that acceptance of it would have brought about the eventual abdication of my birthright. I might well have been pleased to accept a more equitable arrangement.

Relieved that my eagerness to take on a partner was fast waning, my father commented with familiar frankness, 'Once he got his feet under the table, Mr Prichard would soon have us dancing attendance on him. There isn't the income to provide for a greedy outsider, let alone one who is not prepared to put in a penny piece himself.'

Six years later Mr Prichard was appointed headmaster of Port Regis School in Dorset, a school that hit the headlines when Princess Anne and Captain Mark Phillips chose to educate their children there. It would be wrong of me to attempt to disparage David Prichard's accomplishments. A prep school mogul of his era, he succeeded in making Port Regis into one of the most highly thought-of schools in England. Had he joined me as my partner, his dynamism and commercial flair would almost certainly have speeded up the process of the school's expansion, but he and I would undoubtedly have clashed.

The decision to discard the partnership idea in no way solved the many problems I had to tackle. My pessimistic belief that I was incapable of doing what was expected of me could only be allayed by a vote of confidence being given in my favour. I was unknown, unproven, timorous and raw. There was not one good reason why parents would wish to assign their sons to the uncertainties of my charge.

Adopting the notion that honesty was the best policy, I gathered together five of my pupils' parents, all of them fathers, so as to make them aware of my anxieties. Chauvinistic though it may sound, women in those times did not intrude on the male preserve of decision making, as a consequence of which my first committee consisted exclusively of men. I chose as my advisers five fathers with professional backgrounds, whose concern for the well-being of the school we had never doubted. They were well qualified to offer opinions and ideas that represented the views of the majority of the parents. Because their local influence was considerable, it cannot be overestimated how important it was for me to capture their support.

A meeting took place at my home. To help promote an atmosphere of informality, I provided everyone with a glass of sherry before we settled down to the business of the evening. Knowing that discussions would focus on my suitability, I had nothing to lose and everything to gain by speaking candidly.

I told them of my trepidation at being forced to take on my father's responsibilities long before it had been intended. I told them that, having investigated the option of taking on a partner, the dangers, in our view, cancelled out the possible advantages. My final words summed up the sincerity of my intentions.

'I know I'm young and inexperienced, but I have always loved the school and there is nothing I'm not prepared to do to help build on what we already have. You have my assurance that not a stone will be left unturned in my attempts to make Arnold Lodge the very best it can be.'

Sitting in silent judgement, the five wise men transmitted with telepathic immediacy their feelings of suspicion. The oldest of the group, a portly man with a double-barrelled name, chewed thoughtfully at his pipe; a second chain-smoked aggressively; the others fidgeted or twitched with manifest unease.

I was convinced that I knew what each of them was thinking. *How in heaven's name can this youngster, a mere whippersnapper, think he has earned the right to control and guide our treasured offspring?*

Tensions were eased when one of the group's members, a solicitor, took it upon himself to be the committee's chairman. It was soon apparent that the five of them had already met and that they knew exactly what they wanted.

'We see little point in your taking on a partner,' he began. 'The only sensible course is for you to carry on as you are, but we shall be on you like a ton of bricks if you mess things up!'

The offer of their grudging support was gratefully accepted. Intimidated by the knowledge that critical eyes would scrutinise my every movement, I knew there was nothing for it but for me to prove myself.

Thereafter the committee met once termly. Occupying snug chairs in our private sitting room, alcoholic refreshments readily available, and with no prescribed agenda, we discussed a variety of issues relating to the school. The meetings often degenerated into frivolous affairs that resembled more an evening's revelry of boisterous Round Tablers than a sober attempt to produce a panacea for the school's ills. As a goodwill exercise, however, these light-hearted occasions were of the greatest benefit.

Four years later, by which time the school was expanding rapidly, we decided to formalise the meetings. Despite our reluctance to dispense with the cosy get-togethers, we were nonetheless aware that our crude methods of operating a clannish consultative group were in need of reform. We hotly debated whether or not to invite a mother to join the committee's ranks. With feelings running high and tempers frayed, the traditionalists reluctantly surrendered.

The group's most reactionary member scoffed at the decision. 'For there to be a *woman* on the committee', he proclaimed pontifically, 'is an idea I find utterly revolting!'

The first woman to join us was a medical practitioner. An articulate left-wing intellectual, she gave her male counterparts a run for their money. Finding fault with archaic practices, she manoeuvred us into re-examining the school's ethos.

To reflect the more open society in which we were living, the committee later included some senior teachers and an increasing proportion of mothers. In the absence of a board of governors, I felt it important for all branches of the school to be represented.

This modest democratisation helped to give me the backing needed to accelerate an ambitious programme of improvements.

Soon after the partnership idea had been rejected, a disagreement with my father very nearly caused me to abandon the school and to leave him and my overburdened mother to their own devices. I was well aware that my workload was colossal. This ineluctable fact I accepted as a necessary liability. What I was not prepared to allow to happen, however, was for me to neglect my own security. My father and mother now owned the school business and buildings in equal shares. It concerned me that, were either of them to die, death duties would erode their lifetime's efforts. When my father offered to make me a partner in the business, he ignored the vital matter of the ownership of the buildings. Until these were gifted to me, there was the prospect that penal taxation might one day ruin us.

I put pressure on my parents to make all the assets over to me. I also stated my desire for future property purchases to be written in my name. Recognising the serious repercussions that would undoubtedly ensue without a tax planning strategy, I presented my father with an ultimatum.

'In your state of health', I said, 'it's crazy to leave things as they stand. I'm not prepared to work all the hours God sends, unless measures are taken to protect my long-term interests.'

'You're even more grasping than our Mr Prichard,' retorted my father. 'If you think we're going to hand everything over to you at the drop of a hat, you've got another think coming.'

Despite the conflicting emotions that overwhelmed my thoughts, my father's unwillingness to recognise the precariousness of our situation strengthened my determination to hold my ground. He had wrongly assumed I would, given time, accept the status quo. He had underrated the level of my resistance to any form of trade-off.

There are two distinct aspects to my character. The soggy, inoffensive, urbane façade conceals a ruthless streak. A tough negotiator, I learnt early on that life was no sinecure. I knew perfectly well that if I did not fight my own battles, nobody else would fight them for me.

Shocked by my intransigence, my father could not understand why I was behaving so heartlessly. Parental loyalty had always been of paramount importance, but now I also had a wife to consider. After much wrangling, it was with reluctance that my father accepted the soundness of my arguments.

In addition to my becoming a partner in the business, all the assets were made over to me. Provided my father and mother lived for the period of seven years, the family would avoid having to pay any death duties. It was indeed a brave step they had taken. It left them without safeguards and vulnerable to my whims, a sacrifice I could only refund with honesty.

And so it was, through a weird combination of fate and nepotism, that I was able to claim, quite wrongly it so happens, that I was the youngest ever prep school head. I now know of at least two others, who were similarly elevated at a younger age than me.

It is as well my stamina was in no way depleted. I was going to use up vast amounts of energy during the days that lay ahead, days that were to bring few triumphs and many heartaches.

Staff Happenings

It was not that my father was a ladies' man, but he seemed less able to retain the services of his male staff than he was their female equivalents. Unmarried women teachers took the trouble to transform the most modest accommodation into a home from home. Having established an ample base for themselves, these women wanted little more than the satisfaction of performing a worthwhile job.

Three of the spinsters who devoted years of selfless service to the school were Noni Young, Eileen Crofton and Winifred Fairbrother. Noni was best known for her fine collection of handmade puppets; throughout the war when entertainment of any kind was scarce, she staged imaginative puppet shows for the pupils. Froebel-trained Eileen Crofton made her mark by revitalising the junior school at a time when the privations of war were most keenly felt.

Winifred Fairbrother's contribution was outstanding. A brilliant teacher with limitless patience, she committed the best years of her life to the school. When she died in June 1966, following a long illness, wrought-iron gates were erected in her memory next to the science block. Shortly after she retired, she praised my parents in a letter in the school magazine that highlighted her own faithfulness and generosity of spirit. 'Those of you who have known Mr and Mrs Hall for any length of time', she asserted, 'will realise that their unfailing sympathy, consideration, hard work and integrity have been the source from which so much has come.'

These warm-hearted words indicated that Winifred Fairbrother enjoyed a deep friendship, as well as a professional association with my parents. It is the more astonishing, therefore, that not once in over twenty years did my father allow himself to break down the barriers of reserve when in her presence. He addressed her formally as Miss Fairbrother until the day she left.

My father was calculably impatient, reckless even, when it came to the treatment of his staff. A short fuse caused him to upset the people he most relied upon. As far back as my early childhood, I can remember constant changes of personnel unsettling our tightly bound community.

On the occasions that an employee nettled him, my exasperated father would complain, 'I can handle the boys, I can handle the parents, but I'm *damned* if I can handle the staff!'

There was one master whose thirty years of service made him the great exception. Woodwork specialist Eric Hyam would not have subscribed to the belief that my father was an intolerant employer. So strong was Eric's sense of loyalty that nothing would have induced him to work for a man for whom he showed no liking or respect. Manifesting the fastidiousness of the true professional, Eric accepted nothing but the best from his pupils. He believed passionately that time spent in his workshop was an investment for the future and that practical skills were a prerequisite for each and every boy. The quality of craftmanship on show at annual woodwork exhibitions was so impressive that Arnold Lodge became a leader in this field.

After the comings and goings of five unsatisfactory Latin teachers in as many years, eighteen months prior to his coronary my father was advertising the same post yet again.

'We can't keep on having changes,' I grumbled. 'What we need is stability, but without proper salaries and increments we shall always have a restless staff.'

'Your problem', rejoined my father, 'is that you think money grows on trees. To spend what simply isn't there is a sure recipe for disaster!'

Throughout the 1960s teaching vacancies in private schools exceeded the supply of good-calibre applicants. As valuable as gold dust, gifted teachers were able to dictate the terms of their employment. Impoverished schools had no option but to select from a motley batch of cast-offs.

First to be interviewed was a young, fresh-faced Oxford graduate, whose glowing testimonials made him a strong candidate. Unimpressed with the school's conditions and amenities, he accepted a more tempting offer somewhere else.

With Christmas almost upon us, the January vacancy remained unfilled. My father, who complained bitterly that schoolmasters were a dying breed, could not understand why bright young men did not jump at the chance of a residential post.

'Just think of it,' he would say. 'Everything found, with no deductions for board and lodging. The salary cheque is merely pocket money!'

It was unrealistic of my father to compare conditions in his own school with his experiences as a resident master way back in the 1920s. Ill-judged optimism caused him to regard free accommodation as a strong inducement to potential staff. The cheerless room on offer to the next incumbent, with minimal storage space, denied the occupant the scope so much as to swing a scraggy cat. In no way would claimants be impressed with this so-called benefit.

Nobody would deny that a school staff is the better for having a number of characters to enliven the community. We do not easily forget the colourful personalities we encountered during our schooldays, whether they were teachers, ancillary staff or the more memorable of our peers.

My house at Repton employed a gardener whom we called Bugger Stacey, because bugger was the one word he used to describe just about everything. The 'houseman', Birdy, who at the age of eighty still cleaned daily fifty pairs of shoes, waited at table and stoked the boiler, had one leg-pull we must have heard a thousand times. 'It's a nice day for the race,' he would say. 'What race, Birdy?' we would ask, not letting on we already knew the answer. 'The human race,' poor Birdy predictably replied with simple innocence.

Not to be remembered for the influence they exerted over us, these two men were memorable nevertheless for their idiosyncratic quirks, qualities that are lacking in today's intolerant, hyped-up populace. I vividly recall a number of my teachers, but it was often the nonconformist oddballs who implanted the lessons and the ideas that have been of greatest benefit.

Had my father sought to appoint a psychotic for the vacant Latin post, Mr Campbell would have been the ideal choice. A middle-aged Scot of sombre bearing, with a face the texture of parchment, he had travelled all the way from Aberdeen for the interview. Out-of-date references indicated that Mr Campbell was highly accomplished in the academic sense. His teaching record, however, was remarkable only in that he was one of those gentlemen, described by my father as 'rolling stones', who incessantly changed his job. When asked why he had moved from school to school so frequently, Mr Campbell, by now greatly ruffled and on edge, began to tremble and shake.

My father commented uneasily: 'I see there are no references to cover the last five years of your employment. Would you please tell me where you have been working in the recent past?'

Not only did Mr Campbell's shaking become ungovernable, but he began also to stamp his feet and shout with imbecilic fury. Such was his extraordinary behaviour that we began to wonder whether he had spent the missing years in a mental institution.

We were relieved when Mr Campbell departed for Aberdeen early next morning. In the normal way, my mother left the appointment of teachers to my father; on this occasion she was justified in voicing her concerns.

'I hope you're not even *thinking* of appointing that uncouth Scotsman,' she said to my father.

'Of course I'm not, he's clearly very ill. Has he done something diabolical?'

'If you call wetting his bed and fouling up the lavatory diabolical, the answer is yes. To have a man like that living in is out of the question!'

A courteous letter was sent to Mr Campbell by my father. 'In view of the strong field of applicants,' he wrote, 'it is with regret that I am unable to offer you the post and I apologise for any inconvenience you may have suffered. Please find enclosed my cheque to cover the full cost of your train fare.'

By return of post, my father was delivered an unstamped envelope with an Aberdeen postmark. The contents spilt onto his desk like unwanted confetti.

After pocketing the cheque, Mr Campbell's insane method of retaliation had been to mutilate my father's letter into shreds and return it to the sender.

'I shudder to think what might have happened had I appointed him,' declared my father. 'The man's eaten up with so much anger that he's capable of murder. We must be thankful he's safely out of reach!'

So desperate was my father to begin the new term with a full complement of teachers that he could not afford to be too finicky. He had made up his mind that, providing the next candidate possessed no conspicuous defects in his character, he would offer him the job.

A bespectacled young man of phenomenal height presented himself for interview; standing alongside him, my father looked like a dwarf. After ushering the visitor into our family's lounge, my father whispered in my ear, 'It would need a fearless boy to take advantage of this Titan!'

On coming down from university, Sussex born and bred John Herbert had taught temporarily at a coaching establishment in Hove. With a good honours degree and respectable reference to support his application, he provided a welcome answer to my father's prayers. Not only was he a skilled chess player and modest pianist, he shared my father's enthusiasm for cricket, all of which were bonuses. We needed a youthful addition to our team of staff, someone who was keen, active and unversed enough to be adaptable. Such a paragon was found in John.

Not wishing to put John off unduly, my father omitted to show him the tiny bedroom in which he would reside. Aware of John's scepticism and unwillingness to commit himself, my father indulged in the rare extravagance of tempting him with a more than ample financial package that included annual increments. This offer John accepted.

John Herbert appeared to settle in happily enough, though it was clear from the outset that he was not one to wear his heart on his sleeve. Despite my inability to assess what were his initial impressions or glean whether he was content with his lot, instinct told me that, like most of his predecessors, he would not wish to remain on the staff for long. Who would have predicted he and I were destined to build up a successful school in a professional relationship that was to last our entire working life?

John is a perfectionist. His determination to make rigorous demands of himself stems in part, I suspect, from the puritanical influence of the evangelical chapel he attended as a child in Eastbourne. Finding it hard to accept fallibility in others, he has no time for slipshod standards and vehemently opposes short-term expedients.

It was soon apparent to John that the only way pupils were going to secure a respectable level of attainment in Latin was for him to begin again from scratch. With gentle insistence, he tried to instil in every boy the habit of hard work, without which scholastic progress is unachievable. Combined with thorough preparation, punctilious marking of written work and the badgering of shirkers, his efforts slowly paid dividends. Achieving varying degrees of academic proficiency, in accordance with their abilities, John's pupils received a scrupulous grounding in all the subjects he taught.

He carried out administrative tasks with a precision and skill that nobody could fault. He rescued me from the ordeal of having to prepare the timetable, a commitment he undertook voluntarily for a quarter of a century. For many years John was my dependable right-hand man, but it was as housemaster responsible for the boarders that he gained most pleasure. Not having the distraction of a wife and family, he devoted the vast proportion of his waking moments to his chosen vocation. Never once did he begrudge the countless hours he spent on call during weekends and throughout each night. He fought vigorously to improve the boarders' comforts and recreational facilities and was a force to be reckoned with whenever I failed to remedy imperfections he exposed.

The school's rapid expansion caused me to reduce my own teaching programme. More and more of my time was spent in dealing with areas of work, in preparation for which I had received no training whatsoever. Public relations, finance and staff management were key functions that were essential for me to try to master. As the front man, it was my responsibility to fill empty beds and desks, in order to generate sufficient income to cover running costs, which included payment of interest on any loans and capital repayments. John Herbert's never-failing presence at the hub of things freed me to push paper, conduct interviews and attend meetings. It was greatly reassuring that he could be relied upon to direct day-to-day matters in my absence.

It took me some time to get to know John. His enigmatic reserve is hard to decipher and I must confess that initially I found his unapproachability quite daunting. Cautious in his judgement of others, John makes certain that those seeking his approval work hard to earn it. Once captured, his solid-as-a-rock allegiance is well worth having. For me to have harvested his lifelong trust is a gift I treasure.

My father had often warned me that once I assumed control of the school I would find it a lonesome path to follow. 'Be careful not to burden friends or staff with your problems,' he advised. 'One of the penalties of being the boss is that you aren't allowed to have your own worries: it's your job to solve other people's!'

I was so well practised in suppressing emotions and camouflaging my vulnerability that I duped observers into believing I was a hard-headed taskmaster, devoid of sensitivity. I thought it far better to be regarded as a cold fish than to manifest publicly a susceptibility that would be construed as weakness.

It took me some while to fathom John out; in consequence, our friendship developed cautiously. After my faith in his trustworthiness had been firmly rooted, I was able to discuss with him doubts and fears I would not have entrusted with any other colleague. John knew I was a depressive and that I suffered dramatic swings of mood. When pressures were driving me to the limits, my recovery to rationality was more than once restored through his flair for disentangling the seemingly insoluble.

There is one flaw in John's character. In common with other diligent members of the teaching profession, he suffered from 'end-of-term-itis', a debility ascribed to those who are prone to crabbiness and tetchy outbursts when tired and overwrought. Woe betide anyone who crossed him whilst he was afflicted with this malady. I owed it to him to show forbearance on the few occasions he allowed his fiery tongue to get the better of him. A reprimand would merely have exacerbated these incidents into full-blown rows. John's value to our frangible establishment was far too great, however, for me to risk the chance of losing him.

The humorous side of John's character is kept well hidden. Reserving his dry wit and ready sense of fun for his closest friends, he can be highly entertaining when the spirit moves him. He and I share a defect; we are irrepressible gigglers.

The first time that our giggling raised eyebrows was at a house music competition. A young violinist was treating the audience to an excruciatingly painful rendering of a familiar piece, with discordant squeaking and scraping sounds that offended the ears of those with the misfortune to be listening. When John and I caught each other's eyes, we were unable to control our levity. The more aware we became of the disapproving glances, the more flagrant were our giggles.

I was overwhelmed with embarrassment at school assemblies whenever John yielded to one of his giggling fits. The trouble was that we often saw a comic absurdness in situations that eluded the majority. This was all very well for John; he did not have to stand up and enunciate prayers, harangue, make pronouncements and pontificate before a pupil audience. As soon as I felt his big frame shaking uncontrollably beside me, the only way for me to conserve a semblance of dignity was to pinch my arm until it bled.

Once fortnightly, I conducted junior school assemblies, at which I read a story that I adapted to the comprehension level of the youngest children. There was one mortifying occasion during Lent when I chose temptation as my theme. My story was to have been preceded by the following introduction:

'This is the season of Lent, the name given to the six weeks before Easter when we remember how Jesus fasted in the wilderness and was tempted by the devil.'

Realising that many of the tinies would be unfamiliar with the word 'fasted', I planned to explain it meant eating and drinking enough to be kept alive and not a lot more. My mind was concentrating on the explanation of the meaning of 'fasted', which with an innocent slip of the tongue I mispronounced 'farted.' Some of the children tittered nervously; the lady teachers, despite exercising considerable self-restraint, could not contain their blushes. A more accomplished man would have made light of the gaffe and begun again. I ploughed on pompously, glaring icily at the sniggerers, determined to complete my spiel.

'Jesus had been in the wilderness for forty days,' I continued, 'and during that time he farted as he wrestled with great problems.'

To have made the blunder once was bad enough, but to have repeated the irreverent error was indefensible. It was as well that John was not there to witness my ineptitude, because if he had been, his ill-timed giggling would have finished me completely.

A staff upheaval occurred during John's second term with us. My father had not forgiven Tom Southam for failing to insure the borrowed props for the annual play when the complete set was destroyed by fire. Shortly after the fiasco, Tom was asked to move from his spacious upstairs bedroom to a poky basement alternative. He strongly resented being downgraded to poorer living conditions, presupposing quite wrongly, as it so happened, that this was due to vindictiveness on my father's part. Relations between the two men became more strained than ever.

Tom spent most evenings in a bar at the nearby Clarendon Hotel, where he incessantly bored fellow drinkers with complaints about his place of work. This was foolish of Tom because my father, too, frequented the Clarendon. Holding impassioned views on the subject of professional correctness, my father was outraged to learn that his senior master was flagrantly declaring his disaffection by casting aspersions on the school. With the intention of hauling Tom over the coals, my father summoned him to a meeting in his study.

'It has been reported to me that you are frequently heard to run the school down in the Clarendon Hotel and at a number of other places in the locality,' began my father. 'Are you able to deny this?'

'It is true I do talk a lot about Arnold Lodge, but I most certainly do not run the place down.'

'If you don't criticise the school in public, why would complete strangers tell me you are being openly disloyal?'

'I have no idea.'

'Isn't it time you explained to me what it is you object to here?'

'Any criticisms I may have implied are said with the intention of bringing about improvements.'

'Improvements, eh. It would be most interesting to know exactly what improvements you have in mind.'

'Ever since I joined the staff, I have known that something is wrong with your entire ethos. I can't put my finger on it, other than the regimentation and formality, the petty rules and regulations, none of which benefit the pupils in any way. The whole system is so archaic that it needs a thorough overhaul.'

'Now let me tell *you* something,' thundered my father. 'You've been a round peg in a square hole from the day you joined us. Has it never crossed your mind that the only problem here is you?'

Constructive dismissal or not, Tom had, in effect, been given his marching orders. Soon after the altercation, he attended an interview at a school whose identity he refused to divulge, lest my father attempted to queer his pitch with an unfavourable testimonial. Returning in exultant mood, he gleefully announced that the job was his. He enthused so much over the merits of his future school that his colleagues were made to feel quite envious. My concern was that Tom's departure to pastures greener might unsettle John Herbert sufficiently for him to want to reconsider his own employment plans.

The question as to which of us should succeed Tom as senior master was a sensitive one. John Wightman, who had given staunch support during his six years' service, was too old to be considered. It was nepotism at its very worst when my father appointed me. The way in which John Herbert was going to react to the news mattered more to me than the doubts of cynical dissenters. Implying an apology, I asked John: 'Do you think it's wise that I've been chosen?' With accustomed bluntness he replied: 'I'm sure you'll cope; there's no one else!'

John may have damned me with faint praise, but it was enough to show me that I had his backing.

A keep-fit fanatic, John Wightman was in fine physical shape for a man of seventy. Rising at crack of dawn, he worked long hours and with a tireless energy that outpaced the stamina of many younger than himself. The accident took place during one of his brisk evening strolls. Colliding with a lamppost, John was so badly concussed that it was with the greatest difficulty that he was able to make the short journey back to the school. He was ordered to bed by the doctor, who said that under no circumstances was he to attempt to get up until the dizziness and blurred vision had subsided.

Notwithstanding my mother's protests, John insisted next morning on resuming his normal programme. Apart from feeling bruised and battered, he assured her that his recovery was complete. With only one more rehearsal before the end of term concert, the thought of his incarceration in the sickbay was inadmissible to John.

Shortly after the concert, John complained of a headache and nausea. The intensity of the headaches increased to such an extent that he soon lay languishing in a hospital bed. A ruptured artery in the main mass of his brain caused him to describe his torment with surprising eloquence. 'There's a ball of fire exploding in my head,' he wailed repeatedly. The suffering he endured became so traumatic and the damage so pervasive that those of us who cared deeply for John were relieved when finally he died. A fastidious, self-respecting person, he would never have come to terms with being a dependant had the stroke left him vegetable-like, para-lysed, confused and incoherent.

This was my first ever encounter with the ending of a life. The speed with which it happened caused me, after years of preclusion of the gruesome topic from my thoughts, to submit to life's impermanence and the inescapability of death.

At a moving memorial service, particular reference was made to John's fortitude. Michael Griffith, our parish curate, and coincidentally a friend of John's family, is quoted from his address as saying: 'That he was not lacking in courage is revealed by the fact that he won the Military Cross in the First World War. He showed courage of another and perhaps greater kind, when after twenty years of service in the education of Egyptian and other boys, he was turned out of Egypt, with the loss of all his money and worldly goods and had, as it were, to start again.'

A fund was set up in recognition of John's service to the school, as a result of which prizes are awarded annually in his memory.

It was two days after John Wightman's memorial service that my father was struck down with his heart attack. The breathlessness had become more noticeable of late and mother-in-law concerns had added to his problems. For eleven years with saint-like patience he had put up with Grandmother's cantankerous presence in our household. Her self-seeking dominance had disrupted our lives so much that everything we wanted to arrange depended on her say-so. On the few occasions that my parents planned a holiday, she insisted on being there with them. Managing to conceal the resentment he must have felt, my father was far less skilled at containing the stress than he was at noble posturing.

When he succumbed to the life-threatening illness, it would not have been possible to imagine a more horrific opening to the summer term. I had begun to come to terms with the fact that as transients we dwell on earth with a short-term lease, the expiry date to be determined by mystical forces that are beyond our reasoning. The only control we could exercise over my father's future, if he had a future, was to relieve him of his everyday cares as best we could.

The most pressing need was to rearrange the timetable, so as to cover the teaching he had undertaken. As a temporary expedient, an old boy of the school had been taken on to fill in some of the gaps that had been created by John Wightman's death. Former public school science teacher, Alan Wilson-Jones, an elderly eccentric, affectionately known as Willy Bones, increased his teaching quota to provide for the arithmetic and algebra. Brushing up on my negligible mathematical skills, it fell upon me to deal with the geometry. It was all very amateurish. Amateurism reached its peak, however, when, in the spirit of a Laurel and Hardy movie, John Herbert and I presided over the weekly singing lessons. John strummed on the piano, whilst I conducted and enjoined the songsters with boisterous energy.

The way in which I was hoodwinked into appointing a dissolute schoolmaster to take over the mathematics from my father underlined the need for me to learn from my mistakes. In my defence, though, it must be explained that mathematicians were hard to come by and I was well aware that able teachers of the subject would find little of appeal in any contract I was able to offer them.

Response to advertisements for suitable staff members had again been disappointing. I finally interviewed a sprightly man in his late middle years by the name of Sewell, who was, so he said, a nephew of Anna Sewell of *Black Beauty* fame. He stated in his curriculum vitae that he was forty-nine, although he admitted that life's knocks had given him the appearance of a man of sixty. He was wiry, pale faced, with short, spiky, greying hair. Smooth-tongued and highly intelligent, he had for many years been head of mathematics at Farnborough Grammar School in Hampshire. For fear of losing this chance to appoint a man who epitomised excellence, I struck whilst the iron was hot and succeeded in procuring his acceptance.

I was foolish not to question why a seasoned professional would choose to move from a secure post with status to a struggling prep school. It is to my eternal discredit that I failed to contact any of Mr Sewell's referees or to scrutinise his ante-cedence. By engaging him with nothing more concrete with which to sustain my judgement than an exiguous instinct was a risk I never should have taken.

On the wall of his bed-sitting room Mr Sewell hung an enor-mous oil painting of himself that portrayed his well-groomed person draped in scarlet finery. He invited me to study the picture, knowing I could not fail to admire the distinctive academic gown that enveloped him, a gown that is only worn by those on whom has been conferred the highest degree awarded by a University.

'Had you known I was a PhD,' he remarked audaciously, 'you would never have appointed me!'

Thereafter we accorded Mr Sewell the title of Doctor, which we later abbreviated to Doc. At the very least, Doc's noteworthy qualifications added tone and status to our list of staff.

It was soon apparent that Doc was addicted to alcohol. His partiality for brandy caused him to spend most of his off-duty moments in a pub. What was surprising was that his mind retained its razor-sharp alertness, even after he had been drinking heavily. Intellectual conceit and a wicked sarcasm were features of his character that were greatly magnified whenever he was drunk, traits that in no way endeared him to his colleagues. As far as I could judge, Doc's ability to cope in the classroom was not affected unduly by his intemperate habits. Treating his teaching commitments with a shallow indifference, however, he showed minimal concern for the progress of his pupils.

Aware that Doc's appointment was likely to prove disastrous, I decided to ask his previous headmaster for a belated reference. My fears had indeed been justified. After a number of unseemly incidents, the root cause of which was his habitual drinking, he had been dismissed from Farnborough Grammar School five years before reaching the retirement age of sixty-five. He had not only lied about his age at the interview, but had also given me a distressing account of a broken marriage. Depicting himself as the henpecked, misunderstood husband, he had managed to evoke my sympathy. As soon as it had been confirmed that Doc was an unscrupulous degenerate, I should have sacked him on the spot. Instead, I adopted a 'wait and see' policy, in the naive hope he would attempt to mend his habits.

The further decline of Doc was more dramatic. Apart from his drinking, his next most urgent need was to find a woman. He met a widow ten years his senior by the name of Dorothy Palin, who managed a local confectioner's business. She offered the attraction of her own private bar in the flat above the shop. Doc was in his element after this stroke of good fortune and in next to no time the couple were engaged. They went abroad for their honeymoon. From some idyllic spot in Italy I received a postcard on which Doc had written the rhapsodic message: 'Blissfully happy'.

By the time the lovebirds had returned to England, the marriage was over. Doc begged me to provide him once again with a roof over his head; all I was able to supply was a room barely large enough to hold a bed.

During the early stages of the couple's separation, Mrs Sewell reverted to her previous name and, when in communication with Doc, signed herself D Palin. Doc found her formal abruptness hilariously funny.

In her desire for an instant divorce on the grounds that the marriage had not been consummated, Mrs Sewell employed a

Leamington firm of solicitors, Wright Hassall, to act on her behalf. Doc approached me one day, armed with a copy of a letter sent by Wright Hassall to his solicitors. 'Right Arseholes have informed me that their client is demanding a divorce on account of my wilful refusal,' he chortled. 'Nothing would have induced me to make love to that repulsive woman!'

Despite having been at least twice bitten, Doc was never shy. Through a dating agency he captured the heart of a replacement lady, who this time was less than half his age. Because she was still married she changed her name by deed poll and the two of them set up home together in rented accommodation quite near to the school. Doc's debts were mounting, his reputation as a drinker was now commonly known and pupils' parents were complaining about the poor quality of his teaching. After two years on the staff I gave Doc a term's notice to leave our employment.

Doc was soon successful in obtaining a post overseas. He and his common-law wife set off for new horizons. There was adverse publicity, two years later, when it was reported that Doc had pleaded guilty to charges of indecently assaulting a thirteen-year-old French boy at Bracklesham Bay in Sussex. He had also taken indecent photographs of the boy, who was so frightened that he had sought help from his father in Paris. Doc was fined one hundred pounds and was lucky not to go to prison. At a court hearing in mitigation he claimed that 'difficult domestic circumstances' had caused a lapse in his otherwise exemplary professional record. And later still, by which time he must have been over seventy, he was known to have been teaching under the name of Dr Byrne at Winterfold House, a Roman Catholic boarding preparatory school tucked away in the heart of the Worcestershire countryside. I never did discover what became of Doc after that!

Service industries have always been labour-intensive. The reputation of a school such as ours reflects the qualities of its bursar, secretaries, caretaker, cleaners, matrons, caterers and dinner ladies, outdoor and maintenance staff, as well as the many teachers and peripatetic specialists. Having made a pig's ear of my first key appointment, it was essential for me to reject impulsive tendencies, in favour of analysing all future employment applications with due vigilance.

My parents had lived a shoestring existence ever since their arrival in Leamington. Lack of money continued to hamper the school's progress throughout the three years that followed my succession as headmaster. The only staff of merit I was able to appoint during this period were those who were rash enough to place reliance in my optimism. What was uncanny was that I somehow knew my aspirations for Arnold Lodge would be fulfilled one day, a belief that deserted me but rarely.

Work-shy teachers, tempted by the smaller classes and lack of accountability within the private sector, were often prepared to accept a lower wage in exchange for what they hoped would prove to be the softest of options. For this reason, standards of competence among teachers in independent schools varied more than with most other sections of the country's workforce. I was never going to succeed in attracting top-flight applicants until I was in a position to offer all my teachers the same basic salaries and conditions as their state school counterparts.

By January 1969 pupil numbers had doubled in the space of six years and now totalled two hundred, forty-five of them boarders. My bank manager approved the business plan I had drawn up, with the result that a medium-term loan enabled a new gymnasium and classroom block to be built. The acquisition and renovation of a large adjoining property provided the scope for further expansion. I was by this time sufficiently confident of our financial stability to apply for the school to participate in the government teachers' superannuation scheme, an action that facilitated staff recruitment markedly.

I planned to go much further than this. In order to recognise the exceptional input made by certain teachers and indispensable administrators, I awarded occasional bonuses, whilst departmental heads were paid responsibility allowances. I never went overboard with my generosity, but nobody could accuse me of being niggardly. Those who worked for me knew they would receive their salary entitlements on time and in full, no matter what. Shallow popularity was not what I was after. What mattered was that, if I were to earn the respect of my employees, it needed to be because they could rely on me to render them fair dealings.

The upgrading of residential staff accommodation was another priority. I provided within the school complex a number of self-contained flats and some decent-sized quarters with conveniently placed bathroom and kitchen facilities. Eventually nine such units were in occupation. No rental charge was imposed, my philosophy being that the school community as a whole benefited by our having a number of committed professionals living and working on the campus.

Open-handedness was taken too far, however, when I purchased a house, together with the furniture, for a newly appointed mathematics master and his family. When it came to light that he had been selling some of the furniture to finance his drunken exploits, he finally made off, leaving behind a surly wife and his four children. For the period of two years I received no rent from my sitting tenant and it was not until the house was sold at a deflated price that the problem was resolved.

Another benefit in kind was the substantial fee reduction I offered for staff children. Teachers who opted to participate in the scheme were asked to pay only ten per cent of the consolidated fee, which covered the cost of all the books and meals that were provided. After a battle with the Inland Revenue, it was agreed that, since the school was suffering no more than a notional loss of income, the concession would not incur recipients with taxation on the benefit.

I can understand exactly what my father meant about not being able to handle his staff. Teachers are a law unto themselves, believing as they do that the world owes them a living. Some of the most prized teachers I have ever employed, aware that their special talents were central to the school's success, were capable of using this knowledge as a blackmail tool for their own advancement.

Had I adopted a tougher stance over employment matters, there is no doubt that the turnover of staff would have increased appreciably. For the most part, I chose to tolerate the barrack-room lawyers, the empire-builders, the puffed-up bigots, the prima donnas and garrulous time-wasters, on condition that their value to the school outweighed the negative effects of their irritations and deficiencies. Those who possessed no saving grace whatever were expeditiously removed.

Wedding Bells

Back from Nice, Stella and I met as often as was possible. So important to me was this newly acquired friendship that I could not conceive the emptiness of a life in which Stella played no part. I worked late into the night on weekdays so as to merit time off on the occasions we were free to meet. She sometimes came to stay with me in Leamington and when not on duty at school at weekends I would go to see her in Twickenham.

It delighted me that Stella adapted so easily to the role of partnering a zealous schoolmaster. Her brief encounters with some of my pupils emphasised an easy charm that complemented my less relaxed demeanour. As well as the obvious physical and emotional attractions, she possessed essential wifely qualities. I was convinced it was only a matter of time before we would be engaged.

Booking into a cheap hotel whenever I visited Stella, I waited in vain to be invited to stay overnight in the flat she was borrowing from her parents. She was a well brought-up young lady, whose mother's trust in her was absolute. A tactile person, Stella unwittingly gave out seductive signals, arousing within me ungentlemanly instincts. She had not so far allowed us to progress beyond the bounds of basic foreplay, even though I sensed she yearned for the sexual release that was vetoed by her strict Greek influences.

One Saturday, I had to make do with a dismal lodging house in Richmond that catered for the elderly. Poor ventilation, the stench of urine, degenerating bodies and overcooked vegetables gave me first-hand experience of what it would be like to reside in a sub-standard old people's home. It was not unreasonable to hope that, taking pity on me, Stella would offer the attractive alternative of allowing me to share her bed.

The afternoon was agreeably spent in Richmond Park. We spoke of our plans and secret longings; not once did conversation falter. An accomplished cook, Stella prepared an intimate and palatable supper by candlelight. Romance dominated our thoughts as we braced ourselves for the lascivious awakening we had dreamt of in our imaginings. There was no doubting I was helplessly besotted with her. Lying beside the fire in the darkened living room, clasping each other tightly, we caressed and tormented, exploring the undiscovered regions with a wanton eagerness that convinced me that this time Stella would surrender her virginity. Encouraged by her seeming desire to acquiesce, I poised myself for the ultimate discovery.

'You are to stop right now,' she ordered, shattering my hopes of attaining the zenith of true manhood. Forced to desist when on the brink, it was with much self-restraint I prevented pent-up passions from erupting.

'You're nothing but a prick-teaser,' I slated her angrily. 'Why bother to lead me on if you haven't the guts to see it through?'

'I have *never* tried to lead you on. I'm a hot-blooded Greek girl with natural inclinations. I will give myself to you in time; it is pointless for you to attempt to rush me.'

Stella's calmness infuriated me. At the crucial moment, it was of little consolation to be told that maybe one day she would deign to permit me to make love to her. Would I have to wait days, weeks, months, even years or was betrothal a requirement? I was not sure I had the patience to endure the uncertainty much longer.

Convinced that the high moral code instilled by her continental background was the reason Stella had been holding back, I contrived a compromise solution. By occupying her spare bedroom I would escape the horrors of the geriatrics' boarding house, whilst not doing the indecent thing of sleeping with her. In the hours of darkness when the flesh is at its weakest, there remained the slenderest of hopes she would dispense with inhibitions in an amorous rapprochement.

'Do I really have to leave your nice warm flat to go back to that miserable boarding house?' I asked.

'We've gone over this already. You know why you can't stay here.'

269

'I'm not asking to *sleep* with you. It's just that it seems daft for me to have to stay in a smelly dosshouse when there's a second bedroom here.'

'You're not going to stay here. And that's final.'

Patent lack of judgement caused me to think Stella was over-doing her self-righteous attitude simply because it was the ladylike custom expected of her. I did not for a moment believe she was as resolute as appearances suggested. These misconceptions led me to behave in a way that was entirely out of character.

'I fail to see what harm it will do if I sleep in your spare room. I'll keep the door unlocked in case you want to join me,' I said presumptuously.

'I thought you were a man I could trust and look up to. You're destroying what I thought we'd got, something that was precious. Stay the night here if you wish, but if you do we're finished.'

Had I seriously believed that Stella meant what she said, I would have returned to the Richmond boarding house without a murmur. Instead, I stubbornly abused her wishes. Confident that the affinity with which we had been blessed stemmed from the surest of foundations, I felt empowered to test the limits of her constancy. Oedipus-like, I expected her to pamper me as a mother would her offspring, to absolve mistakes, to condone my senseless actions.

At breakfast next morning, Stella suffered my presence with a sullen frostiness I took to be the reprimand that undoubtedly was warranted. An hour later she was behaving towards me in much the same way as she had always done. Taking the softening of her mood to mean I had been forgiven, I began again to conjure up thoughts of the contented future I was still quite certain was predestined for us. Smiling radiantly and after an embrace no less profuse than all the others, she waved a jovial farewell as I began the evening drive to Leamington.

For some weeks a telephone conversation with Stella had been a daily ritual.

'How's things?' I asked when next we spoke.

'I've had a busy day at the college; apart from that, nothing much has happened.'

'I'm free the weekend after next to come to Twickenham.'

'No, you're not, *not* to visit *me*! I made it clear I would end the relationship if you insisted on staying in my flat. I am *not* going to see you again. Not *ever*.'

'Surely you don't mean it. I did apologise and thought you'd given me a second chance.'

'I've lost the respect I had for you. I do not wish to speak to you or meet with you again. To ring me is a waste of time. It's over!'

The line clicked dead, followed by a melancholy silence that seemed interminable. Stella's harsh words had in one breath erased all hopes of condonation.

Deprival of Stella caused an insufferable despair to smother me with blackness. I looked back with feelings of remorse at the corroded happiness, the squandered opportunities. Debilitated by low morale and overwork, I retired to bed with an attack of influenza. Two unexpected happenings helped to annul the effects of the depression. One concerned a tempting offer; the other was the arrival of a get well card from an unrevealed admirer.

The front of the card pictured a fluffy kitten. The wording bolstered my spirits with the comforting disclosure I had gained a friend.

> Sorry to hear you've been unwell. Hope you will soon be better.
> Love
> Pussy

No matter how hard I racked my brains, I was unable to detect the identity of my feline sympathiser.

The tempting offer was made during an unforeseen telephone conversation with a Leicester bandleader.

'This is Dick Jones, a fellow teacher,' announced the caller. 'Robert Godfrey, an Exeter student chum of yours, tells me you blow a cool clarinet. How would you like to join my band?'

'I haven't had a blow in ages; in fact, I'm so rusty my lip wouldn't last out for more than a few minutes.'

'Daily practice would soon remedy that.'

'I just don't have the time.'

'From what I hear you're the kind of guy that relishes a challenge. You'd lose nothing by sitting in for just one evening.'

'I can't believe you'd want to risk hiring someone you've never heard play.'

'Relax, man! We're not booked for the Albert Hall. Bob's recommendation is more than enough for me.'

Dick went on to explain he had led a popular mainstream jazz outfit in London before moving to the Midlands to become head of physical education at a Leicester comprehensive school.

'I play trumpet,' he continued. 'The rhythm section's as solid as a rock and you'll be riveted by the trombone playing. All I need is a clarinettist. What about it?'

School work was taking pride of place over everything; for this reason, I had never considered making a musical comeback. Dick's powers of persuasion succeeded in weakening my defences, but it was his inexhaustible enthusiasm that brought home to me how much I missed being part of the jazz scene. With conflicting feelings oscillating between euphoria and panic, I agreed as a trial run to perform a gig with the band at a Leicester nightspot.

Dark haired and with the sturdy build of a rugby player, Dick was in his early thirties. We met in the bar of a squalid dance hall on the first floor of a city-centre building. After he had introduced me to the other musicians, he led us on to the stage to kick off with the inaugural number. Dick blew his horn with dazzling competence. The potent thrust of his playing and the fervour of his leadership inspired the five 'session men' to emulate his dexterous musicianship. Swinging with startling accord, there was nothing wrong with the more uneven elements of the band's performance that could not have been put right by disciplined rehearsal. Given expert management, the Dick Jones Band was capable of making a name for itself on the national circuit.

In common with many jazz musicians, I deluded myself into thinking the quality of my playing was enhanced whenever I had a skinful. I drank heavily that first night in Leicester and very nearly fell asleep at the wheel of my car on the homeward journey. Leicester was a long way to travel to a gig before the M69 was established. After three such excursions, it was evident that burning the midnight oil was already interfering with my teaching. A worse scenario was that my strawberry-jam remains were in danger of being scraped off some godforsaken highway on the way back to Leamington.

An exuberant Dick telephoned to confirm the arrangements for a gig in Nottingham.

'The band's going down a bomb,' he exclaimed excitedly. 'We've got bookings in Sheffield and Cardiff, with the possibility of London. My head will loan us the school hall for practice sessions on evenings when it's vacant. Once we've ironed out all the flaws the recordings are showing up, I'm going to pack up teaching to be a full-time pro. If you decide to throw in your lot with us, I know you'll not regret it!'

I would be telling a downright lie if I said the idea of freeing myself from the shackles of the family school had no appeal. Parental pressures were such that it was out of the question for me to be allowed the luxury of a choice. There was nothing for it other than for me to erase all thoughts of becoming a professional jazzman.

A not dissimilar opportunity had come my way a year earlier. Ray Lawrence, my drum tutor of days gone by, was building a successful dance band empire that was acclaimed throughout the Midlands. On busy evenings, he managed up to half a dozen bands, travelling as far afield as Scotland. Serving a wide-ranging clientele, it was his high-class contacts whose patronage he valued most. Without wishing to reduce his bread-and-butter work, Ray decided to expand the scope of the services offered to his most important clients, among whom were the Duke of Kent and other members of the aristocracy. He asked me to front a band that was to cater solely for society weddings, country house parties and the like, believing that, as a public school product, I would add a cultivated charm to the events. Little did Ray know that I was embarrassingly sheepish when mixing with the ruling classes, which is why I found it easy to decline.

'Pussy', my mysterious well-wisher, turned out to be Elizabeth, the girl with whom I had struck up an instant amity at a cocktail party some months earlier. After a spell working in London, she was now living in Warwick with her mother and stepfather. Greatly flattered that a young woman of such elegance should concern herself with my welfare, I was surprised how quickly my injured spirits healed.

Ever since our first meeting, I had been fascinated by Elizabeth's untouchable aloofness. I suspected her refined veneer obscured a complex character. To be able to discover what lay behind her inscrutability, I could see it was going to require a long, hard effort before I made much headway.

Not wishing to put all my eggs in one basket, I decided to fight shy of forming an exclusive attachment so soon after the Stella disappointment. Much as I wanted to develop the friendship with Elizabeth, I adopted a safety-in-numbers policy. I also met Susan, a light-hearted girl, who never failed to be a bubbly companion. As a free agent, I was able to ask out other females, as and when the spirit moved me. The world was my oyster and, as far as matters of the heart were concerned, I was answerable only to my conscience.

The Arnold Lodge Ball whose organisation I had handled on my own for the last four years was to be held in six weeks' time, on 5 January. The advantage of being answerable to nobody other than myself was that, not only was it a more productive use of labour, it short-circuited a variety of pitfalls.

Two bands had been booked twelve months in advance and, by September, announcement letters had been dispatched to all the old boys and parents of current pupils. My public relations objective was to try to build in people's minds the perception of Arnold Lodge as a thriving, forward-looking, à la mode establishment, with which it was desirable to be associated. The fact that the reality could not have been further from the truth was a state of affairs I hoped would soon be remedied.

The ball was advertised on a lavish scale, considering the less bold marketing approaches of the 1960s. Clad in their striking maroon caps and blazers, my boy volunteers helped me distribute hundreds of display posters to shops, cinemas, libraries, hotels, pubs and restaurants throughout the district. By the time our mission was completed, we must have entered every shop of any consequence in the towns of Leamington, Warwick, Kenilworth and Stratford.

It defies belief that the promotion of the event, on which so much time and energy had been expended, should escape the attention of any other than the truly blinkered. If our efforts succeeded in increasing the number of tickets sold, so much the better; what mattered more was that people with no previous knowledge of the school should recognise its name in future. These were pioneering days that required inventive methods. The drip-feed publicising of the school's virtues to the local populace made little impression as a short-term measure, but the policy was to pay dividends in the years ahead.

For all the razzle-dazzle that accompanied the ball's publicity, the occasion was nothing more than a pretentious 'hop' at which the men togged themselves up in dinner jackets and the women in long dresses. For an admission fee of twelve shillings and sixpence, strict tempo dance music was to be provided by Ray Lawrence in person with his Grosvenor Orchestra, which would make way for a traditional jazz band during the forty-minute interval.

Buying drinks at the bar was always something of a scrummage; despite this shortcoming, we generally succeeded in getting large quantities of alcohol to our tables. What was extraordinary was the more we drank the better we danced; by the time we were in our cups the quality of our footwork was stupendous. Excitement would once again reach fever pitch when the balloons drifted down in colourful splendour onto the dance floor after the singing of 'Auld Lang Syne'. For two frenzied minutes we would fight for, tear at, stamp on and sit upon the inflated balls with greater aggression than at the most out-of-hand children's party.

For the two weeks preceding the ball I thought of little else. Boring the pants off everyone, I gave my listeners an elaborate account of what I had laid on for their benefit. Many were bullied into buying a ticket; those who did not suffered the excruciating experience of being bombarded with a blow-by-blow version of my plans for the next extravaganza. I had no qualms whatever in using every means at my disposal to trumpet the glad tidings to the whole of Warwickshire.

I had been getting on so well with Elizabeth and Susan that the dilemma of not knowing who to invite as my partner presented me with a problem. Unable to make a decision, I was relieved to discover an extra female was needed to make up the numbers in my party. Heavy snowfalls on the day itself caused road conditions to be treacherous. As Susan lived some miles away in an isolated area, my parents thought it better to offer her a bed for the night than risk my having to drive her home on icy roads after the jollifications were over. I gave Susan's mother my personal assurance that I would take good care of her daughter and would get her back safely in the morning. Through this stroke of chance, it fell upon the spare man in our group to act as Elizabeth's escort.

Distanced by so many years, much of what happened at the ball has long since been extinguished from my memory. Crystal clear, however, are my recollections of the contrasting attitudes assumed by Elizabeth and Susan that same evening. It told me a great deal about their characters and of my own confused emotions.

On the occasions I had taken Susan out, her geniality expressed itself in ways that always left me happy and contented. Pleasing to the eye rather than beautiful, her sparkling smile radiated warmth and kindliness. The product of a stable home, she was fun loving, straightforward and dependable.

In no way was Elizabeth a humdrum person. During her childhood the family had enjoyed an opulent lifestyle in a fashionable London neighbourhood, mixing with the rich and talented. What had been a stormy marriage came to an end when her German mother divorced her husband, leaving Elizabeth and her brother, Ian, in a state of bewilderment and shock. Matters worsened after her mother remarried; her second husband, Josef Unger, a German Jew, regarded his newly acquired stepchildren as nothing more than nuisances. Bitter and resentful, Elizabeth felt she had been let down by the ones she loved.

Susan was an engaging ball companion, whose good-natured friendliness was infectious. A social asset in every sense, there was nothing about her conduct that could have caused offence. Whether dancing or hobnobbing in her usual friendly manner, she participated with ebullient good humour and a gleeful twinkle in her eyes.

Elizabeth's escort waited on her attentively, exuding an ingratiating charm that for some strange reason angered me. Far from responding to his displays of affability, Elizabeth was in no mood to socialise; in sullen silence, she watched my every movement with hawk-like scrutiny. Registering her displeasure by sabotaging the enjoyment of the other guests, she remained distant and morose. Then suddenly I desired Elizabeth with a burning passion that was eating out my heart. For all her spoilt-brat tendencies, underneath there was a sensual, loving, desperately unhappy girl. I wanted to be her knight in shining armour, to recast the doleful face of this Mona Lisa replica.

'Susan's a delightful girl,' my mother ventured breezily. 'She'll make someone a lovely wife, the kind of girl I'd have liked as a daughter, appreciative, well mannered, a contented, chirpy soul.'

Motivated by her desire to eliminate Elizabeth as a competitor for my affections, my mother stressed Susan's attributes with an earnestness that gave the game away. Her attempts to influence my judgement reinforced a stubborn longing on my part to become better acquainted with Elizabeth, irrespective of the minefields that were bound to block our way.

I was determined not to scare Elizabeth off by making the same mistake that had caused Stella to abandon me. By allowing the friendship to develop at an unhurried pace, I hoped in the fullness of time to be able to piece together some of the fragmented elements of her puzzling background.

Relieved that Elizabeth was beginning to relax in my company, I felt able to be more intrusive with my questioning.

'What caused your parents to split up?' I enquired.

'My father was incredibly ambitious. His Scottish canniness and Italian recklessness produced a dangerous combination. He was very successful for a time, but when he became greedy and began taking risks, the world fell apart and we lost everything. You learn who your friends are at such times; most of ours ran away and hid. It was a bitter pill to have to swallow, especially for my mother. She never took any interest in my father's business dealings, providing the bills were paid. It never occurred to her there was ever any question of his going bust.'

'So the financial collapse led to the divorce?'

'Not exactly, but it did have a bearing on what happened. My parents had little in common, a problem that was compounded by the large gap in their ages. They were always quarrelling.'

'At what point did your stepfather meet your mother?'

'He didn't break the marriage up, if that's what you mean.'

'Am I right in thinking he's a lawyer?'

'Although he qualified as a lawyer in Heidelberg he's now an academic, professor of International law at Birmingham University. After fleeing from Germany to escape the Nazis, he had to read law all over again in London. Give him his due, he's worked hard and done very well for himself. Living under his roof is quite another matter; he rules the household like a Victorian tyrant, which is why my brother, Ian, hardly ever visits.'

Instinct told me that what I had heard from Elizabeth so far was a mere drop in the ocean, compared with other more shocking revelations that would follow. It was vital for her to be able to unburden herself as part of the cathartic process.

It is clear from my father's detailed diary entries that he kept tabs on my social activities with a precision I would never have imagined. Meetings with Elizabeth during the weeks following the ball were by no means frequent. The friendship continued to develop nevertheless in an atmosphere of magnanimity and trust that brought pleasure to the two of us. Concerned though I was about Elizabeth's emotional hang-ups, we had no plans to tie the knot, neither were there interfering influences to hinder the natural flow of the relationship. All that changed when we found ourselves in the midst of a most bizarre drama, a drama which was to alter irrevocably the pattern of our lives.

Never before had Elizabeth looked so downcast, pale and disconnected. It is true she often seemed flustered and anxious, but on that fateful February evening her strained eyes bore signs of an indifference that was baffling and distressing. Arriving at her home to take her out to dinner, I was about to ring the front doorbell when Elizabeth, who had been waiting in the darkened hallway, crept out furtively.

By the time we had seated ourselves in a modest eating place just round the corner, she could contain herself no longer.

'My stepfather has threatened to throw me out of the house, unless I stop seeing you,' she said with a cold dismissiveness that was quite unnerving.

'You can't be serious. I'm sure his only motive is to harass you.'

'I promise you he means every word of it. Whenever he has an obsession, he's far too stubborn to admit he's wrong and carries out any threats he makes, regardless of the consequences. Believe you me, if I don't obey his wishes, I'll be out on the street, bags and all, first thing tomorrow morning.'

'The man must be a nutcase. He's behaving like an autocratic potentate way back in the Middle Ages. Who the hell does he think he is? What on earth can I possibly have done to have caused him to hate me with such venom?'

'He's been ranting and raging these last few weeks whenever your name is mentioned. He's got it into his head you're a male prostitute and a provincial snob and says I'm not to associate with you any longer.'

'That's outrageous. I would have thought a trained lawyer would know better than to make false accusations about someone he doesn't even know. I'll have him up for slander. He must have a crush on you or something. Once I'm removed from the scene, he'll have you to himself; I'm sure that's what he's after. What other explanation *can* there be?'

'It certainly isn't that; he doesn't even like me. He sees the situation as a good excuse to get shot of me for ever. After I'm gone, he can get on with living his life in the way he wishes, without having constant reminders of my mother's former marriage.'

'It's absolutely scandalous. You can't give in to his selfish demands, you really mustn't. Doesn't your mother have a say?'

'She has no option but to go along with what he wants. My stepfather is the boss and she knows there's nothing she can do about it. I'm not going to allow him to dictate to me who I can or cannot see, so there's no alternative other than for me to return to London and get a job. We can keep in touch and meet discreetly.'

It was not until some weeks later that I discovered what Elizabeth's stepfather was getting at when he described me as a 'male prostitute and provincial snob'. I had met him only briefly before Christmas at a party in Warwick at which Elizabeth was helping to serve the drinks. Accompanying me as my partner had been Louise, a journalist from Stratford. Louise and I were no more than the vaguest of acquaintances, which made Professor Unger's extraordinary accusations the more astonishing. He was scandalised to think I had the gall to be seen in public with another female, having taken out his stepdaughter in the past. Free to come and go with whomsoever I wished, I had no intention of making an emotional commitment at this stage. Nobody had the right, least of all the intolerant professor, to prescribe or veto my choice of friends.

The final outrage, as far as Professor Unger was concerned, was when he thought he had caught me in the act of committing yet another indiscretion, this time at Leamington railway station. I had been awaiting the arrival on a train from Paddington of Maria, a young Dutch girl, who was about to commence a six-month contract working as a domestic at the school. Hard though it would have been to have orchestrated a more innocuous happening, Elizabeth's stepfather once again jumped to the wildest of conclusions, dubbing me a philanderer of the vilest order. What infuriated him even more was that I failed to acknowledge him as he passed me on the platform. Guilty I most certainly was of failing to recognise him, whereas the imputation I had ignored him had not a grain of truth. My birth and upbringing were as provincial as they come; snobbishness, however, has never been a failing of which I can with any fairness be deemed culpable.

As anticipated, Elizabeth was thrown out of the house by her stepfather the morning after our surreptitious meal together. She removed herself post-haste to London, where she took up residence in a flat in Belgravia and quickly found a job. Horrified to think I had been the cause of her unhappy state, my protective instincts were aroused towards her in a way that was beginning to amount to love. If there is a lesson to be learnt by parents, it is that there is no better way of drawing two young people together than by forcing them apart. Professor Unger's grim action was soon to bring about the opposite effect to what he had intended.

From now on Elizabeth and I communicated daily. She was allowed the dispensation of an intermittent weekend home in Warwick, on which occasions we met in secret. One Saturday in the middle of March, the inevitable happened, validated by the following memorandum in my father's diary: 'Jonathan took Elizabeth out to lunch and for the rest of the day. He later announced his engagement to her and we are delighted with his choice.' What my parents did not know was that our decision to get married was little more than a gesture of defiance. The spiritual obligations and the compatibility issue were vital matters we had yet to contemplate.

Three weeks previously Elizabeth had attained the age of twenty-one. Realising there was nothing further he could do to prevent her from marrying, her stepfather accepted the decision with cynical ill will. My future in-laws invited my parents for a drink one evening, an invitation that characteristically excluded me. I gleaned little as to what form the discussions took, except that Professor Unger was keen to quiz my parents about my educational background. Discovery that I was a trained teacher with no university degree must have come as music to his ears. I can well imagine how he would have waxed eloquent on the subject of his most hated adversary to his highfalutin' friends.

'Elizabeth has met an arrogant upstart and is foolish enough to have agreed to marry him. She'll rue the day, because it's not a hope in hell of lasting. Every time I set eyes on the bounder, he's with a different woman. Not only is he a male prostitute, he's a provincial snob as well. And do you know what? He does not have the wit to have gained a university degree. All he has achieved after the large sums of money spent on his education is a certificate from a teacher training college I've never even heard of. He's helping his father run a tinpot school in Leamington, with no prospects for his future betterment.'

Professor Unger's curfew was lifted to the extent of allowing me to go out with his stepdaughter once the engagement was official. Never to be forgotten is the occasion her mother had the temerity to invite me inside the house; on seeing me there, her husband, who looked as if he was about to burst a blood vessel, proceeded to crush his wife against a wall whilst in the process of ejecting me with monstrous savagery out onto the pavement. His appalling temper also gave rise to notoriety at the university, where he was known to have terrorised a number of his students. I wondered what could possibly have caused a man with such intellectual merits to behave so brutishly.

The wedding was to take place on the last Saturday in August. Multifarious arrangements had to be made, the most pressing of which was our need to find a place to live. Concerning ourselves overmuch with practicalities, Elizabeth and I spent remarkably little time analysing what each expected of the other in our married life together. Deficient of the maturity to make a go of it, we were naive enough to see in our chosen partner an escape route to a better way of life. So we trundled on regardless, anticipating a heaven-sent union, ignorant that unselfishness was the cardinal component required for bringing this about.

The day before the wedding, I went to see Elizabeth's step-father in the hope I might be able to explain some of the misunderstandings which had caused so many heartaches in the past. I rang the bell of the tastefully renovated former shop in the centre of Warwick, where he and Elizabeth's mother lived. On seeing I was the one to have intruded on his privacy, he reacted to my presence in his customary warlike way.

With trepidation I began my carefully rehearsed apology.

'If I've done anything to upset you, Professor Unger, I really am very sorry. I hope you will be able to find it in your heart to forgive me for having caused offence. Elizabeth and I are getting married tomorrow and it is important for all of us to try and get along as friends.'

Without giving me the chance to complete my speech of conciliation, he issued a callous order I shall not until my dying day forget.

'Get away from my house, you bloody bastard, and never come back!'

I had imagined he would have wanted to make the best of the unpalatable situation for his wife's sake by behaving in a civil way towards me. The hurt caused by his unwillingness to absolve me of any misdemeanours he believed I had committed made me painfully aware that hatred of this magnitude had irrational origins for which there could never be a cure.

My dutiful best man insisted on doing everything by the book. He was frantic with worry when, having been beguiled by David Howell Jones into taking liquid refreshments at a nearby pub, I escaped his custody an hour before the wedding.

The marriage was conducted in Warwick's lovely collegiate church of St Mary's. Elizabeth's mother registered her displeasure at what she saw as an appalling mismatch by snivelling grief-stricken sobs throughout the service. Superstitious members of the congregation would have had cause to regard her emotive outbursts as an ill-starred omen.

A bedraggled, disparate crew, we stood outside the church in the pouring rain waiting for the photographs to be taken. We then proceeded drearily on foot in a funeral-like procession for the fifty or so yards to the house for the reception. My family, friends and guests greatly outnumbered Elizabeth's, reflecting the strained atmosphere under the Unger roof. Professor Unger absented himself for the entire day; Elizabeth's father, who gave his daughter away, attended in his place.

When finally the two of us began our honeymoon journey, I felt utterly alone, wondering what act of lunacy could have led us to imprison ourselves in a relationship with nothing but the barest of foundations. There was to be no turning back from the solemn undertakings we had made: 'To have and to hold from this day forward, for better, for worse; for richer, for poorer; in sickness and in health; to love and to cherish, till death us do part.'

Two double brandies had given me the courage to cope with the ceremony itself. I was going to need a great deal more than alcohol to sustain me in the days ahead.

Afterword

A permanent recognition of the efforts made on behalf of the school by my parents, the Douglas and Eileen Hall building was officially opened by the Rt. Hon. Mrs Margaret Thatcher, MP, the secretary of state for education and science, on the 20 October 1972. It was a great sadness that my father did not live to see the completion and inauguration of this very fine project.

In her speech, Mrs Thatcher made reference to the school's facilities by commenting, 'I think this is one of the best equipped prep schools that I have ever seen.' She went on to say: 'I know that our inspectorate hold this school in very high regard and it is of a very high reputation. I am certain that the things which are demonstrated here, not only in the formal education, but in the way in which the headmaster, and his father before him, constantly plough back the profits to revivify the school for the next generation, are an example we should all emulate.'

Four years before I stepped down as principal, by which time there were four hundred pupils on the school roll and further land and buildings had been acquired, specific reference was made in my speech day address to the accomplishments of some of my time-honoured colleagues.

'The school has benefited by having had few changes on the teaching staff over a number of years,' I proclaimed. 'I spoke on speech day last year of John Herbert's remarkable record. He is now completing his twenty-sixth year here. In addition, a further nine members of the teaching staff have been with us for between twenty and thirteen years, a record of loyal service and continuity for which we are grateful and gives us cause to be very proud.'

Critics challenged my vainglorious remarks by saying that it was healthy to have regular staff changes and that teachers who entrenched themselves too deeply in a post were in danger of becoming complacent, stale and ineffective. Change has its place, but to prevent the abstraction of intrinsic values from the school community, some of the enduring features must always be retained.

From humble beginnings we at Arnold Lodge had travelled far. The teachers I saluted in my speech were among the many men and women responsible for developing the school into one of the best of its kind and without whose true-heartedness and skills it would have remained an also-ran, pedestrian establishment.

The school suffered four years of financial penury under Graham Hill and very nearly closed. Revitalised through the aegis of The Education Partnership, Arnold Lodge, as their flagship school, is once more a pace-setter in the private sector. A network of computers has been installed with a high-powered server, enabling all lesson plans, assessments and personal files to be accessed by each pupil via a coded password process. Parents are able to follow the curriculum experiences of their children by logging on to the network from the comfort of their homes.

The school must never cease to be receptive to new ideas and remain appreciative of the need constantly to update the quality of the service on offer. It is only when it fails to fulfil this need that there will be an end in sight.

> If you can dream – and not make dreams your master;
> If you can think – and not make thoughts your aim:
> If you can meet with Triumph and Disaster
> And treat those two impostors just the same;
> If you can bear to hear the truth you've spoken
> Twisted by knaves to make a trap for fools,
> Or watch the things you gave your life to, broken,
> And stoop and build 'em up with worn-out tools.

(The above extract from Rudyard Kipling's 'If' has been included with non-exclusive permission of A P Watt Ltd on behalf of the National Trust for Places of Historic Interest or Natural Beauty)